PAPIST DEVILS

Robert Emmett Curran

PAPIST DEVILS

CATHOLICS IN
BRITISH AMERICA,
1574–1783

THE CATHOLIC UNIVERSITY OF
AMERICA PRESS ◆ Washington, D.C.

Library of Congress Cataloging-in-Publication Data
Curran, Robert Emmett.
Papist devils : Catholics in British North America, 1574–1783 /
Robert Emmett Curran.
pages cm
Includes bibliographical references and index.
ISBN 978-0-8132-2583-8 (pbk. : alk. paper)   1. Catholic Church—
North America—History.   2. Catholic Church—United States—
History.   3. Catholic Church—Maryland—History.   4. Catholic
Church—Maritime Provinces—History.   5. Catholic Church—
West Indies, British—History.   6. North America—Church his-
tory.   7. United States—Church history.   8. Maryland—Church
history.   9. Maritime Provinces—Church history.   10. West
Indies, British—Church history.   I. Title.
BX1403.3.C87 2014
282'.7—dc23   2013042110

TO EILEEN

CONTENTS

ILLUSTRATIONS

PREFACE

In December 2010 Trevor Lipscombe, as director of the Catholic University of America Press, asked if I had any interest in putting together a proposal for a brief history of Catholics in British America, a subject that he found to be a fascinating one but little treated by historians. I immediately conveyed my distinct interest in such a project. Indeed, I proceeded to tell him, three decades earlier I had secured my initial sabbatical at Georgetown University to begin a study of the Maryland Catholic community during the so-called penal age (1689–1776). That research was still in its early stage when the president of the university asked me to write the history of the institution for its upcoming bicentennial. That had effectively ended my project on Maryland Catholics in the penal age, but, I assured the director, I still retained a keen interest in it and welcomed the opportunity to do something on a broader scale for Catholics in the colonial era. Little did I realize how much broader that scale of the Catholic experience in the British Atlantic empire would prove to be.

My starting assumption was that Maryland was the heart and soul of any history of Catholics in British America. That, after all, had been the pattern set in earlier historical treatments: a central focus on Maryland, the locus of the vast majority of known Catholics in the thirteen colonies that became the United States of America, with side glimpses at the other two colonies, New York and Pennsylvania, that had some Catholic presence. More problematic to me was where to begin the story. It occurred to me early in the project that any context, to be truly illuminative, had to trace the Catholic experience in British America back to the place of origin for the vast majority of those Catholic settlers in

America—that is, the British Isles. To understand the Catholic exodus from England, Ireland, and Scotland that took place over the nearly two centuries that constituted the colonial period meant a starting point of the English Reformation that had, in turn, so shaped the Catholic community that survived it and the colonies in the New World that England founded.

Exploring the British roots of the American Catholic experience in time raised questions about the geographical framing of any comprehensive survey of that experience. English colonies in the Atlantic world included many more than the thirteen that eventually carried out the first successful colonial revolt in the Western world against an imperial power. In fact the colonies that became the United States of America made up but half of those that Great Britain ruled in the Atlantic world on the eve of the Revolution, from Quebec, St. John's, and Nova Scotia in the north to the Floridas, Bermuda, and the West Indies in the south. Quebec and the Floridas were both recent acquisitions but the rest were not. Nova Scotia had a large settlement of French Catholics, the Acadians, who found themselves caught between the imperial powers of France and Great Britain for most of the first half of the eighteenth century. In certain islands of the West Indies (Barbados, St. Kitts, Montserrat, Jamaica) Catholics were at least a significant minority of the population. In the seventeenth century, indeed, there were more Catholics in the British Caribbean than there were on the British North American mainland. The late development of institutional life in those islands has tended to render invisible the formidable Catholic presence there. Thanks to the path-breaking work of such historians as Donald H. Akenson, Hilary Beckles, Sally Schwartz, and Sonia Johnson, it is possible now to reconstruct a good deal of the Catholic experience in the West Indies and thus fill in that portion of the story of Catholics in British America that has been absent in previous tellings.

As for the time span of the book, the dates in the subtitle, 1574–1783, mark the beginning of British Catholic colonization in the New World and the formal end of British rule over the North American colonies that became the United States of America, respectively. In selecting the latter date I have carried it past the usual end point of the outbreak of colonial rebellion in 1775 to include a chapter on the American Revolution and an epilogue on the colonial legacy. The Revolution proved to be a culminating as well as liberating event for Catholics in the thirteen colonies, particularly Maryland and Pennsylvania, where most were concentrated.

The introduction sets the context for Catholic colonization by tracing the post-Reformation experience of the three major Catholic communities in the British Isles—the English, Scotch, and Irish—and how that experience nurtured Catholic colonization projects in the last quarter of the sixteenth century and the beginning of the seventeenth. Chapter 1 focuses on the Calverts' emergence as colonizers, their motives in undertaking plantations in Newfoundland and Maryland, the composition of the initial settlers in the Chesapeake adventure, and the pattern of settlement that developed in the first decade of that colony. Chapter 2 examines how the Calverts' vision of the relationship between church and state led to their separation of the two spheres and the establishment of religious liberty. It explores Jesuit motivations for coming to the colony, their adaptation to the plantation economy as a means of supporting their ministry, and the issues of authority, tradition, and power inherent in the controversy that developed in the 1630s between the proprietor and the Jesuits. Chapter 3 covers the fifteen-year period of turbulence (1645–1660) during which the Calverts and shifting opponents in Maryland mirrored the struggle between crown and Parliament in England. It follows Lord Baltimore's efforts to survive the civil war, first by casting his lot with the crown, then, with Parliament's triumph, through shrewd ecumenical policies. When these efforts failed to keep him in power, he finally succeeded by making his case on economic and political grounds with the new sovereign, Oliver Cromwell, who enabled him to regain his colony.

The substantial minority that Catholics constituted in the British West Indies is the focus of chapter 4. Dominant in this Catholic community were the Irish, émigrés by force or economic push factors. Very limited economic mobility proved to be the lot of most of the Irish in the West Indies in the seventeenth century with the exception of Mont-

serrat, where the Irish were a majority of the white population. Chapter 5 examines the political stability and economic progress that peace
brought to Maryland during the three decades of restored Stuart rule. It
also traces the emergence of a second colony, New York, to have a significant Catholic institutional presence in British America. In both provinces tensions mounted in the 1680s between Catholic proprietors and
largely non-Catholic subjects over Catholic-dominated administrations,
provision of ministry for Protestants, Indian threats, and other issues.
Chapter 6 reveals the intercolonial nature of the Glorious Revolution
in England by its repercussions throughout the British Atlantic world,
particularly in Maryland, New York, Barbados, and Montserrat. In all
these colonies the revolution brought an end to the religious liberty and
economic progress that Catholics had been experiencing—in the case
of Maryland Catholics, for more than a half century. Over the next half
century penal laws marginalized Catholics more and more within society
by the steady reduction of their political and economic rights. For many
Catholics in the West Indies, because of the discriminatory legal system
in combination with socioeconomic developments and natural disasters,
outmigration to the mainland became an increasingly popular recourse.

Chapter 7 focuses on the demographic and economic changes in
Maryland at the turn of the century that consolidated wealth in the top 2
percent of the population, a cohort in which Catholics, whose landholdings the existing penal legislation did not directly threaten, came to be
disproportionately represented. This Catholic elite was epitomized by
Charles Carroll of Annapolis and Richard Bennett III, who successively
over the course of the first half of the eighteenth century were the richest merchant-planters in the province. Over the first two decades governors attempted to employ penal legislation to curtail the economic and
political power that Catholic merchant-planters enjoyed, mainly through
proprietary offices that they continued to hold, thanks to the Calverts,
who were still the legal owners of the land, although politically no longer
sovereign after 1689. When Lord Baltimore regained the rule of his province by renouncing the Catholic faith, Carroll, the leader of the Maryland
Catholics, overreached in attempting to move the proprietor to restore
the Catholic elite to their old privileged position. The stark consequences

of this miscalculation were the loss of the franchise for Catholics and a confirmation of their outcast status in Maryland. Chapter 8 examines the adaptation of the Maryland Catholic community to its new position in society—how it affected its spiritual culture and fostered among the gentry a tradition of transatlantic education for their children. It also tracks the spreading and diversification of that community, through migration and immigration, into Delaware and southeastern Pennsylvania. Chapter 9 explores the persistence and power of anti-Catholicism throughout British America as a defining force for society. Several factors, including impending war with France and a religious awakening, revitalized anti-Catholic sentiment throughout the colonies. In Maryland it expressed itself chiefly through a revival of penal legislation against Catholics, increasingly seen as subversive threats. The Acadians on Nova Scotia, however, posed the greatest internal threat to security for many British Americans. That fear plus the opportunity for a highly valuable land grab led to the forced removal of thousands of long-settled Acadians from their homeland and their cruel dispersal throughout the colonies to the south. When formal war finally broke out with France in 1756, anti-Catholic paranoia escalated in the colonies; in Maryland an unprecedented double tax upon Catholics prompted many of the wealthy among them, including Charles Carroll, to consider abandoning Maryland for more hospitable territory in Spanish or French America.

How the outcome of the Seven Years' War with France accelerated the movement for most British Americans on the North American continent from dependent colonials to citizens of a united republic is the subject of chapter 10, with particular focus on the role that Catholic issues played in that transition and on the factors that led Catholics to choose a side or not in the civil war that eventually created a new nation. The last chapter, chapter 11, looks at the American attempts to bring other British colonies in the North Atlantic into their rebellion—specifically the abortive invasions of two colonies with more or less Catholic populations, Quebec and Nova Scotia. It surveys as well the participation of Catholics, both native and foreign, in the struggle. Finally, the epilogue attempts to show how the colonial experience of the Catholic community affected its development, institutional and attitudinal, in the early national period.

Those I would very much like to acknowledge for their part in bringing this work to print include Trevor Lipscombe, who first suggested it
and was throughout a source of wisdom and encouragement; Tricia T.
Pyne, archivist of the Associated Archives of St. Mary's University and
Seminary, who not only was an inexhaustible font of bibliographic leads
but also a reader of the entire manuscript with the discerning eye of an
outstanding historian of the Catholic colonial experience; the second
(anonymous) reader whose comments and recommendations were particularly valuable to me; Pat New, director of interlibrary loans at Eastern Kentucky University, who, in the course of my research, managed
to secure many, many volumes, including some I considered virtually
inaccessible; and Aldene Fredenburg, my copy editor, whose keen eye
for inconsistencies, faulty sentence structure, and vague language vastly
improved the style of the manuscript. To all of them I am most grateful.

Feast of the Immaculate Conception
December 8, 2012

PAPIST
DEVILS

INTRODUCTION

THE CONTEXT OF
COLONIZATION

CATHOLICS IN A STATE
OF SIEGE

On March 27, 1625, Charles Stuart, son of James I, succeeded his father as king of England, Scotland, and Ireland. His
pomp-filled coronation, occurring two days after the beginning of the new year (the Feast of the Annunciation in the
seventeenth-century calendar), carried the promise of a new era
for the nation's Catholics, the tiny community of gentry, artisans, and farmers in pockets of London and several northern
counties that had somehow survived the systematic efforts to
destroy them over the past several generations. Hardly anyone
in that community was old enough to remember Mary Tudor,
the last Catholic to occupy the throne, nearly seventy years
before. Mary's successor, Elizabeth I, had consolidated in her
kingdom the Protestant Reformation that her father, Henry
VIII, had haltingly introduced in 1534, only to have his oldest
daughter, Mary, restore Roman Catholicism as the religion of
the land when she succeeded her brother in 1553. Mary had moved
swiftly to stamp out Protestantism in her realm. Her sister,
once in power, moved more deliberately, but, over the course

of her nearly half-century reign, enacted a much deadlier toll upon Catholics.

The Act of Uniformity that Elizabeth had passed in 1559 was the keystone of the penal legislation that effectively outlawed the profession and practice of Roman Catholicism in England. Resistance on the part of Catholics to the new order came swiftly. Emigration was the response of hundreds of scholars at Oxford and elsewhere who took refuge in institutions on the Continent, particularly in the Netherlands, where they waged polemical warfare with defenders of the Church of England and, beginning with William Allen, who founded the English College at Douai in 1568, trained priests as missionaries for the reconversion of their mother country.

Other resistance was more directly militant. In 1569 earls in the northern tier of shires that would become the Catholic heartland led an unsuccessful uprising to replace Elizabeth with Mary Stuart. Two years later Pope Pius V's bull, *Regnans in Excelsis*, excommunicated and deposed Queen Elizabeth for her apostasy, explicitly sanctioning attempts to overthrow her. The bull inspired no immediate plots to dethrone Elizabeth (there would be several in the 1580s), but it did occasion a new series of penal legislation, two of which acts made it high treason for anyone to question Elizabeth's place as queen or to be trained abroad as missionaries to England. Rome's response was to threaten excommunication against any Catholic who acknowledged the deposed queen. Parliament answered in kind by holding the charge of treason over any Catholic who followed orders from Rome. Many Catholics, finding their convictions at odds with the laws, adopted as a mode of survival the vacillating stance of church-papists, publicly professing to be members of the Church of England to avoid the penal laws while secretly practicing Catholicism.

Some Catholics, particularly those who had sought refuge on the Continent, continued to advocate the militant solution that the earls had failed to achieve. The émigré Jesuit and former Oxford don Robert Persons promoted rebellion with the support of the leading Catholic power, Spain, as the path toward restoration. Others, continuing to believe that the English masses were still inertly Catholic (only needing to be awakened by effective evangelization to take the initiative to restore the old order), argued for this more democratic, if ultimately violent, solution from the premise that the ruler derived his authority not by divine right, but from the consent of the commonwealth. Others relied on the pope's political power as the final authority. When either pope or people judged that a sovereign had acted badly, there was just cause to remove her by force. Such radical calls to arms were not just frustrated appeals of expatriate clergy in Douai or Rome; there seems to have been significant, if not widespread, support within the Catholic community for such a solution, at least into the 1580s. The most serious attempt at a violent overthrow was the attempted invasion of the Spanish Armada in 1588. When that enterprise ended in disaster, it marked the culmination of the drive to restore by force the *status quo ante* Elizabeth.

By the mid-1590s Catholics such as Persons were professing their political loyalty to the Queen and calling for toleration, not repression, as the government's policy toward their coreligionists. Any conversion of ruler and people would come now through persuasion, not force. Toleration and evangelization through persuasion were conditions that Catholics increasingly promoted as they abandoned the illusion that the country was still at heart Catholic. With great reluctance they slowly but surely came to accept the cold reality that Catholics in England were now a permanent minority, and a small one to boot.

They also came, in practice if not in aim, to recognize the limits of evangelization. The mission to reestablish Catholicism in England had begun in 1574 with the arrival of the first priest with missionary faculties. Over succeeding decades scores of secular priests, Jesuits, and Benedictines from Louvain, Douai, and Rome followed. Initially they regarded their mission as a necessary, but temporary means of preserving the church in England until her restoration under a Catholic ruler. By 1610 time and experience convinced most of the missionaries, as they had the Catholic apologists, that the surviving Catholic community, perhaps forty thousand to fifty thousand in a general population of four million, was not the nucleus of a national Catholic restoration, but rather a minuscule sect that would remain so for the foreseeable future. Subtly the mission became primarily a ministry to that community's needs.

With Elizabeth having no descendants, the crown passed to King James of Scotland. James's Catholic ties had spurred in 1603 even greater hopes than those sweeping through Catholic England in 1625—hopes that James's assumption of the English throne would finally bring an end to the war against Catholics that Elizabeth had waged for most of her long reign. James, after all, had been baptized a Catholic. As king he had cultivated a Catholic party at the Scottish court; had, in practice, adopted a policy of toleration for his Catholic subjects. He had manifested a desire to make peace with the Spanish, the perennial suspected source of any English Catholic conspiracy. Then, too, James's wife, Anne of Denmark, had become a Catholic convert in 1601, two years before the call went north for the king of Scotland to rule over the lower kingdom, as well. Topping it all were rumors of James's impending return to the religion of his birth. All this had fed Catholic expectations that the new ruler would, at the very least, free Catholics from the civil disabilities that marked them as internal aliens whose religion made suspect their loyalty to crown and country. The more hopeful looked forward to a Catholic again being on the throne after nearly a half century.

It, of course, proved not to be. Whatever ambiguous encouragement James might have given to individual Catholics about the prospects of his conversion, he had no intention of becoming a Catholic. When the new king took no steps to change the condition of Catholics in his realm, Catholic hotheads concocted wild plots involving kidnapping or assassination of the king to gain toleration and restoration of a Catholic to the throne. In gratitude to the Catholics who exposed the plots, James granted relief for a year from the penal laws and released some Jesuits from prison, only to reverse course sharply under pressure from Parliament. In February 1604 he stunned the Catholic community by denouncing the "Papist religion" in a speech to Parliament and ordering all priests to leave the country. The subsequent execution of two priests, as well as the renewal of the anti-Catholic laws, occasioned the Gunpowder Plot, the hare-brained scheme of several Midlands Catholic gentry to blow up Parliament in November when the king came to open its session, thus eliminating the source of the persecuting legislation, as well as its executor. When the government predictably learned of the plan, its net swiftly

The Kingdome of England (1637)

gathered in for execution not only Guy Fawkes and the other would-be terrorists, but innocents as well, including the superior of the English Jesuits, Henry Garnet.

The government exploited this aborted plot as the justification for new penal legislation for the Catholic community. The Penal Laws of 1606 imposed upon all Catholics an oath of allegiance to James as well as a denial of the doctrine of regicide and of the pope's authority to depose rulers through excommunication. The oath thus became a litmus test of Catholic loyalty. Many reluctantly took it. A second law restricted the travel of Catholics to a five-mile radius of their homes and banned them from practicing the professions of law and medicine. The new legislation was, at best, unevenly enforced, both over time and across the Catholic community. Still, twenty-three recusants, not counting those involved in the Gunpowder Plot, were put to death under the laws during James's reign—considerably fewer than James's predecessor had dispatched, to be sure, but a figure dispiriting enough to a Catholic community that had thought its long nightmare was at last over. The Catholic community continued through the first quarter of the century in the state of siege that it had known since Elizabeth's days on the throne.

THE CATHOLIC COMMUNITY
IN ENGLAND AND WALES

John Bossy has argued in his classic study, *The English Catholic Community, 1570–1850*, that the English Catholic community was a new entity created by the missionaries who had descended upon England beginning in the 1570s—an entity disconnected from a medieval English church that had essentially died by the early years of Elizabeth's reign.[1] Christopher Haigh, in his study of post-Reformation religion in Lancashire, *Reformation and Resistance in Tudor Lancashire*,[2] admits that it was a new creation, but one that built upon surviving elements of medieval Catholicism kept alive by religious traditionalists, both priests and laity, in Lancashire, Yorkshire, the Welsh Marches, and elsewhere well before the missionaries began to arrive in force from the Continent. As Michael A. Mullett has argued, these "Marians," priests who had served under Queen Mary, were the "rebuilders of a religious community managing to survive an unprecedented disaster."[3] Continuity was a precondition for resurrection.

By the early seventeenth century this revived Catholic community had consolidated itself largely into certain traditional areas of the seven northern counties. As Edward Norman has noted, there was an inverse correlation between counties in the vanguard of socioeconomic change and those with a strong Catholic presence.[4] Put differently, the more conservative a region was in its economic and social ways, the greater the likelihood that Catholicism would survive there. No county was more Catholic than Lancaster in the Uplands. Indeed, in 1600 there were arguably more Catholics in this comparatively small area than in the rest of the North put together. Stock raising was the principal occupation,

1. John Bossy, *The English Catholic Community, 1570–1850* (New York and Oxford: Oxford University Press, 1976).

2. Christopher Haigh, *Reformation and Resistance in Tudor Lancashire* (New York: Cambridge University Press, 1975).

3. Michael A. Mullett, *Catholics in Britain and Ireland, 1558–1829* (New York: St. Martin's Press, 1998), 10.

4. Edward Norman, *Roman Catholicism in England from the Elizabethan Settlement to the Second Vatican Council* (Oxford and New York: Oxford University Press, 1985), 32.

and the gentry were numerous. Lancashire was the one jurisdiction in which Catholicism had a public face, with masses being celebrated in parish churches. In the Midlands the strong majority of Catholics were to be found in the western shires, particularly Staffordshire, Warwickshire, and Worcestershire. South Central England, particularly Sussex and Hampshire counties, housed much of the Catholic nobility: the Arundells, the Paulets, the Montagues, the dukes of Norfolk. The rest of southern England, the epicenter of economic development, counted relatively few Catholics, except for London, where the foreign embassy chapels provided the opportunity for a heterogeneous group, most prominently those Catholics connected to the court, to practice their religion.

Wales, the most isolated region of Great Britain, had, despite strong traditionalist instincts, submitted to Elizabeth's reformation without significant resistance in most parts. There was, however, a small core of opposition rooted in southeast Wales, in the counties adjacent to England, the area governed by the Council in the Marches. Monmouthshire was its hub, being to Welsh Catholicism on a smaller scale what Lancashire was to the English. Here too was a community dominated by the gentry and the occasional lord, including the Earl of Worcester in Monmouthshire.

GENTRY CATHOLICISM

The focal points within this clustering were the gentry houses that harbored priests and served as liturgical centers. With the gentry estate as the nucleus of the local Catholic community, authority had passed from the clergy to the lay aristocracy. Given the fragile conditions under which Catholic life existed, with priests under the threat of capital punishment for even being in the country, this transfer of authority was inevitable. But these gentry comprised but a minority of the Catholic community. Farmers, laborers, tradespersons were its majority. The estate-centered Catholic congregation usually included the resident family and relatives and the household staff, which tended to range from a dozen to more than fifty servants, depending on the size and wealth of the place, as well as tenant farmers and farm workers. By the 1620s the household staff was ordinarily composed of Catholics only, a marked change from the mixed staffs of the previous century. A religiously homogeneous household meant more security for the gentry in housing priests and performing religious services. Gentry matriarchs had been responsible for the change. With a uniformly Catholic household came a strict regimen of religious observance, ranging from Mass to litanies, under the direction of the matriarch, from day's beginning until its end. Surrounding the estate were usually other Catholic farmers and farm workers who depended on the manor house for their religious needs.

This Catholic community, unlike the larger society, continued the pre-Reformation tradition of observing the feast and penitential days that crowded the liturgical calendar. Feast days numbered no fewer than forty. Days of fasting and abstinence took up more than a third of the year. They formed a very prominent part of the annual cycle of seasons. Here, women played an important role in deciding the menus of feasting or restraint as keepers of the Catholic culture of the household. That was perhaps one reason more women than men converted to Catholicism. Gentry women had particular influence as nurturers and protectors of the resident priests. For gentry women a resident priest, who depended on the mistress of the household for his security and sustenance, could be a useful ally in contesting the authority of the male head. Then, too, wives, precisely because they lacked rights and property, enjoyed a certain freedom and immunity in the exercise of their religion that the penal laws denied their husbands. There was much less pressure upon women than upon men to become church-papists in order to protect the family from the penal laws, and far fewer women did. In any event these nominal conformers, who had constituted an important portion of the Catholic community in the late sixteenth century, by the 1620s were virtually extinct, the majority having finally subscribed, publicly and privately, to the state religion. But the male dominance of the church-papist status was clearly a factor in women coming to play the central role in the religious affairs of estate Catholicism.

Under the penal laws Catholics were required to be baptized and married in the Church of England. To what extent they should abide by the laws (have both Anglican and Catholic rites, marry and baptize in secret) was a matter that perplexed the community until well into the eighteenth century. Catholics preferred the clandestine performance of the Catholic rite for both life passages, despite a £100 fine for priests who performed them. In mixed households, more common among those below the gentry, the head of the household apparently decided in what religion the child would be baptized. Even those undergoing Catholic baptisms frequently had their names entered in the local parish books, either through a second Anglican baptism or through a parson willing to record a Catholic baptism as though he himself had performed it. Separate marriage was much less a problem in an age in which clerical presence was not considered necessary for the administration of the sacrament.

By the 1620s it had become the ordinary practice for the Catholic gentry and nobility to send their sons across the Channel for their collegiate education, particularly to St. Omer's, the Jesuit college founded in Flanders in 1590 for recusant children. In the same decade English women established their first religious community on the Continent. By 1640 there would be nearly a score of English convents in France and the Lowlands, to which hundreds of the daughters of the gentry went to study; most remained to become members of the Benedictines, Carmelites, and other orders that maintained the houses. An increasing number of the graduates of St. Omer's and other schools stayed on the Continent to study for the priesthood. During most of the first six decades of the seventeenth century, the sons of the gentry constituted two-thirds of the English seminarians. That upsurge in vocations was a major element in the remarkable growth of the Jesuit mission in England.

There was substantial growth in the Catholic population over the first quarter century, although calculating the precise size of that community at any particular date has eluded historians' efforts. When Charles became king in 1625 it likely stood somewhat below fifty thousand. Conversions were one reason for the growth, both in the general Catholic population and in the size of its clergy. Converts constituted one-third of the English seminarians on the Continent. The increase in the clergy, particularly among the Jesuits, was even greater than conversions in the community itself. The overall number of clergy doubled in that quarter century, a growth far outstripping the general increase of Catholics.

The Jesuits, fewer than twenty in 1600, sextupled their ranks by 1623, the year a Jesuit province was established for England in recognition of the large body of Jesuits now at work in the island. In that same year Rome appointed the eponymous William Bishop to govern the Catholic community as a vicar apostolic.

The appointment of a bishop marked a decisive turn in the controversy, which reached back into Elizabeth's reign, about the polity and nature of Roman Catholicism in England. Should the structure of church governance in England reflect its missionary status, with authority ultimately based in the papal missionary congregation, *Propaganda Fide*, and priests operating semi-autonomously in the unsettled religious situation? Or should the Roman Catholic Church in England be organized in parish units, under the jurisdiction of a bishop—units that had traditionally characterized national Catholic communities in Europe, including England until Henry VIII's break with Rome? The Jesuits and priests of religious orders in general considered as essential the missionary status with the freedom it assured them from episcopal control. The secular clergy (nonreligious-order priests) wanted a return to the canonical structure of parishes under the administration of diocesan bishops. Rome's initial effort in 1598 to establish a local authority without a diocesan structure, an archpriest with very limited jurisdiction over the Catholic community, proved unsatisfying to both sides, especially the secular clergy. Two years into George Blackwell's administration a group of secular priests appealed to Rome to replace the archpriest with an ordinary bishop who would have normal authority within his jurisdiction. These "Appellants," as they came to be known, succeeded eventually in persuading the pope to dismiss Blackwell in 1607, but neither an ordinary bishop nor an apostolic vicar was sent in his place. Nearly two decades elapsed before William Bishop was appointed as vicar apostolic. Bishop set in motion the establishment of a diocesan structure, including the organization of the clergy in a chapter, but his death nine months after taking office put an end to this reform. His successor, the autocratic Richard Smith, failed miserably in trying to rein in the independence of both the gentry and the Jesuits. It was the latter's turn to win Rome's ear. In 1631

Pope Urban VIII ruled in favor of the Jesuits over the question of their freedom to go about their ministry without interference from Smith. The pontiff chastised the prelate for undermining the community's unity. That same year the Jesuits and gentry succeeded in removing Smith altogether when he was forced to flee to the Continent to avoid a government prosecution instigated by certain Catholic laymen. For whatever reason, Rome never replaced him (he lived as a refugee in Paris for nearly a quarter of a century, until his death in 1655). For the next fifty years the gentry retained their traditional power within the community. The Jesuits, for their part, continued their pattern of operations that had marked their activity in England over the past half century.

CATHOLICS IN SCOTLAND

The revolution that John Knox and a majority of the Scottish nobility made against the queen regent, Mary of Guise, and the established religion of the country, Roman Catholicism, culminated shortly after the queen's death in 1560 with the Scottish Assembly declaring Calvinism the national religion and outlawing the formerly established one. In its wake the revolution left a country-wide destruction and demolition of churches, monasteries, and ecclesiastical structures. This massive uprooting of medieval Catholicism from the Scottish landscape served as an outward sign of the discontinuity between the Catholic past and Protestant present that the rapid triumph of reform throughout most of Scotland had managed to instill in the consciousness of Scots. Most natives quickly internalized the new religious construction. Despite the attempts of two Stuart Scottish monarchs, Mary and her son, James VI, to undo the revolution, either by the restoration of Catholicism or some Protestantism a good deal to the right of the Genevan brand that John Knox had introduced, the Reformation not only survived in Scotland, but became a more hegemonic religion than anywhere else in the British Isles.

Even so, within this Calvinist-dominated society, there persisted a core of Catholics. As in England, Scotland had its own corpus of penal laws to underscore the new reality that Catholicism was a religion whose practice the government had the obligation to discourage and punish in order to complete its demise. Excommunication, with its cutting off of the victim from society, was a major tool in dealing with recusants (Catholic nonconformists). Imposing the Calvinist confession of faith on all would-be members of the Scottish church very effectively reduced the number of church-papists in the country. The same profession was forced upon priests. Those who refused risked losing state-provided incomes or even worse. The Scots preferred shaming rituals, rather than executions, to check the ministry and influence of recusant priests. Nonetheless, more than a few priests went to the scaffold. No wonder recusant clergy sought refuge in France in the late sixteenth century. Some monasteries relocated themselves on the Continent, where they pursued their scholarly and contemplative traditions.

By the early seventeenth century Catholicism had, to a large extent, survived only in the Gaelic north and west. This most traditional area in the Highlands of the country had proved to be very resistant to the inroads of Calvinism and reform. It held the greatest prospects as a mission for the Dominicans, Capuchins, Franciscans, and Jesuits, who began targeting the region at the beginning of the century. By 1625 their success had resulted in the stirrings of a strong Catholic awakening in the Highlands that ensured a continuing Catholic presence in at least a portion of this staunchly Protestant region.

IRELAND

Ireland was the one country in the British Isles where attempts to implant the Reformation not only failed, but occasioned a strong revival of Catholicism. Proselytizing of the natives by English and Scottish missioners was virtually impossible, except among the Old English (descendants of earlier Anglo-Norman immigrants). The Gaelic population was overwhelmingly illiterate, and the would-be converters were unable to speak the native language. But it was the emerging symbiosis of religion and national identity, a key promoter of reform in Scotland, that in Ireland ultimately ensured that Catholicism would remain overwhelmingly the religion of the people. An English occupation that, beginning in the late sixteenth century, involved the progressive confiscation of land, relo-

cation of its owners elsewhere, and loss of their political power all tended to unite the several ethnic groups of natives in opposition to the government and the Protestant religion it was attempting to impose upon
the overwhelmingly Catholic population.

The English presence in Ireland dated from the late twelfth century,
when Henry II invaded the island and settled Anglo-Normans, Welsh,
and English colonists throughout much of the country. In the following
century large numbers of Gaelic Scots, who had been imported by the
natives as mercenaries to combat the Anglo-Norman settlers, immigrated to Ireland. Both the Anglo-Normans, or Old English, and the Scots
tended to acculturate into the host society, particularly in the countryside; intermarriage with the Irish was common. The decline in population that Ireland, along with Europe in general, experienced from the
fourteenth century on accelerated this assimilating process. By the fif-
teenth century a distinctive Old English presence had become very largely an urban phenomenon, especially in the area around Dublin, which
came to be denoted as "The Pale."

Until the sixteenth century the English crown's rule in Ireland was
felt very lightly, if at all, beyond "The Pale." The dominant Gaelic Irish
society was a pastoral, semi-nomadic one in which cattle were the most
prized commodities. A fragmented, fluctuating, contentious ruling class
of major and minor lords controlled land in a chaotic and ruthless manner that rendered the lot of freeholders and tenants a rather miserable
one. The lords also effectively controlled the church, inasmuch as they
tended to supply the clerical ranks. And with clerical marriage still widespread, despite its outlawing by a local church synod in the twelfth century, clerical families supplied many, if not most, of the priestly vocations,
and were as much beneficiaries of feudal tithes and payments as were the
secular lords. The upshot was a constellation of semi-independent fiefdoms, with token fealty to the English crown.

That all changed in 1541 when Henry VIII formally declared himself the sovereign of Ireland and extended English law to his dominion
across the sea as a way to bring order into what the English perceived to
be quite an anarchic society of savages. Central to this disorder was the
crazy-quilt pattern of landholding. The king introduced a system of "sur-

render and regrant" in which the lords would surrender their traditional rights and lands to the monarch, who would in turn acknowledge their ownership according to the English laws of possession and inheritance. The goal, in a sense, was to make the boundaries of the Pale coterminous with the country itself, to nationalize the laws and workings of this English hub. The idea might have looked perfectly fine on paper, but, given the chaotic reality of Gaelic landholding, attempts to apply the system inevitably offended many lords who lost land in the process and led to a spate of disputes among lords that plagued the ruling class for the rest of the century, particularly in Ulster, which was the heart of Gaelic Ireland.

Very late in the century the lords realized that they had signed away their independence by taking part in the land-transmission program. The Rebellion of 1594, led by the head chieftain, Hugh O'Neill, was their response. But O'Neill's attempt to unite the Gaelic tribes in a successful ousting of their perennial occupiers ultimately fell victim to Irish factionalism and inadequate support from Spain. The Treaty of Mellifont that ended the Nine Years' War in 1603 effectively completed the reorganization of Ulster that the occupiers had begun in 1570. The division of the province into nine counties or shires essentially shifted authority from the Gaelic chiefs to English administrators. In their ensuing attempt to reclaim power, several of the leading earls, including O'Neill, fearful of English reprisals to preempt another uprising, fled the country in August of 1607 and eventually found refuge in Rome. Hundreds of Irish students and thousands of soldiers would choose exile on the Continent in this period, joining expatriates of the English Catholic community who had set the pattern decades earlier. Schools in Spanish- and French-controlled areas of Europe served as refuges for Irish clergy and as training centers for future priests. As the English recusant community had established educational institutions and seminaries on the Continent, so too did the Irish. Irish colleges were established in Douai in 1594 and in Louvain in 1607. Other institutions of learning were founded in Lille, Tournai, and Antwerp.

Gaelic resistance to the crown, culminating with the flight of the earls and the short-lived revolt of Sir Cahir O'Dougherty, the most important chief remaining in Ireland, provided a rationale for the general confiscation of Irish land in Ulster and beyond. In 1600 the 1.2 million or so in-

habitants of Ireland were almost entirely Gaelic in origin. Those of English or Scotch descent accounted for only 2 percent of the population.
The plantation policy that England introduced shortly after the end of
the Nine Years' War dramatically changed that over the course of the next
century. By 1700 the non-Gaelic portion of Irish society had jumped to
more than 27 percent. Under the new plantation system, inaugurated in
1608, about half of the land grants went to Scottish undertakers. Clearly
the provisions of the plantation policy were observed more in the breach
than otherwise. Despite the injunction against leasing to Catholics, many
of the new settlers, occupying vast tracts of 1,000 to 3,000 acres that they
could not efficiently "undertake" or work, kept many of the Irish on their
old homesteads as tenants. Moreover, several hundred of the Irish elite
managed to retain their land titles, which comprised about a fifth of the
territory. In the end few outside of those who had been actively involved
in the rebellion were expelled from Ulster. But the Ulster Plantation constituted a real revolution in land ownership. By 1630 the Gaelic Irish still
made up the vast majority of the population in the province. The minority
settlers, however, held by far most of the land. The Irish, for the most part,
had been reduced from lords of the land to renters who could be displaced
at will. And Ulster was only the largest section to be affected by a plantation policy that by the 1630s had spread through much of Ireland.

For the Old English the new dispensation introduced by James eventually meant a loss of political hegemony as well as a widespread decline
in landownership. The Irish Parliament may have had little impact outside the Pale, but for the Old English it had been a vital safeguard of
their interests. They had been the chief beneficiaries of the crown's initial
seizure of monastic lands. Thanks in large part to this windfall, despite
constituting less than 2 percent of the population, the Old English held
no less than one-third of the country's land. They enjoyed even more
disproportionate political power, holding nearly three-quarters of the
seats in the Irish parliament. But if they had good reason to be loyal to
the crown, particularly to the Stuart household, they were loyal Catholics, as well. Moreover, any application of the penal laws had its worst
effect upon the Old English, since they were so concentrated in the cities,
where the laws could be most effectively implemented. At the beginning

of James I's reign they had attempted to secure the king's toleration of their religion and a recognition that their ancient town charters guaranteed their full rights as citizens. The Irish government retaliated by enforcing the penal laws in Dublin, forcing the newly elected Catholic mayor and aldermen out of office. King James answered their petition by ordering all Catholic clergy out of Ireland. Protests by Irish Catholic gentry led to arrests and imprisonment of prominent Catholics for failure to attend Church of Ireland services. For several years the government carried on this persecution of the Catholic community, until the Privy Council put a stop to it in 1607. Eight years later the government renewed the enforcement of the penal laws, only on a much larger scale that affected the principal towns in Leinster and Munster. Scores of Catholic officeholders were imprisoned for refusing to take the Oath of Supremacy. For its collective opposition to the government policy, Waterford lost its charter and was reduced to the status of disfranchised village. Such government aggression, rather than weakening the allegiance of the Old English to Rome, tended rather to alienate the Old English from the crown.

The plantation revolution was part of the Anglicization of society that the crown had committed itself to in the first decade of the century. Anglicization also meant Protestantism. Office-holding within the central government was confined to those able and willing to take the Oath of Supremacy. Along with the creation of the Ulster Plantation, the government created eighty-four new boroughs with representation in the Irish parliament. The imported settlers of this redistributed land in the north and west of Ireland thus became the largest group of "New English," who by the 1620s held a comfortable majority of seats (132 to 100) in the Irish Parliament. From the middle of the 1620s on, the Old English attempted to change this political equation, largely by persuading the crown to suspend a large part of the penal mechanism through the exercise of certain "King's Graces," which amounted to a policy of practical toleration of Roman Catholicism and the recognition of Catholics as full citizens. Eventually this effort failed, which left the Old English with a fateful choice to make about their ultimate identity and allegiance. But, in the mid-1620s, that lay in the future.

CATHOLICS AND COLONIZATION

As a community under attack, colonization would have seemed to have had a distinct appeal to Catholics as an escape from their condition in England. To a few in the community it did, but they found little support from their fellow Catholics, particularly as long as Catholics harbored hopes for restoration. As early as 1568 a Catholic noble, Sir Thomas Gerrard, developed plans for a Catholic refuge in Antrim, Ireland, a semi-autonomous settlement that would serve as an English buffer against the native Irish to the west and the transplanting Scotch to the east. Despite Gerrard's patriotic intentions, the English government rejected his plans. Six years later Gerrard joined another Catholic nobleman, Sir George Peckham, along with a Protestant, Sir Humphrey Gilbert, in seeking to establish in the New World a colony very similar to the one Gerrard had proposed for Northern Ireland. Gilbert obtained a charter from the crown and, after one failed voyage in 1578, the trio prepared for another attempt at settlement in 1582. This occasioned an informant to warn the secretary of state, Francis Walsingham, "There is a muttering among the papists that Sir Humphrey Gilbert goithe to seeke a newefound land; Syr George Peckham and Syr Thomas Gerrarde goithe with him. I have heard it said among the papists that they hope it will prove the best journey for England that was maide there."[5] It is unlikely that the secretary shared the informant's conviction that there was something sinister lurking beneath the Catholic interest in Gilbert's voyage. Walsingham needed no warning. Peckham and Gerrard had already sought his permission for recusants to join the overseas venture, with the provision that they would pay all outstanding fines before departure or promise to do so once they had established themselves in the New World. As an added incentive for Walsingham to give his approval, the nobles informed the official that one-tenth of their party would consist of those who could not support themselves in England. Once having established a foothold in America, they would leave a group there as the nucleus of a permanent

5. Public Record Office, Patent Roll, 21 Elizabeth, part 4, membr. 8, June 11, 1578, quoted in Thomas Hughes, *History of the Society of Jesus in North America: Colonial and Federal; Text*, vol. 1, *From the First Colonization Till 1645* (New York: Longmans, Green, 1908), 147.

colony. That colony, somewhere around Rhode Island, would be a feudal kingdom, with Gilbert as lord proprietor and governor and Peckham
and Gerrard as sublords, ruling over tenants on the lords' vast manorial
estates (2 million acres each).

Whether Walsingham granted permission and whether any other
Catholics joined the undertaking is unknown. We do know that the
Spanish ambassador to England, Bernardino de Mendoza, very much
opposed the scheme (it would weaken Spanish claims to all of North
America as well as lessen the potential of the English Catholic community as a potential internal ally of Spain in overthrowing Elizabeth) and
used his contacts within that community to make clear that Spain would
challenge any settlement situated on land that the pope had already
granted it. Nonetheless, Gilbert, after a year's delay, finally set sail to reconnoiter the intended settlement site in June of 1683. He apparently
never made it farther than Newfoundland, where the loss of a ship
forced him to abort the journey and return home. On the homeward
voyage his own ship sank, with all aboard it.

Despite this terrible loss, Peckham pressed forward with his settlement plans. He managed to get some commitment from prominent ex-
plorers Francis Drake and Martin Frobisher, as well as a few London
merchants. Together they published a pamphlet in December 1683, *A
True reporte of the late discoveries ... of the Newfound Landes*, which delineated the compelling reasons that it was "honest and profitable" to settle
in the region between 30 and 60 degrees latitude, reasons ranging from
the evangelization of the natives, to the wealth that colonists would realize from the abundant natural resources they could exploit on their extensive estates, to their patriotic duty to establish an English presence in the
New World. But by the time the *True reporte* was released, the exposure
of a new Catholic plot against the queen set in motion yet another wave
of persecution of Catholics, in which Peckham himself was imprisoned.
This crackdown, followed shortly by the outbreak of war between England and Spain, effectively ended any Catholic colonization efforts for
the next two decades.

In 1605 another Catholic nobleman, Sir Thomas Arundell of Wardour, in collaboration with his brother-in-law, the Protestant Henry

Wriothesley, Earl of Southampton, looked to find a refuge for his afflicted coreligionists and to evangelize the indigenous Americans. At some
point a Cornish Catholic, Tristam Winslade, became involved in the
project. Winslade, a former mercenary in various Continental armies,
including the Spanish, had the notion of recruiting a hundred or so
English Catholic veterans of Spanish service for the proposed colony.
When Winslade sought Robert Persons's advice in Rome, the English
Jesuit advised him to drop the plan. Politically it was impractical to think
the government would consent to allowing a group of Catholics to begin a settlement in the New World. In addition, emigration of any scale
would further weaken a Catholic community that was weak enough as
it was. Finally, it was questionable to Persons whether the Spanish, with
their great interest in evangelization of the Indian, would suffer quietly
any English competition in the New World.[6] Indian evangelization was
the one goal of the would-be colonizers that clearly touched the English
Jesuit. "[T]he intention of converting these people liketh me so well, and
in so high a degree as for that only I would desire myself to go in the
journey, shutting my eyes to all other difficulties if it were possible to
obtain it."[7] As it was, Persons promised that if they could raise any support for the plan in England or Spain, he would do what he could for
them in Rome. Whether Arundell and Winslade took Persons' advice is
unknown.

At the same time that Persons was making his response, in March
1605, Arundell sent out a ship, the *Archangel*, under Captain George
Waymouth, who explored Monhegan Island and the Maine coast as
possible sites for the colony. After an extensive reconnaissance of the St.
George River, during which they made contact with the Penobscot Indians (indeed, brought back forcibly to England five of the natives to serve
as guides for future expeditions), they arrived home in mid-July, having

6. James Hennesey, "Catholicism in the English Colonies," in *Encyclopedia of the American Religious Experience: Studies of Traditions and Movements*, edited by Charles H. Lippy and Peter W.
Williams (New York: Charles Scribners Sons, 1988), 1:345.

7. Robert Persons, "My Judgment about Transferring English Catholiques to the Northern Par-
tes of America for inhabitinge those partes and converting those barbarous people to Christianitie,"
March 18, 1605, in Hughes, *History of the Society of Jesus in North America*; Vol. I, Part I (documents)
(New York: Longmans, Green, 1908), 3–5.

made the return trip in a little more than a month, proving how easy an Atlantic crossing could be. Waymouth discovered, to his surprise, that Arundell had abandoned his colonization project to assume command of an English regiment in service to the archdukes of the Spanish Low Countries. Waymouth, desperately attempting to attract other investors, published at the end of 1605 *A true relation of the most prosperous voyage made this present yeare 1605 ... in the discovery of the land of Virginia.* He found no takers. Another exposure of Catholic subversion, this one the notorious Gunpowder Plot in November of 1605, had laid waste any possibility of a mass Catholic exodus from England in the foreseeable future.

When Lord Arundell, three years later, had a change of heart and revived earlier plans for a New England settlement, his attempt to secure a patent for the region predictably went nowhere. Two decades later, with Charles on the throne, circumstances were taking shape in a way that was reviving Catholic colonization efforts, now undertaken by an in-law of Sir Thomas.

CHAPTER 1

"TO SEW THE HOLY FAITH IN HIS LAND"

The Calverts and the Beginnings of Catholic Settlement

GEORGE CALVERT

By the 1620s religious allegiance had become a more stable phenomenon than it had been, certainly, in the previous century. Conversions (or apostasies, depending on your viewpoint) were a less common occurrence among Anglicans, Catholics, and Puritans. But if converts were in decline across the religious landscape, they could still have an impact upon the faith community they joined, as George Calvert's (re)conversion in 1625 certainly had upon the Catholic community and its involvement in colonization.

Born in 1579 or 1580 of an old Yorkshire family in one of the Catholic strongholds of the north, Calvert, raised Catholic by his parents, at twelve, under pressure from government officials, conformed to the established religion. Attending Trinity College, Oxford, which Calvert began a year later, might well have been a factor in his conforming. Following Oxford he studied law for three years at Lincoln's Inn, then spent two years, 1601 to 1603, touring the Continent. Through the probable influence of a cousin, Calvert became a protégé of Sir Robert Cecil, the powerful secretary of state and privy councilor. Calvert, starting as Cecil's secretary, advanced steadily within the royal bureaucracy, acquiring considerable wealth from his various offices in the process. In 1610 he became a clerk of the Privy Council with a new patron, the Earl of Salisbury. In that position Calvert regularly crossed paths with King James, who was so taken with the clerk's language skills, work habits, and prudence in administration that the king had him research and translate his tract against a Dutch theologian. When Cecil's successor, the Earl of Salisbury, died, Calvert took over a number of Salisbury's responsibilities, including carrying out sensitive missions for the crown to Ireland and the Continent.

Finally, in 1619, James named him one of his principal secretaries of state, which post ironically isolated him from the king and his council and forced him to give up the lesser offices that had provided such a rising source of income for him. As a substitute for this loss of connections, Calvert turned to his home county of Yorkshire to build up a network of supporters and allies, none more important than Sir Thomas Wentworth. Wentworth's patronage brought Calvert election in 1620 to the House of Commons, where he became one of the king's principal spokesmen while continuing to serve as his secretary of state. As friction increased between king and Parliament over James's quest for a Spanish alliance and other issues, Calvert bore the brunt of the anti-crown animus. Over the next several years Calvert's standing within the court declined sharply as power subtly shifted from King James to Crown Prince Charles. Early in 1625 Calvert submitted his resignation as secretary of state (having garnered £3,000 from the sale of the position, an entirely ethical transaction in Jacobean England).

At about the time of his resignation it became known that Calvert had returned to the religion of his childhood, but that reconversion had not been the cause of his leaving government. It was rather the reverse: his decision to resign because of his loss of influence within the royal circle had provided the opportunity to resolve his struggles over his

George Calvert (1578/79–1632)

conflicted religious identity. For years, perhaps since his forced conversion, Calvert had been, as his biographer put it, a man "with 'the face of a
Protestant and the heart of a Papist.'"[1] A series of events, including his
wife's sudden death in 1622, had brought that conflict to a resolution. If

<hr />

1. John D. Krugler, *English and Catholic: The Lords Baltimore in the Seventeenth Century* (Baltimore and London: Johns Hopkins University Press, 2004), 75.

Calvert harbored fears that becoming a Catholic would cut him off from the government he had so loyally served, those fears proved unfounded. The king allowed him to remain on the Privy Council and bestowed on him an Irish title, Lord Baltimore, and a grant of 2,300 acres in County Longford to match.

CALVERT THE COLONIZER

Calvert at last was free to pursue his longstanding interest in colonization. As early as 1609 Calvert, in a patriotic gesture, had made a modest investment in the Virginia Company of London and, for profit motives, a much more substantial one in the East India Company. In 1620 the prospects of expanding the king's overseas realm and exploiting the natural resources of the area led Calvert to acquire the southeastern peninsula of Newfoundland from Sir William Vaughan. In the summer of 1621 he sent an expedition there to scout its economic potential. Reports of a rich variety of staples—timber, hemp, tar, iron—encouraged Calvert to seek to develop a permanent settlement there. The following summer he dispatched fifty men to begin commercial cod fishing as well as to construct a village and manor house. Two years later Calvert obtained a royal charter for the province of Avalon, which showed all the signs of his own devising. The charter granted an extraordinary set of powers: the same rights and privileges that "any Bishop of Durham within the Bishopprick or country palatine of Durham... hath at any time heretofore had."[2] The rights and privileges that these borderland bishops had enjoyed were the gold standard of royal grants. Among their powers were the creation of titled nobility, the establishment of manors and lordships, the prosecution of war, the instituting of martial law, the enactment of laws and ordinances, the establishment of courts, the regulation of trade, the imposition of taxes, the incorporation of cities, and the establishment of churches. No one under the king had more power and authority than the Bishop of Durham.

For two years Calvert ignored the Newfoundland project. Then in

2. Hughes, *History of the Society of Jesus; Text,* 1:177.

1625 he returned to it, now bringing a new perspective, as a Catholic, to the prospects of a settlement. As Simon Stock, a discalced Carmelite whose services Calvert had enlisted for the undertaking, wrote in February:

Among… others whom I have here converted to Our Holy Faith there is a lord of a land some three weeks' distance by sea from Great Britain, where Our Holy Faith has never been preached. And in the spring this gentleman means to return to his land with his servants… and desires to take with him two or three religious to sew the Holy Faith in his land.[3]

Stock was wrong. Calvert had not yet been to Newfoundland. Nor did he get there in 1625. Charles, the new king in whose ascension the Catholic community had such hopes for the betterment of their condition, had initially seemed to be all they had dared hope he would be. In one of his very first acts Charles suspended the penal laws under which Catholics had struggled for so long. For Catholics the Stuart monarch could not have sent a clearer signal that a new day was at hand. When he appointed a Catholic to the high post of chancellor, that dawning seemed even more of a reality. But very quickly Parliament and its allies had forced the king to reactivate the state's by now highly developed anti-Catholic machinery. Penal laws were not only once again enforced but enforced with ruthless efficiency. Priests were imprisoned. Privy Council members, of whom Calvert was still one, were ordered to take the oath of supremacy and oath of allegiance. Calvert, refusing to take the first and asking for more time to consider taking the latter, submitted his resignation from the council.

In these circumstances Calvert postponed his trip to Newfoundland until the following spring. Instead, he went to explore his Irish estates, extending over nearly 4,000 acres. He left behind Simon Stock to lobby Rome for clergy for Avalon and to recruit Catholics to join Calvert in the undertaking. As a Catholic, Calvert wanted a significant community of his coreligionists, including priests, in Avalon. Stock proceeded to launch a two-year campaign to persuade curial officials in Rome of the

3. Simon Stock, letter to the Congregation of the Propagation of the Faith, London, February 8, 1625, in *The Coldest Harbour of the Land: Simon Stock and Lord Baltimore's Colony in Newfoundland, 1621–1629*, by Luca Codignola (Kingston and Montreal: McGill-Queen's University Press, 1988), 77.

paramount need for the church to "establish missions in all those lands which the English hold in America."[4]

That a Catholic was founding a colony in Newfoundland was a marvelous opportunity for the Church to secure a presence there. Newfoundland would be the bridgehead from which missionaries could easily make their way eventually to the other British colonies and beyond. In the region of Newfoundland, Stock claimed, a mariner had recently discovered the long sought-after Northwest Passage. Newfoundland was the ultimate gateway to Asia, long an evangelical target of the Holy See. How much of Stock's hyperbolic story Rome believed is unknown. He was at the time virtually their only source on America. Eventually the Congregation of the Propagation of the Faith (*Propaganda Fide*) did make two priests available for the Avalon mission.

Called back into government service when England found itself in wars against both France and Spain, Calvert postponed the trip to Newfoundland until the late spring of 1627, when he decided he could wait no longer. It was obvious, as he told Sir Thomas Wentworth, that the place was being run badly. If he could not personally turn things around, he had to put an end to the operation, despite all the wealth he had poured into the venture. Calvert and a mixed company of Protestants and Catholics, including two secular priests, set sail on June 1. Satisfied that the situation at Avalon was stable, Calvert returned to England that fall. The following spring, together with family, relatives, and at least thirty other Catholics, he retraced his route to Newfoundland to take over the direction of the colony.

A year and a half later Calvert concluded that, despite his heavy investment (£20,000 to £25,000), Avalon was not the place to build his colony. "There is a sad face of wynter upon all this land," he wrote the king.[5] Half the hundred people in the settlement were habitually sick from the unforgiving climate. At least nine had died. The soil he found too rocky for productive farming. And England's war with France had

4. Stock to the Congregation of the Propagation of the Faith, London, May 31, 1625, in Codignola, *Coldest Harbour*, 84.
5. Krugler, *English and Catholic*, 102.

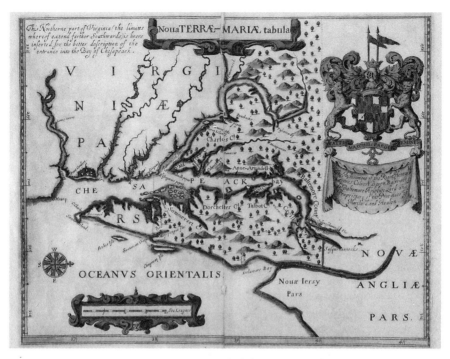

Nova Terrae Mariae Tabula (originally 1635)

spilled over to the island's waters where Calvert, with six ships supplied him by the crown, had to fight off hostile forces. He considered simply abandoning his colonial ambitions but on second thought decided to try his fortunes in a milder clime farther south. From Avalon he petitioned the king for a grant of unsettled land in the Chesapeake area, just north of Virginia, territory that had originally been part of the grant to the now defunct Virginia Company of London. "I may yet do the King and my Country more service there," he explained, "by planting of Tobacco."[6] In the late summer of 1629, leaving behind two small settlements at Fer-

6. Lawrence C. Wroth, *Tobacco or Codfish: Lord Baltimore Makes His Choice* (New York: New York Public Library, 1954, quoted in David Beers Quinn, *England and the Discovery of America, 1481–1620* (New York: Alfred A. Knopf, 1974), 395.

ryland and Petty Harbour, Calvert, together with his family and a majority of the settlers, weighed anchor to reconnoiter that possible site.

Calvert's stay in Virginia proved to be a very brief one. Arriving in
September, Lord Baltimore and his party received a chilly reception.
William Claiborne and the other Virginia officials knew too well that
the king's former secretary had been one of the principal parties responsible for the nullification of their charter five years earlier. When Calvert
proceeded to divulge his intention of transferring his settlement from
Newfoundland to the Chesapeake, the air got chillier. If the Catholic
Calvert wanted to develop a part of Virginia, he would first have to take
the oaths of supremacy and allegiance. The baron proposed taking an al-
ternate oath of his own devising, but Virginia officials declared that unacceptable. So Calvert, leaving his family and the other Avalon émigrés
behind, headed back to England to pursue a charter, despite Virginia's
opposition.

Claiborne, meanwhile, turned to England as well to utilize his thick
connections to thwart Calvert's plans. They quickly proved to be very
effective. Awaiting Lord Baltimore at home was a letter from the king
in which he urged Calvert to give up his colonizing dreams and return
to the government where he was needed, advice that Calvert found his
friends echoing. Lord Baltimore would have none of it. Having seen the
richness of the Chesapeake country made him all the more determined
to plant a colony there. For a time everything seemed to conspire against
that happening. The ship carrying his wife and servants back to England
sank off the coast of Ireland with the loss of all aboard. His household
was ravaged by the bubonic plague that swept over London in the summer of 1630. Calvert had exhausted his money. The king, from whom
Baltimore hoped to receive grants as well as a charter, was in the same
condition.

TERRA MARIAE

Still, Calvert persisted in his efforts. On Halloween 1631 he at last secured one of the *sine qua nons* for the launching of the venture: the grant
from the king of an annual pension of £1,000. Four months later he

gained the other, when the Privy Council approved the preparation of a charter for Calvert's Terra Mariae, or Maryland. The name derived from the king's suggestion that the colony be named "Marianus" in honor of the queen, Henrietta Maria. When Calvert pointed out that that was the name of a Jesuit who had written "against monarchy," a euphemistic reference to Marianus's defense of regicide, they settled on "Terra Mariae."[7] The charter granted to Lord Baltimore all the undeveloped ("not yet cultivated and planted") land between Delaware Bay and the Potomac River. As Calvert had requested, the charter contained the same powers and privileges as the Avalon charter. In Maryland, as in Avalon, Baltimore was to be an absolute lord.

Calvert did not live to receive the charter he had fought so long to obtain. For nearly a decade he had suffered occasional illnesses. The winter in Newfoundland had weakened him further. In mid-April 1632, at the age of fifty-two, he succumbed to his ills. Two months later his son and heir, Cecil, got word that the charter had been impressed with the royal seals.

The twenty-six-year-old Cecil, who began to live as a Catholic about the same time as his father, took up his father's work of planning for the colony, assisted by a Jesuit, Andrew White, who, at George Calvert's urging, had joined Lord Baltimore in London sometime in the spring or summer of 1630. Calvert and White had begun a correspondence in the fall of 1628 when Calvert was in Newfoundland and White was teaching theology at the Jesuit college in Liège. What initiated this exchange we do not know, but it marked the beginning of the Calverts' relationship with the Society of Jesus that would constitute the official face of Catholicism in British America.

There were a number of reasons for George Calvert to have sought a substantial Jesuit participation in his colonization project. The Society had a fundamental commitment to provide men for the missions of the church. The English province had a surplus of men, something Calvert had already discovered from the two Jesuits the Society had made available for his colony in Newfoundland and from White's availability to

7. Hughes, *History of the Society of Jesus; Text*, 1:236.

Cecil Calvert (1605–75)

serve Calvert as planner and publicist. The English province had a financial surplus that could provide vital funding for the expedition. And for
the Jesuits Maryland ultimately offered a place of refuge should they find
themselves ordered out of England, the penalty for losing the struggle
with the English secular clergy over the nature and future of the church
in that country. At the time they were clearly winning, having succeeded,

with George Calvert's vigorous involvement, in forcing William Bishop to flee England, thus bringing an end, for the present, to episcopal governance of the English Catholic community, including the Society of Jesus. But who could tell what the future held?

The Calverts, drawing upon the experience of the Catholic community since the Reformation came to England, brought a singular perspective to the shaping of a colony that affected both its economy and its religious life. With his conversion Calvert, as we have seen, began to incorporate the Catholic community into his plans for Avalon. His father-in-law, Lord Arundell, who had been one of the leaders of the attempt in 1605, may have been an influence in shaping his planning, particularly in regard to the feudal nature of the community. To attract and protect Catholics there he put into practice a policy of religious toleration for both Catholics and Protestants. For Maryland the planning, begun by George and carried on by Cecil, became more comprehensive. The Calverts wanted a settlement, first of all, that would be profitable. Maryland represented a very expensive investment from which father and son expected a lucrative return. But if the quest for profit was primary, the Calverts' concern to construct a society where Catholics could participate fully was genuine enough.

To an extent, George and Cecil Calvert hoped to replicate the landholding pattern of feudal England. The Catholic adventurers that they hoped to attract would form the nucleus of the feudal pattern of manorial settlement and governance that the Calverts envisioned for their colony. The manorial system would indeed be the structure to ensure that Catholics would be both free and at peace with their neighbors. As Catholicism in England had survived largely because of the relative security and freedom that the gentry manor houses provided, so a more comprehensive and legally sanctioned manorial system would, they hoped, ensure that the colony would flourish economically and religion remain private (see chapter 2). "Maryland," John D. Krugler has noted, "was to be the manor writ large."[8] As for governance, the Calverts envisioned a

8. Krugler, "Lord Baltimore, Roman Catholics, and Toleration: Religious Policy in Maryland During the Early Catholic Years, 1634–1649," *Catholic Historical Review* 65 (1979): 74.

limited participation of the property holders. There would be a governor
and council, the latter appointed by the proprietor from the manorial
lords, as well as a parliament composed of the freeholders.

To attract potential men of wealth and standing to invest in the venture, as well as to join it, Cecil Calvert published in the winter of 1632–
1633 *A Declaration of the Lord Baltimore's Plantation in Maryland*, the
first of three tracts to appear over the next three years. The pamphlet,
written by White, laid out the proprietor's objectives. The primary goal,
White claimed, reflecting his own priority rather than Baltimore's, was
the spreading of Christianity, particularly to the natives. Crucial also was
the extension of England's presence within the New World, a not-so-
subtle affirmation of Catholic loyalty to the crown. Finally, the objective
that they hoped would reel in both planters and investors: the harvesting
of the abundant natural resources of the region that promised prosperity
to those who joined the venture. The tract delineated the generous terms
under which adventurers could acquire land. For every five servants
brought into the colony, a person would be granted 2,000 acres.

THE FIRST ADVENTURERS
AND SETTLERS

The campaign of the Calverts to secure investors and to recruit Catholics and Protestants of wealth and social standing for Maryland proved
to be very disappointing. Investment in the joint-stock company set up
to support the colony provided but half the needed shares. Baltimore
himself had to absorb the rest. In addition, he had to furnish passage
for twenty-five servants that he had expected others to sponsor. That
the response from the potential Catholic adventurers should have been
so tepid should not have surprised them. Since Charles's early anti-
Catholic campaign that he had been forced to undertake, the condition
of the Catholic community had undeniably improved; at court Catholics
had unprecedented influence. For the Catholic nobility, Maryland had
nothing to offer. For the gentry, the prospect of transferring their manorial existence from England to the Chesapeake seemed highly impractical.
John Bossy suggests a deeper source of their reluctance: the tendency of

Catholics to identify their religion, in which sacraments and other sacred objects figure so vitally, very strongly with place and tradition—to invest them with a sacred character, as it were.[9] Such people were poor prospects psychologically for transplanting themselves across the Atlantic. Thus, besides Cecil Calvert's two brothers and the two Jesuit priests, there were only fifteen or so of the nobility and gentry, most of whom were Catholic. The nobles, in addition to the Calverts, included the younger sons of Sir Thomas Gerrard and Sir Thomas Wiseman, as well as two sons of Lady Ann Wintour. Among the Catholic gentry were the two chief officers of the colony, the commissioners Jerome Hawley and Thomas Cornwaleys. Virtually all of them came from families with a history of interest in colonization or with a connection to the Calverts. Thomas Cornwaleys was fairly typical. A devout Roman Catholic who was committed to planting his religion in Britain's dominion within the New World, Cornwaleys, as an ambitious second son with limited prospects at home, saw compelling advantages in casting his lot in Maryland, particularly with Calvert promising him trading privileges there and a license to build a mill, as well as a seat on the provincial council. The Cornwaleys and Calverts were related by marriage. Cornwaleys's father and grandfather had both invested in earlier colonial ventures. Cornwaleys himself made the second-largest investment in the Maryland enterprise.

The Calverts made no attempt to secure the artisans and other laborers needed for Maryland, perhaps realizing the difficulty of finding enough Catholics of those classes. Instead, they relied on the gentlemen adventurers to transport enough servants (in order to qualify for land grants) to provide a work force for the colony. When the 400-ton *Ark* and 40-ton pinnace *Dove* prepared to sail from Gravesend in November 1633, there were 125 or so servants onboard, nearly all of them Protestants, mostly males between the ages of sixteen and twenty-five. The governor, the two commissioners, and the Jesuits controlled the service of at least two-thirds of them. By various estimates the Jesuits accounted for anywhere from twenty-some to forty-four of the servants.[10] We do know

9. Bossy, "Reluctant Colonists: The English Catholics Confront the Atlantic," in *Early Maryland in a Wider World*, edited by David Beers Quinn, 159 (Detroit: Wayne State University Press, 1982).
10. Hughes, *History of the Society of Jesus; Text,* 1:264.

that over the first six years of the colony's history they were responsible for bringing in at least fifty servants, more than any other adventurer. They also seem to have been responsible, either from their own resources or from those of lay spiritual advisees, for a large portion of the funds raised to make the journey possible.

Once at sea the ships stopped at the Isle of Wight, where most of the Catholics, including the Jesuits, apparently came aboard to avoid taking the oath of allegiance that was required of all those leaving England. Then came a calm that prevented the ships from clearing the harbor. "We were not without apprehension," White later wrote:

[f]or the sailors were murmuring among themselves, saying they were expecting a messenger with letters from London, and from this it seemed as if they were contriving to delay us. But God brought their plans to confusion. For that very night, a favorable but strong wind arose; and a French cutter, which had put into the same harbor with us, being forced to sail, came near running into our pinnace. The latter, therefore, to avoid being run down, having cut away and lost an anchor, set sail without delay... And so that we might not lose sight of our pinnace, we determined to follow. Thus the designs of the sailors, who were plotting against us, were frustrated.[11]

The providential-minded priest noted that it was the feast day (November 22) of St. Clement, who had been martyred by being tied to an anchor and cast into the sea. Now God was displaying his power anew by the losing of an anchor. White was sure that Clement was protecting them as they began their voyage to the New World.

They were at sea a little more than seven weeks, a rapid crossing in the seventeenth century, despite encountering a hurricane that nearly wrecked them. Still, ocean travel was a trying experience: cramped, water-soaked quarters; a Spartan diet of biscuit, cheese, beer, perhaps dried meat. There had been stays of several weeks at Barbados and Guadeloupe, so it was late February when they finally reached Virginia. Lord Baltimore had instructed them to seek landfall at Accomack, on Virginia's Eastern Shore of Chesapeake Bay, where they were to engage a pilot to guide them to the territory granted by the charter to Calvert. Under no circumstanc-

11. Andrew White, *Relatio Itineris in Marylandium* (Baltimore: Maryland Historical Society, 1874).

es were they to land at Jamestown, Calvert no doubt remembering the hostile reception he had had from Virginia's officials four years earlier. For whatever reason, the adventurers ignored Baltimore's injunction and landed at Jamestown. There they found that most Virginia officials, including William Claiborne, were no more welcoming than they had been to Calvert. Fortunately, the disposition of the governor of the colony toward the newcomers was a pole apart from that of his council. He entertained them for more than a week, gave them valuable information about the region, and promised to provide provisions for their support. Apparently the governor was hoping through his openness and generosity to gain the assistance of Baltimore, a known favorite of the king, in recovering money owed him by the crown. In early March the expedition pushed up the Chesapeake for the Potomac. On one of the islands in the lower Potomac, they first landed in their new homeland. They named the island for St. Clement.

ESTABLISHING A PRESENCE

Following Lord Baltimore's instructions, Governor Calvert first set out to establish good relations with the Algonquin tribes that inhabited the region. Sailing up the Potomac to Piscataway Creek, where the nominal ruling tribe had its village, about fifteen miles below the fall line of the river, Calvert and his party encountered an armed group of Piscataways lining the riverbank. Devastating attacks upon the tribe by both Europeans (Virginians) and Amerindians (Erie) over the past decade had bred hostility to all outsiders. When Calvert sought permission from Wannas, the tayac (emperor) of the Piscataways, to establish a settlement in the area, the chief was utterly noncommittal, telling Calvert essentially that it was his choice to make. Calvert took that as a suggestion to look elsewhere and headed back downriver, satisfied that the promise of trade and protection against the threatening northern tribes (the Erie and Susquehanna) would ensure the good will of the Piscataway. Nearly ninety miles south, just down from St. Clement's Island, the governor received a much friendlier reception from the Yaocomicos, with whom he exchanged cloth and tools for thirty miles of land from the tribe (land, it should be noted, that the Indians had already decided to abandon as too vulnerable to attacks by the Susquehanna swooping down the Chesapeake Bay).

On the site of the Yaocomicos's former village, on a bluff overlooking a tributary of the lower Potomac River, the settlers built a palisade, whose crude wooden structures within probably housed the majority of the settlers over the first three years. From the enclosure, which they named St. Mary's, the settlers went out to work their crops in the surrounding open fields.

Maryland initially experienced a less lethal seasoning of its settlers than Virginia had during its infancy. To begin, Lord Baltimore's people had arrived in early spring, in time for the planting season. The site they had purchased from the natives contained rich soil that yielded a good harvest of corn and other vegetables. Unlike the initial Englishmen to inhabit Virginia, they experienced no starving time. Still, the unaccustomed climate extremes and diseases of the region took their toll on probably more than a fifth of the newcomers. During the particularly harsh winter of 1638–1639, sixteen colonists succumbed, including Jerome Hawley, the commissioner. Malaria, yellow fever, and other diseases claimed scores over the first decade, including the Jesuit lay brother, Thomas Gervase. Another Jesuit died from an accidental shooting. By 1639 only six gentlemen adventurers of the original twenty remained. Of the first fourteen Jesuits who came to Maryland, more than half had died by 1646.

Despite the deaths and departures, a steady stream of immigrants throughout the late 1630s and early 1640s brought an annual increase in population of 10 percent. Baltimore was able to recruit additional adventurers, more of them Protestants than the original group, and they all brought people with them. Most prominent among the Catholic newcomers was the Brent family, Giles and his sisters Margaret and Mary, who arrived in the colony in November 1638. The well-connected Brents of Gloucestershire had converted to Catholicism in the mid-1620s. Three of the sisters had entered a recusant convent at Cambrai. The remaining two, along with their brother, decided to make their future in Maryland when Lord Baltimore appointed Giles Brent treasurer of the province.

Most of the immigrants were not gentry but indentured servants, over-whelmingly male. Indeed, the general population remained male-heavy (about six men to every woman), the imbalance being more pronounced among servants than freeman, more among freemen than gentry.

The temporary concentration of the population at St. Mary's during the first three years might have reflected the primacy of fur trading in the economic goals that the planners had set for the colony. But the fur business quickly brought not lucrative profits but a financial crisis. The supply of furs in the region, it turned out, was quite limited. Most of the furs they were able to gather rotted in St. Mary's harbor awaiting shipment as the *Dove* underwent repairs of damage incurred during the voyage from England. When the *Dove* finally sailed with the remaining furs, it sank at sea; with it went any hope of redeeming the investment they had made to launch trade operations. The fur business continued on a very limited scale but was never the major source of revenue that the Calverts had expected.

A more likely explanation for the delay in taking up manorial lands was the expectation that Cecil Baltimore would be arriving in the very near future to direct the development of the province. When it became obvious to Baltimore that he needed to remain in London to protect the interests of his colony, he authorized his brother, Leonard, to proceed with the granting of land under updated conditions of plantation.

MANORIAL MARYLAND

The first grants were enormous: 12,000 acres each to Thomas Cornwa-leys, Richard Gerrard, Jerome Hawley, and John Saunders. Gerrard sub-sequently, perhaps by prearrangement, passed on to the Jesuits his grant, St. Inigoes, just south of St. Mary's. Others, such as Giles Brent and Thomas Gerrard, received smaller grants ranging from 1,000 to 6,000 acres. By 1642 there were sixteen manors that had been laid out—some 31,000 acres that represented over four-fifths of the land that had been patented. These manorial lords also gained, under the same conditions of plantation, 10 acres each of town land, which amounted to 90 percent of the property that constituted St. Mary's. The proprietor's intention

was that the lords, as in England, with town houses as well as rural estates, would be the central figures in both town and countryside. The
lords' surplus town holdings, Baltimore figured, they could lease or sell
off as the value of land increased with the growth of the colony.

These urban lordly residences never materialized. Indeed, St. Mary's
failed to develop as a commercial center. Given the bulk of tobacco bales,
easy access to water was a necessity for shipment. The labyrinth water-
ways of the region provided docks at individual plantations where tobacco could be loaded onto oceangoing vessels; there was no need for
a central port. During the first decade of Maryland's history, however,
St. Mary's did function as something more than the place where the governor lived and the legislature assembled once a year. Before the shipping of tobacco from waterside plantations became the norm, the town
served as the colony's port and financial center as well as its capital.
Stretching out from the town north and south were the manors whose
merchant-planters dominated the economy, from the cultivation of tobacco that had quickly become the chief source of revenue in Maryland
to the control of the credit that financed it. As Lois Green Carr, among
others, notes, "They held the most important government positions and
directed the spread of settlement. They owned the factors of production—land, capital, and most of the unfree labor—and they dominated
local marketing and credit networks.... To a point, the manorial system
operated according to plan: most of the wealthier gentlemen took up
manors, and most of the more ordinary settlers lived on those manors as
servants or as freedmen—that is, ex-servants."[12]

Thomas Gerrard took up his manorial grant north of the capital, at
Mattapany, on a bay he called St. Clement's, the same name he gave his
estate. Given his English gentry background, he probably intended for
his manor to be populated with dependent tenants, as the estates of the
Catholic aristocracy in England had been. The problem in Maryland was
a lack of men with the freedom to rent or to work as laborers. In 1642,
five years after taking over St. Clement's, Gerrard still had but three ten-

12. Lois Green Carr, Russell R. Menard, and Lorena S. Walsh, *Robert Cole's World: Agriculture
and Society in Early Maryland* (Chapel Hill: University of North Carolina Press for the Institute of
Early American History and Culture, 1991), 10.

ants but twenty indentured servants. There was one distinct benefit that accrued from the acquisition of servants for a limited period of labor (four or five years). Thanks to the Conditions of Plantation, the more servants one was responsible for bringing into the colony, the more land one was eligible to receive. So Gerrard, whose initial grant in 1638 was merely 1,000 acres, increased that sixfold in 1642. By 1651 Gerrard's property encompassed over 14,000 acres, too large a tract in fact for Gerrard to come close to fully developing so long as there was a dearth of freemen to sign on as tenants.

Tobacco quickly became the staple of commercial agriculture. Despite planters' initial doubts about the soundness of investing in a commodity whose prices were known to fluctuate wildly, tobacco had proven to be a boon for the economy from the beginning, as the colonists had begun production at a time of rising prices. Indeed, as early as 1637, the staple was functioning as the currency of the colony. Gerrard had quickly cleared hardwoods and pines from his property to plant tobacco over a broad swath of his land. Within five years of the colony's founding in 1634, Maryland was exporting 100,000 pounds of tobacco from large plantations like St. Clement's. But St. Clement's was more than a plantation worked by servants and tenants. It was a judicial center as well as an economic center. As Baltimore intended, Gerrard established a manorial court that had jurisdiction over the inhabitants of the immediate area. As the possessor of a manor, Gerrard was among the elite eligible for appointment to the provincial council, which he eventually received. As Lorena S. Walsh notes, "settlers in the St. Clement's area looked to the manor house at Mattapany to provide protection, direction, and legal services."[13] The Catholic Gerrard was planter, judge, provincial ruler, and lord of his manor.

The manor, despite Calvert's intention, never became the dominant land unit in the colony, the underpinning of an agrarian aristocracy. In 1642 the sixteen manors accounted for over four-fifths of the patented land. That, as it turned out, represented the high-water mark of manori-

13. Lorena S. Walsh, "Community Networks in the Early Chesapeake," in *Colonial Chesapeake Society*, edited by Lois Green Carr, Philip D. Morgan, and Jean B. Russo (Chapel Hill: University of North Carolina Press for the Institute of Early American History, 1988), 204.

al Maryland, as the pattern of landholding changed dramatically beginning in the 1640s.

There were factors very much working against the manor becoming
the socioeconomic center of Maryland society. The pressing need for labor meant that servants, once having fulfilled their term of indenture,
could build up enough capital from the high wages paid farm laborers
to acquire the land and tools to become farmers themselves. In 1642 over
half the labor force in Maryland was free, not indentured. In that same
year a quarter of the adult males owned land. The headright system
established by Lord Baltimore in the 1630s awarded hundreds of acres
to every family immigrating to the province. Such land availability was
made even more attractive by the nature of tobacco cultivation, which did
not require the large-scale production of a plantation. The colony's dominant staple could be raised on a middling-sized farm. The single-family
farm or plantation, not the manor, would be the future of Maryland's development. Upward mobility, not hierarchical stasis, would increasingly
characterize its social order over the next several decades. By the latter
part of the century there would be some justification in Maryland's reputation as the "poor man's best country."

During this first decade, in which Calvert's dream of establishing a
neo-feudal society of manorial fiefdoms came closest to being realized,
the proportion of Catholics also peaked at the beginning of the 1640s
at something like a quarter of the four hundred persons in the colony.
Immigration and conversions accounted for the increase of Catholics in
a population that was growing by 10 percent a year. It was in this first
decade also that Lord Baltimore's vision regarding the place of religion
in the society, including the relationship of church to state, took flesh in
the policies and practices that emerged in the newest colony, partly as a
consequence of the bitter controversy that developed between the proprietor and the Jesuits whom he had urged to join his enterprise to meet
the religious needs of settlers and natives.

CHAPTER 2

"HOLY CHURCH SHALL HAVE ALL HER RIGHTS, LIBERTIES, AND IMMUNITIES"

Church and State in Early Maryland

RELIGIOUS LIBERTY AND THE COMMONWEAL

Cecil Calvert had issued instructions to his brother, Leonard, the governor of the new colony, that all acts of Catholic worship were to be done privately. The proprietor's stricture did not prevent the Catholic minority among the settlers, including the governor himself, from formally inaugurating their colony with the celebration of a public Mass by Andrew White on St. Clement's Island on March 25, 1634, the Feast of the Annunciation and, as noted earlier, the first day of the new year. After Mass in solemn procession they carried a great cross to the highest point of the 400-acre island. There it was planted as a towering sign that Roman Catholicism had come to Chesapeake country, while Governor Calvert, the commissioners, and the other Catholics, on bended knees, chanted the litany of the Holy

Cross. As would be true so often in Maryland, policy did not translate easily into practice.

The other public ritual that took place shortly after the voyagers landed in Maryland was a communal oath-taking. Lord Baltimore, to undercut any charges that a colony whose proprietor and principal settlers were Catholic could not be loyal, had everyone take an oath of allegiance to the king. Unlike the oath required of all those departing England, Calvert's said nothing about the pope. Unspoken was the assumption that loyalty need not be confined to a single sphere, the political, but could morally function in separate spheres—that is, the political and the religious, with different objects of one's allegiance.

Among the powers and privileges that the Maryland charter bestowed on Cecil Calvert was the right to erect churches. There was one stipulation, however. Any such church erection had to be done "according to the Ecclesiastical Lawes of our Kingdome of England." David Quinn has suggested that this provision created a dilemma for Calvert: either he could establish the Anglican Church in Maryland or adopt a policy of separation of church and state.[1] Calvert chose the latter, and would have done so even without the religious bind in which the charter put him.

In the conventional thought of the seventeenth century, the separation of church and state was a contradiction in terms. Religion was considered too central to the total life of a society to admit more than one faith. To admit religious freedom was tantamount to admitting social anarchy. The Reformation had broken the unity of Christendom, but a more local ideal of unity had taken its place: the principle of *cujus regio, ejus religio*—that is, that the ruler of a particular state determined what the religion of the people would be. One simply could not divide one's political loyalty from one's religious allegiance. Uniformity was the norm in both the political and religious realms. The ruler was the enforcer of both tables of God's commandments: those that related to worship as well as those dealing with the social order. This was particularly the case in England, where the sovereign was the head of the church as well as of

1. David Beers Quinn, ed., *Early Maryland in a Wider World* (Detroit: Wayne State University Press, 1982), 27.

Settlement of Maryland by Lord Baltimore

the state. Penal laws were measures designed to pressure Catholics into conformity with that reality.

Implicit in the Calverts' planning for Maryland was the commitment to religious liberty. That had been the policy in practice at Avalon, where Protestants and Catholics gathered under the same roof but in separate rooms to worship. As noted in the introduction, since the end of the sixteenth century Catholic writers had been advocating toleration as the crown's standard for dealing with religious dissidents. By the 1630s this was a well-established position, one with which Calvert almost surely was familiar. For several reasons he chose to implement it in his new colony. He knew from the outset that it would have a religiously pluralistic population (Catholics, it turned out, were a small minority from the beginning). Toleration, in this light, was a prudent entrepreneur's way of protecting his investment in the New World. As a 1649 pamphlet, *Objections Answered Touching Maryland*, defending the religious toleration of the colony put it, to force allegiance to a particular religion was to undermine the state itself, since those who feign religious beliefs for political or social ends cannot in the end be trusted.

There was no way under English law that Calvert could make Roman Catholicism the established religion in Maryland. More importantly, there is no indication that Calvert preferred this possibility. As an English Catholic Lord Baltimore shared the realization, implicit as it might have been, that a separation of church and state was the painful reality the Catholic community had known for nearly a century. In his colony such a separation would be the unstated relationship between religion and government. The Assembly in March of 1639 appeared to enact this policy into law when it passed an act that declared that "Holy Churches within this province shall have all her rights and liberties." Was the ambiguity a deliberate attempt to obfuscate the religious situation in Maryland? It seems not. The act as originally proposed read, "Holy Church shall have all her rights, liberties, and immunities safe whole and inviolable in all things."[2] "Churches" was probably nothing more than a scribe's nodding. But whatever the language of the law might suggest, there was to be no established church in Maryland.

Court records indicate the lengths to which provincial officials were willing to go to enforce toleration. In 1638 they fined William Lewis, the Catholic overseer at the Jesuits' St. Inigoes plantation, the punitive sum of five hundred pounds of tobacco for forbidding two servants there to read any Protestant books and for declaring Protestant ministers to be instruments of the devil. Four years later Thomas Gerrard found himself in court for having refused the further use of his chapel to his Protestant servants and having appropriated some Protestant books he discovered there. The court ordered him to make the chapel available to them and to put £100 in escrow for the support of the first Protestant minister to arrive in the colony. In Maryland there was to be no conformity in reli-

2. Proceedings and Acts of the General Assembly of Maryland at a Session held at St. Mary's, February 25 to March 19, 1638–1639, *Archives of Maryland*, ed. William Hand Brown (Baltimore: Maryland Historical Society, 1883–), 1:40, 82–83.

gion, even within the private boundaries of manor lands. Just as the proprietor had chosen not to impose any religion upon settlers in his colony, so manorial lords were not free within their estates to enforce religious conformity.

CLERICAL PLANTERS

With the practical separation of church and state there could be no government support of religion, a prospect that Cecil Calvert made clear when he sought to have a Jesuit presence in his colony. If the Society agreed to provide members to minister to the settlers as well as to evangelize the natives, the Jesuits would be treated in the same manner as gentlemen adventurers. They would qualify for land grants according to the number of persons they brought into the province and be responsible for supporting their ministry from the revenue they realized from working that land. In brief, in Maryland, unlike England, they would be clerical planters, not resident chaplains of the manorial lords.

The Jesuits reluctantly accepted this arrangement. Over the first five years of Maryland's history, they accounted for sixty-two persons—Jesuits and indentured servants to work their lands—of the three hundred or so who had arrived in the province. Such a large number of persons imported qualified the Jesuits, under the Conditions of Plantation, to 15,700 acres of manor land and 455 acres of town land. The first land they acquired, St. Inigoes, came not from a grant but by a purchase from Richard Gerrard somewhere around 1637. Two years later they had surveyed three parcels of land due them under the headright system, totaling nearly 9,000 acres along the Patuxent River. In the late 1630s they received land from a new source: the Patuxent Indians. That gift proved to be the catalyst for a long-running controversy between the proprietor and the Jesuits about the "rights, liberties, and immunities" that the Jesuits, as the embodiment of the Roman Catholic Church in Maryland, could expect to enjoy.

Over the course of the next eighty years the Society of Jesus would continue, through the Conditions of Plantation, legacies, and purchases, to acquire additional property. Their several plantations, with a labor force approaching two hundred, would be a prominent part of the colonial landscape in southern Maryland, much more so than on the Eastern Shore where they acquired land in the eighteenth century.

In the former Indian village that the settlers moved into in late March 1634, the Jesuits appropriated a twenty-foot longhouse for a chapel. Here they began their ministry, saying Mass daily for a mixed congregation of Catholics and Protestants, many of the latter eventually converts. Despite Lord Baltimore's instruction that the Catholics not raise the topic of religion with their Protestant brethren, the Jesuits in St. Mary's and elsewhere clearly proselytized, particularly those Protestants who were gravely ill or dying, even if it meant overcoming resistance of family or friends to their efforts. In 1638, for instance, a Jesuit, hearing that a Protestant settler was near death from a snake bite, took himself and a surgeon to the house where the man lay dying, only to be turned away by the head of the household. Undeterred, priest and surgeon waited until the house was dark and surreptitiously entered. There the surgeon treated the victim while the priest persuaded him to become a Catholic. When the man unexpectedly recovered and left his friend's house rather than retract his conversion, the Jesuit took it as God's blessing upon his persistence. Whatever the circumstances, the scale of conversions was impressive: a score or so in 1638; a dozen the following year.

Sometime around 1640 the Jesuits replaced the longhouse with a wooden chapel, where they continued to offer public Mass. As early as 1638 they were giving retreats to laymen in the form of the *Spiritual Exercises* of St. Ignatius. When they took up manorial land at St. Inigoes and along the Patuxent, their houses served as liturgical centers for the local Catholic community. They also began, in the 1640s, to establish missions to serve the outlying communities.

SPREADING THE KINGDOM

As Andrew White had made clear in the advertising pamphlet he had prepared for Lord Baltimore, the conversion of Indians was the primary motivation that brought most Jesuits to Maryland during its first decade—the same impulse that had stirred Robert Persons's feelings about

Piscataway Prayers of Rev. Andrew White, SJ

colonization three decades earlier. Ignatian spirituality nurtured in Jesuits a pressing desire to serve apostolically by seeking out those missions
that were the most promising in advancing God's kingdom against the
forces of evil. To Jesuits in the late sixteenth century, England seemed to
be the front line of that struggle. With conditions improving for Catholics under the Stuarts, the prospect of being chaplains to the gentry
hardly satisfied their hunger for heroic service. It was natural for them to
see in the founding of Maryland a providential opportunity to transplant
that apostolic zeal to a part of the world that God's kingdom had not
yet reached. The English provincial's call for volunteers for the Maryland
mission produced far more than he could send. As one applicant told
the provincial, when he learned of the invitation, "my joy was so great,

that no thought nor word for a long time could come from me which resounded not 'Maryland.'"[3] Another testified that for many years he had experienced "no smale inclination towards such a mission" and begged the provincial to send him "forthwith into those parts, there to spend *et superimpendere meipsum* in reducing those soules so deare to Christ our Lord, and for His sake more deare to me than my very life."[4]

Initially the Jesuits were unable to take up the work that had motivated most of them to volunteer for Maryland. The few Jesuits, never more than five, had first of all to serve the community in their midst, the settlers around St. Mary's and its immediate vicinity, as well as take up the land that would support their ministry. Even if it had been feasible for them to begin their Indian mission in the early years of the colony, Maryland officials, concerned about a general Indian uprising, had declared their villages off-limits. When the fears subsided in 1638, the Jesuits immediately headed out from St. Mary's to carry the gospel to tribes on both sides of Chesapeake Bay. Andrew White moved to Mattapany to work among the Patuxents. John Altham was on Kent Island, where Indians from the northern portions of the bay came to trade. Andrew White was clearly hoping to convert the Patuxent's chief, Macquacomen, who had shown himself the most friendly of the Indian chiefs of the region, as the first step toward the conversion of the tribe. That was the traditional missionary strategy. White did baptize a few of the Patuxents but not Macquacomen. The latter was still well-disposed toward White—indeed, gave him the land around their town, Patuxent, as a sign of his benevolence. Then Leonard Calvert, who feared that the Patuxents might take White hostage in order to make some unknown demand upon the government, ordered White to leave the village. He moved north by canoe some eighty miles to work with the Piscataway, who were now suddenly open to an English presence. The new tayac, Kittamaquund, having alienated a good portion of the tribe by securing power by forcibly removing his brother, Wannas, had good reason to seek allies wherever he could against his internal enemies.

3. Hughes, *History of the Society of Jesus; Text*, 1:461.
4. Hughes, *History of the Society of Jesus; Text*, 1:473.

Soon after White's arrival among the Piscataway, Kittamaquund became seriously ill. After a couple scores of medicine men had failed to
cure him, White bled him and applied a certain powder mixed with holy
water. The chief recovered and shortly afterward sought instruction in
the faith that had given White such healing power. Kittamaquund may
have also hoped that baptism would give him some further claim upon
English support. In any event, Kittamaquund and his queen were baptized the following summer of 1640. The Jesuits' expectation was that,
once the chief and his family were baptized, the rest of the tribe would
quickly follow. To that end White had begun composing a catechism in
Piscataway (he later wrote a grammar and dictionary). Like his Jesuit
counterparts in Canada, White was committed to bringing Christianity
to the natives in their own language. He realized that he and his brethren needed to master the Indian language and culture if they were to
convert them to the Christian faith in any lasting way. Of the Jesuits,
White and Roger Rigbie, who succeeded White among the Patuxents,
came the closest to achieving fluency, but both realized how limited even
their grasp of the native language was.

The anticipated mass conversion did not happen. White himself,
during the protracted ceremony for the chief and his wife (both their
baptism and solemnization of their marriage), had come down with a
chilling fever that forced him to return to St. Mary's and battle the illness
for the remainder of the year. He returned briefly to Piscataway in February, only to suffer a relapse that caused him to abandon the mission for
a second time within a year. A month later the chief died.

White survived his recurring illness. John Altham, not so fortunate,
fell victim to yellow fever, as did John Brock, another Jesuit in the colony.
In July 1641 the current superior, Ferdinand Poulton, died after being ac-
cidentally shot. That same year the Susquehannocks suddenly increased
their incursions into Maryland waters to attack both natives and settlers,
invasions they would repeat in the following two summers. In March
they attacked the Jesuit trading vessel as it crossed the Chesapeake on
its way to Kent Island. In the wave of brutal attacks that the Susquehannocks carried out in 1642, the first English settlement they struck was
the Jesuit storehouse and trading center at Mattapany. That was prob-

ably by design to show the terrible price to be paid for having a special relationship with the Piscataway, as the Jesuits had had from the colony's beginning, when the order had been a major investor in the stock company set up for the fur trade. For good measure the Indians raided it again the following summer. Plundered goods, burned buildings, and several servants dead was the cumulative price for the Jesuits at Mattapany. But the carnage failed to deter the Jesuits from continuing their Indian mission to the Piscataway and the other Algonquian tribes.

With so few missioners available by 1642, however, the Jesuits could no longer afford to establish semi-permanent missions at villages. So they reluctantly had to decline an invitation from the chief of the Anacostans to have a Jesuit live in their village. Instead, in order to reach as many tribes as they could with so little manpower, they adopted the strategy of making short expeditions to villages. A missioner, accompanied by a servant and an interpreter, would set out by canoe, with supplies, gifts, and sacred vessels aboard, along the Potomac or Patuxent for a particular village. At the village the party would erect a tent for their short stay. An altar would be erected for the celebration of the Mass. Catechism lessons, usually through the interpreter, would be given.

Such brief but repeated visits brought promising results. The leaders of several villages were converted. At Portobacco not only the chief but most of his village were baptized. In all, in six years (1639 to 1645) the Jesuits were responsible for more than 130 Indians in the region becoming Catholics, usually after a protracted period of instruction and testing in the faith. What led them to seek baptism? The tangible nature of Catholicism, thick with sacraments and sacramentals, could be one attraction. The message of Christianity, garbled as it no doubt was in translation, could be another. Shaman-like healing power, which White displayed on at least two occasions, could be still another.[5] Considering the language barrier, the shortage of priests, and the inability (lacking the government

5. Besides the cure of Kittamaquund, White saved an apparently dying Anacostan Indian by reading the scripture over him, reciting the Litany of the Blessed Virgin, and applying the relic of the cross that White wore around his neck. White, who expected him to die, left instructions for his burial. A day later, making his way downriver, the priest was overtaken by two Anacostans, one of whom was the "dying" man, now displaying only a small spot where his supposedly mortal wound had been.

support that the French Jesuits enjoyed) to provide substantial goods to the tribes being evangelized, it was a remarkable record.

The Ingle invasion of Maryland in the late winter of 1645 (see chapter 3) brought an abrupt ending to the Jesuit evangelization of the natives, as all five priests were captured and taken out of the colony. When the first Jesuit, Thomas Copley (Philip Fisher) returned to Maryland three years later, the Indians in the region contacted him about visiting them again. "I scarcely know what to do," Copley explained to the superior general in Rome, "but cannot attend to all.... Truly flowers appear in our land—may they attain to fruit."[6] But there were no further harvests, as the Susquehannocks finally succeeded in the ensuing decade to force out of the Chesapeake region most of their fur trade rivals, nine Algonquian tribes who retreated westward. When there were enough Jesuits once again in Maryland to renew the Indian evangelization, few Indians were to be found. The mission that had been the primary reason for the Society of Jesus's commitment to the Maryland venture and the spur for most of the Jesuits who volunteered to labor there proved sadly to have a very short life span.

A NEUTRAL OR CONFESSIONAL STATE

As noted earlier, the Jesuits had very reluctantly agreed to send its members to Maryland without any support from Calvert. They would have the same rights as all the adventurers—nothing more, nothing less. Of course, the reality was that they did have a distinct status. Calvert, after all, had recruited them precisely because they were Jesuits who could minister to the Catholic settlers and evangelize the natives. He made no effort to include ministers of the Church of England. Whatever the reality, the bargain struck between Calvert and the Society of Jesus began to break down within the first two years. The Jesuits' conversion of many of the Protestants among the original settlers troubled Calvert. Such proselytizing, to his mind, was not consistent with the private nature of religion in Maryland. It was also dangerous, providing a perfect opportunity to

6. Philip Fisher to Vincenzo Caraffa, March 1, 1648, quoted in Henry Foley, *Records of the English Province of the Society of Jesus* (London: Burns and Oates, 1883), 1:256.

exacerbate the opposition to Jesuits that in London now included the royal couple. The Archbishop of Canterbury, so went the rumors, was set to petition the Privy Council to strip Calvert of his colony because he had allowed Jesuits there. For their part, Jesuits resented the proprietor's governor restricting, if not prohibiting, their movement among the Indians.

The arrival of the Jesuit Thomas Copley in Maryland in the summer of 1637 soon escalated the tensions to a full-blown dispute. As John Krugler has noted, "The entente could only work if both parties accepted the fiction on which it rested. Baltimore, to circumvent the penal laws, permitted Jesuit involvement on the understanding that the priests would be treated as gentlemen adventurers and fend for themselves."[7] To Baltimore that was the only possible arrangement in the colony of a country that banned Jesuits. Copley brought a different understanding: that Maryland was a Catholic state that should recognize the rights and privileges that church law accorded the clergy.

When the proprietor in 1638 sent a body of laws for the enactment of the assembly that laid out, among other things, the duties of settlers in the colony, Copley protested that several of them imposed duties from which the clergy had traditionally been exempt: participating in the assembly, paying taxes, serving on juries and in the militia. He asked Maryland officials to honor that tradition. John Lewgar, as secretary of the province, clearly at a loss as to how to respond to Copley's request, sought guidance from the man who had appointed him. To what extent, if any, Lewgar asked Lord Baltimore, did canon law and the traditional exemptions and privileges of the clergy apply in the colony? Was Maryland in any way a Catholic colony? Finally Lewgar wanted to know what the basis of law and authority in Maryland was. Was the realm of law in Maryland confined to those enactments of the assembly that the proprietor himself had initiated, or were there other kinds of law that operated in a default manner, apart from any enactments that came from the proprietor? Lewgar (and presumably Leonard Calvert) clearly feared that sweeping away traditional ecclesiastical privileges and customs might be a serious violation of church law. If so, to what extent were Catholics in positions of power accountable?

7. Krugler, *English and Catholic*, 171.

With some prominent Maryland Catholics like Thomas Cornwaleys supporting the Jesuits' position, Lord Baltimore attempted to work out some compromise with Jesuit officials in London and Rome. In the summer of 1638 he reached an agreement with the English provincial that basically granted the exemptions that Copley had sought. That proved to be a very temporary settlement. The new area of contention was the acquisition of property. In late 1639 the Jesuit superior in Maryland, Ferdinand Poulton, attempted to have three large parcels of land patented in his own name, including one manor that likely contained the gift of the Patuxents. The patents were not granted, despite Calvert's initial guarantee that Jesuits would be treated no differently than any other adventurer. The Jesuit claim on the land was not in question. The rub was that Baltimore could not recognize Poulton as the legal owner. Land granted to an individual Jesuit became the property of the order. As the property of an ecclesiastical corporate group it could not be alienated without the pope's special permission. In English law it became "mortmain," a dead hand within the land body of the country. So the English statute of mortmain prohibited any corporate body from owning land. Baltimore was determined to honor that statute in Maryland. To do that, as well as to enable the Jesuits to acquire land to support their ministry, the proprietor had suggested to the English provincial in the previous year that the Jesuits in Maryland use a layman to serve as the legal trustee of their property. The Jesuits, so Calvert concluded from Poulton's action, had scorned that advice.

In 1639 Calvert sent over a new body of laws, one of which gave the proprietor absolute power over the control of property in Maryland. When the assembly failed to enact that particular bill, Calvert in 1641 issued new "Conditions of Plantation," among which was one forbidding the holding of lands by any group or corporation without a special license from the proprietor. And, to make sure that everyone knew what organization he had in mind, he made known that the English statute of mortmain, which prohibited any ecclesiastical body from holding property, applied in his colony. Nor could such a body, under the new conditions, resort to a trustee to hold the land for it. Finally, he required all colonists to take an oath that they would not purchase or receive any land from the Indians.

In response, the English provincial, Edward Knott, informed Calvert that such conditions were unacceptable. Maryland Jesuits could not live under them. Baltimore replied that no ecclesiastical person in Maryland could expect any privileges, exemptions, or immunities other than what they would enjoy in England. But, of course, priests had no legal standing there, since penal law forbade their even being in the country. Knott pointed out to Baltimore that in actuality the condition of the Jesuits in Maryland was not that of ordinary freemen. They did not participate in the assembly, he reminded the proprietor. Left unsaid was that their exemption from the assembly was something they themselves had sought. Instead, the provincial leaped to the illogical conclusion that nonparticipation in the enactment of laws meant that Jesuits could not be bound by them, including those regarding property. Besides, those laws did not apply to Jesuits, whose property fell under ecclesiastical jurisdiction, not civil. Ecclesiastical immunities and exemptions did not acquire efficacy from the permission or approval of the ruler; rather they had an a priori nature that gave them force wherever the clergy lived and worked. As far as the Jesuits were concerned, church law was universal.

A CRISIS AND AN
UNDECLARED PEACE

Not until 1642 did Lord Baltimore learn, from Andrew White, that the Jesuits were already in possession of land, Mattapany, that they had received from the Patuxent chief Kittamaquund. To his brother, Leonard, Calvert expressed his dismay: "you may daily perceive what ways these men go, and of what dangerous consequences their proceedings are to me." Whether they realized it or not, they were challenging the proprietor's position that all the land belonged to him. It was no one else's. To hold otherwise was to impugn Calvert's authority and the king's right to grant the land to him and to jeopardize the entire land system that Lord Baltimore had set up. If people could acquire charter land from other sources, Calvert's ability to control the land grants would be greatly diminished, if not ruined. The Jesuit challenge not only threatened Baltimore's prerogatives and financial well-being; it endangered the very existence of the colony. That civil war between crown and Parliament had broken out in the summer of 1642 only increased, in Calvert's mind, the vulnerability of his colony. So paranoid had the proprietor become in contemplating the catastrophic consequences that Jesuit defiance would likely produce that he began to question the Jesuits' loyalty. He warned his brother that the Jesuits might attempt to arm the Indians as a counterforce to his government.

Furious at the Jesuit position, Baltimore refused to permit any more Jesuits to go to Maryland. In fact, he had determined to replace the Jesuits in Maryland with secular priests who would not pose the same challenge that the religious order did. So desperate was Calvert to carry out the change that he agreed to support at his own expense the two secular priests he managed to find for the mission, something he had never considered doing for the Jesuits. That no doubt only added to his anger when he learned that the seculars, all too soon after they arrived in Maryland, began taking the Jesuits' side in the dispute.

Within Baltimore's own family, saner voices urged restraint. Cecil's sister and brother-in-law counseled him to find a compromise that would end the controversy that had plagued him for five-plus years. The Jesuits, as it happened, were the first to offer one. They would accept no further land from the Indians. What they had already received they would continue to hold. Calvert, beyond any willingness to compromise, continued to press for the surrender of the Indian land gift. To get his position vindicated he submitted the case to a theology professor at Douai, only to have that clerical scholar judge that the Indians had the right to give or sell their land to anyone they wished. At this point Baltimore demanded that the Jesuits cede to him all of their property—not just the Indian gift, but lands they had acquired in any fashion. His justification for this demand was that the Society of Jesus held their Maryland land in clear violation of the statutes of mortmain, which applied as much in Maryland as they did in England.

The English provincial, appraising the situation as hopeless, was ready to meet Calvert's demand for the property. Without the property the Jesuits would have to end their Maryland mission and look elsewhere in British America. Before the provincial could take any action, the Holy Office in Rome, to whom the English Jesuit had appealed for guidance in the controversy, instructed him to resist Baltimore's demands. For its part Rome would not permit any secular priests to accept Calvert's invitation to Maryland.

While this was transpiring in London and Rome, a new property issue had arisen in Maryland. In 1641 Thomas Copley petitioned to patent the 400 acres of town land as well as 3,000 acres at St. Inigoes that the Jesuits had already taken up. Unlike his petition of two years previously, Copley was not attempting to patent the lands in his name but in that of Cuthbert Fenwick, Thomas Cornwaleys's overseer. Fenwick would serve as trustee of the Jesuit property. Remembering his brother's suggestion to the English provincial a few years earlier about using a trustee to satisfy English law, Leonard Calvert issued the grant. Shortly afterward the new Conditions of Plantation arrived that prohibited such an arrangement. When Leonard Calvert reluctantly informed his brother of the grant to a trustee, Baltimore was determined to undo it. The need to support the two secular priests whom he had secured for Maryland presented an opportunity to do so. He had his brother negotiate with the trustee of the Jesuit property, now Thomas Cornwaleys, for the 400 acres that made up the chapel freehold at St. Mary's. That would provide the seculars with both a chapel and a substantial residence. Calvert and Cornwaleys reached an agreement under which Cornwaleys would receive £200 for the property. That was submitted to Lord Baltimore for his approval, only to have the proprietor reject the deal because of its price. The war, which in the spring of 1643 had come to Calvert's county of Wiltshire, had put even more of a strain on Calvert's finances. Perhaps the price *was* beyond his present means. Or perhaps the war on his doorstep (his brother-in-law's castle, a mile and a half distant, was under siege that May) shifted his focus from the controversy, which was now in its fifth year. Whatever the reason, Calvert's turn-down of the sale amounted to a de facto acceptance of what would become the standard means by which the Jesuits acquired and held property over the next quarter century—the utilization of lay trustees. If Calvert had any thought of raising the issue anew after 1643, Richard Ingle's invasion of Maryland at the beginning of 1645 laid the matter to rest permanently.

CHAPTER 3

"ALIENS, SAVAGES, AND ENEMIES OF THE KINGDOME"

Maryland and the
Repercussions of the
English Civil War

BALTIMORE CASTS HIS LOT

Since the summer of 1642 war had raged throughout England
between the forces of the crown and those of Parliament. The
anti-Catholic rhetoric and actions of the Puritan-dominated
Parliament (e.g., seizing two-thirds of the property of Catholics, even if they were not in arms with the king) confirmed for
Catholics their natural inclination to support the royalist cause.
Catholic aristocrats gravitated to the court that Charles set up at
Oxford. In September 1642 the king appealed to Catholics to take
up arms in his behalf. Many of the Catholic elite, including Lord
Baltimore's two brothers-in-law, responded to his call. What the
penal legislation had denied Catholics—the bearing of arms—
the king in dire need of aid from any quarter was now urging as a
patriotic duty. For the first year and a half of the conflict, the royalists seemed likely to prevail. During that phase of the war, even
when it came to his brother-in-law's castle close by Lord Balti-

more's estate, Cecil Calvert had not joined his in-laws in publicly committing himself to the king's cause. Finally, in January of 1644, Calvert cast his
lot. He received a commission from Charles to seize in Virginia any ships
from London, the Parliamentary commercial base, as well as to recruit in
that colony for the king's armies. The commission would not only establish
Baltimore's credentials as an active supporter of the king but would rescue
him from the financial perils that the war had worsened. The prize money
from the ten or so seized ships that could be delivered to the royalist port
of Bristol from Virginia promised to exceed £40,000.

VIRGINIA AND CLAIBORNE

Virginia was a natural target for Baltimore's privateering, since Virginians,
particularly William Claiborne, had opposed from the outset his colonizing efforts in the Chesapeake. From a prominent Kent merchant family,
Claiborne, fresh out of Cambridge, had been appointed surveyor of Virginia in 1621. Over the next decade he exploited various government positions to accumulate the capital to become a principal player in the beaver
trade that in the 1630s became an important part of the Chesapeake's ex-
ports to London. In 1630 he formed an alliance with the Susquehannocks,
who controlled the bulk of the supply of beavers in the region. The following year, with a royal trading license, he established a post on Kent Island,
on the Eastern Shore of the upper Chesapeake, in part to establish there
an enclave for Virginia that would prevent Baltimore from claiming the
territory. By 1634 the hundred-person settlement had an Anglican minister in residence and representation in the House of Burgesses. Of course,
the territory granted Calvert in the Maryland charter included Kent Island within its Eastern Shore portion. Claiborne not only began defending
his rights under the trading license to the area but used his extensive network of business allies in London to influence the Privy Council to undo
Calvert's charter on the grounds that a Catholic settlement would bring
"Aliens, Savages or Enemies of the Kingdome" into the Chesapeake.[1]

---

1. J. Frederick Fausz, "Merging and Emerging Worlds: Anglo-Indian Interest Groups and the
Development of the Seventeenth-Century Chesapeake," in *Colonial Chesapeake Society*, edited by
Carr, Morgan, and Russo, 68.

On his brother's instruction Leonard Calvert invited Claiborne to share in the settlement of Maryland. All he needed to do was take an oath of allegiance to the proprietor in the governor's presence, something no other settler had been required to do.[2] Claiborne declined the offer and began fortifying the island against any possible attempt by the Calverts to take the place by force. When the captain of one of Claiborne's ships in the spring of 1635 was forced to swear on a Latin bible before testifying before the provincial court at St. Mary's, the coercive use of such a Catholic artifact so incensed Claiborne that he sent an armed sloop into the Potomac to redress the offense. The ensuing naval engagement between Claiborne's vessel and two sloops commanded by Captain Thomas Cornwaleys ended in defeat for the Virginians, with five of them dead. A second encounter three weeks later brought another victory for Calvert's forces. As a result of Claiborne's attacks the Maryland Assembly declared him a pirate, rebel, and murderer who was to be arrested and his property seized. Shortly after his second defeat on the Potomac, Claiborne, still a political force in Virginia, teamed with allies there to depose the governor and form an interim government. Claiborne and his supporters vowed to take over Maryland, as well.

His Virginia triumph was short-lived. In January 1637 the deposed governor returned from London with armed support and quickly regained power. Claiborne was stripped of all his money-making offices and removed as commander of Kent Island. A year later Governor Calvert led an expedition that invaded the island and confiscated an estimated £10,000 in goods. Two months afterward a special commission of the English government legitimated Calvert's action by declaring that Kent Island belonged to Lord Baltimore by charter right. Meanwhile, Leonard Calvert secured the allegiance, reluctant as it was, of Claiborne's former subjects by granting pardons for any rebellious actions, recognizing their entitlement to land given them by Claiborne and involving some of them in the governance of the island.

2. Three years later, in March 1638/1639, the Maryland Assembly passed legislation that established a loyalty oath to the proprietor as a prerequisite for holding public office. In 1650 the Maryland legislature extended this requirement to all adult residents of the province; Henry Miller, "Oaths," *A Brief Relation: The Quarterly Newsletter of Historic St. Mary's City* 33 (Holiday 2012): 1–2.

Exiled to England, William Claiborne strengthened his economic and political connections with the ascendant Puritans. He returned to Virginia in 1643, was restored to his old offices, and was appointed major general of militia. The Calverts' Chesapeake nemesis was more powerful than ever, a reality that Lord Baltimore would be forced to confirm on more than one occasion over the next fifteen years.

PRELUDE TO REBELLION

While Claiborne was enjoying the renaissance of his fortunes in Virginia, the proprietor's government was exposing its weakness by its utterly ineffectual attempts to punish the Susquehannocks for their summer raids in the early 1640s. That failure increased the displeasure of the colony's Protestant majority with what it saw as the proprietor's arbitrary rule and the dominant power of the Catholic manor lords and their clients in the government. That majority, overwhelmingly young, male, and unmarried, had no stakes in the traditional patron-client society that Baltimore was trying to replicate in Maryland. Some within their ranks followed closely the tumultuous events in England and saw in Parliament's revolt against arbitrary royal power parallels to their own situation in Maryland. In September 1642, when the Maryland assembly unsuccessfully challenged the proprietor's authority to adjourn their meetings without their consent, to many Protestants the contrast with Parliament's successful effort the previous year in gaining the same concession from the king could not have been starker. What they sought was a catalyst that would convert their unrest into decisive action and legitimate their striking at the palatinate government. They soon found one in Richard Ingle.

Richard Ingle, a thirty-three-year-old shipmaster and merchant, controlled the largest share of the colony's trade with London by 1642. Although ardently anti-Catholic, he had put aside his religious animosity to pursue his business interests in Maryland. When civil war came to England, Ingle became an ardent supporter of the Parliamentary cause. That commitment led the trader, while in port at St. Mary's at the beginning of 1644, to the rash proclamation that Parliament, not Charles I, was England's true sovereign. Ingle's loose tongue afforded Giles Brent, then acting governor in Leonard Calvert's absence, the excuse to arrest him on the charge of holding a commission from Parliament against the king and to seize Ingle's ship, the *Reformation*.

Brent had more than loyalty to the crown behind his sudden action. The Brent family was in heavy debt to Ingle. By charging Ingle with treason, Brent clearly could not only prove his fidelity to king but solve his family's financial problem and perhaps redeem Ingle's ship at Bristol for a handsome prize. That plan soon collapsed when Brent failed to prevent Ingle from regaining control of the *Reformation* and then had to endure four hung juries who were split on whether there was sufficient evidence to convict the trader. Thomas Cornwaleys finally persuaded Brent to release Ingle on the condition that he would return within the year to answer the charges against him. After Ingle departed (with Cornwaleys), Brent had Ingle's estate impounded as a bond against his failure to honor his promise. Upon his arrival in England Ingle received from Parliament the privateering commission—to seize ships trading with royal ports—that Brent had prematurely charged him of possessing.

By the fall of 1644 Leonard Calvert and Richard Ingle were back in Maryland, each with a privateering commission for their respective sides. Both went to Virginia, Calvert to pursue his commission and Ingle, as the evidence suggests, to plot with William Claiborne a joint invasion of Maryland to overthrow Lord Baltimore's government as an enemy of Parliament. Claiborne attempted to raise a force on Kent Island but failed to convince the settlers there that he had the proper authority to oust Baltimore's government.

PLUNDERING TIME

Ingle brought the *Reformation* into St. Mary's in early January 1645. From there he began communicating secretly to the principal Protestant planters his subversive intentions against the Calverts and their "papist" allies. Ingle then suddenly quit the port, presumably having learned that Claiborne was no longer part of the operation. In Virginia he recruited more people for the mission, some of them landowners in Maryland who had relocated in Virginia for political reasons. In mid-February Ingle returned with his enlarged force to St. Mary's.

In port he first seized the only other armed ship, a Dutch vessel loading tobacco. He also captured Giles Brent and held him captive. With these prizes in hand and control of the local waters, Ingle sailed up St. Inigoes Creek to Cross House, Thomas Cornwaleys's manor. As a friend of the absent commissioner Ingle knew that Cornwaleys's house, with its palisade and three cannon, constituted the best fortification in the colony, one he needed to possess before the government could make its stand there. Alighting from the *Reformation*, Ingle and his men surprised Cuthbert Fenwick, Cornwaleys's overseer, who with his family and twelve servants occupied Cross House. Taken hostage aboard Ingle's ship, Fenwick was forced into ordering the armed occupants to surrender the house, which became the center from which the insurgents carried out attacks against the Catholic manors in the region, from the Jesuits' St. Inigoes near the tip of the peninsula to their plantation at Portobacco sixty miles to the north. A large portion of the Protestant freeman, including the assemblymen Thomas Baldridge, Thomas Sturman, and Nathaniel Pope, quickly swelled the ranks of Ingle's force.

After a wave of looting, burning, and taking hostages the raiders would return to Cross House with their plunder and captives. Ingle was particularly intent on capturing Leonard Calvert, John Lewgar, and other officials, along with the five Jesuits in the region. Lewgar and the five Jesuits were all found and put in chains. Leonard Calvert managed to elude their search and desperately attempted to call out the militia to resist the insurgents but found that most of it had gone over to Ingle. With the militia remnant Calvert took refuge at St. Thomas Fort, the palisade surrounding Margaret Brent's house in St. Mary's. The insurgents established their own town garrison at Fort Pope, Governor Calvert's old house, now owned by Nathaniel Pope, who had emerged as a leader of the rebellion. The rebel's site choice was partly for its symbolic value, the house having served as the seat of government, with the assembly and court holding its sessions there. By holding the house the insurgents were staking a claim as Maryland's legitimate government.

The conflict settled into what Timothy Riordan has described as "a pattern of raiding and counter-raiding. Both sides began foraging to support their garrisons and plundering their opponents."[3] The Catholic manors got the worst of it, with most of the estates being thoroughly plundered and buildings burned (as eventually was Cross House, the finest dwelling in the colony). The rebellion spread across the bay to Kent Island, where settlers plundered Giles Brent's estate. One looter in Brent's mansion discovered Catholic books in his loft. "Burn them Papists Divells," he shouted as he tossed down the volumes, which those below promptly did.[4]

AFTERMATH

The governor's force apparently held out at Fort Thomas until sometime in early April. Calvert himself managed to escape into Virginia. With resistance at an end, Ingle made plans to sail to England to obtain from Parliament the legal divestment of Lord Baltimore from his colony as well as to claim his prize money for the captured ship. In mid-April the *Reformation* and the *Looking Glass* headed into the Chesapeake bearing as prisoners Giles Brent, John Lewgar, Andrew White, Thomas Copley, and the other three Jesuits (John Cooper, Bernard Hartwell, and Roger Rigby). The latter trio, so the evidence indicates, was put ashore in Susquehannock country to meet either a natural death from the elements or a violent one at the hands of hostile Indians. If so, they should be counted as North America's first martyrs. None was ever seen again.

Once in London Ingle fully expected to have the court confirm his claim to the Dutch ship and its goods, which in turn would bring him an unprecedented landfall in profits. His four prisoners would all be living evidence of the papist government that was Lord Baltimore's colony. Ingle petitioned both houses of Parliament to nullify Calvert's charter and put Protestants in control of Maryland. A parliamentary committee was subsequently instructed to write an ordinance to that effect. With the war turning against the royalists in the summer of 1645, Cecil Calvert

3. Timothy B. Riordan, *The Plundering Time: Maryland and the English Civil War, 1645–1646* (Baltimore: Maryland Historical Society, 2004), 205–6.

4. Riordan, *Plundering Time*, 210.

had to be pessimistic about the chances of his holding Maryland. The commission he had sought from the king had very likely proven to be the undoing of his colony.

Then Lord Baltimore's fortunes suddenly turned favorable. The ordinance died in committee, probably a result of the court's ruling against Ingle in his claim to the Dutch ship and the plundered goods he had hauled back to England. Parliament would not establish a new government for Maryland, and Richard Ingle would not profit from the "Plundering Time" he had unleashed in the colony.

Brent and Lewgar were eventually set free in London. The two priests were imprisoned to await trial for violating the law that imposed capital punishment on priests coming into the country. Earlier that year another Jesuit had been hanged for returning to England after being banished. White, who had been exiled in the aftermath of the Gunpowder Plot in 1605, was in the same situation (even though he had already returned to England fifteen years earlier and had worked in London without incident). Copley and White both argued in their defense that their return to England had not been by choice but by coercion. Both were released by the court but ordered to leave the country. Copley apparently managed to have that sentence commuted by proving that he was not English by birth (he had been born in Spain), hence fell outside the law. White also stayed in London without the court's sanction, was again imprisoned, and finally left the country for Antwerp in 1648.

REGAINING MARYLAND

Since the ousting of the proprietor's government, Maryland had been in a virtual state of anarchy, with no one in charge. In the second summer after the uprising, the remaining council members offered the governorship to Edward Hill, a Virginian who happened to be visiting the colony. Having an outside Protestant as the leader of Maryland probably seemed to the Catholic counselors the prudent thing to do, given the circumstances. Hill restored much of local government, including the court. He also called the assembly to session.

In Virginia Leonard Calvert was preparing to retake Maryland for his brother. With a small force (fewer than thirty) of Maryland refugees and Virginia mercenaries, the governor retook St. Mary's without any apparent opposition as summer turned to fall in 1646. The following April Calvert led an armed expedition to Kent Island to complete his recovery of the colony. For all those who had rebelled on either shore of the Chesapeake the governor issued a general pardon, contingent upon their taking an oath of fidelity to the proprietor. The intent of the oath was to ensure the peace would be a stable one, with all settlers having a stake in the survival of Maryland. They were all now important.

In the nearly two years of mayhem and chaos four-fifths of the five hundred residents on the Western Shore had either died or fled, the worst consequence of the "Plundering Time." The population could, with planning, grow again. The manorial system, with so many of the estates laid waste, could not survive. Calvert's dream of a seigneurial social order died with the havoc that Ingle and his allies spread across the colony. It also marked the passing of the Catholic oligarchy, the manorial lords who had such control of the economy during Maryland's first decade. As noted in chapter 1, the availability of land, social mobility, and the scarcity of labor made the collapse of the manorial system inevitable. Ingle simply made it happen sooner. The rebellion had nearly destroyed the Jesuit mission, its plantations plundered, buildings burned, its priests driven out. It would take nearly two decades for it to recover.

RETURN OF THE JESUITS

As it was, the mission came very close to ending with the dispersal of its five members in 1645. By the time the Calverts regained control of Maryland nearly two years later, the superior general of the Jesuits, reflecting on their protracted difficulties with the proprietor, had decided to close the Maryland mission. Before his decision reached the English provincial in London in the late fall of 1647, however, Thomas Copley and another Jesuit had already set sail for the Chesapeake. When Copley arrived in St. Mary's at the beginning of 1648 the colony's few remaining Catholics thought they were seeing an apparition. When Ingle carried off the missionaries in chains, the survivors had never expected to see any of them again. Now here was Copley in their midst along with another Jesuit. "Like an angel of God," Copley wrote, "did they receive me." He found them in better spirits than he could have imagined they would be, given the recent travails—indeed, happier than some of their Protestant neighbors "who had plundered them."[5] As a safeguard Copley carried a note from Charles I declaring the priest to be under the king's protection. That pledge, Copley sadly learned all too soon, was one the king could not even fulfill for his own person when the Puritans prevailed in the civil war that had been raging in England for most of the decade.

It was fortuitous that the Society had sent back to Maryland the man who had proven to be its best administrator in the mission's first decade. Copley set about to resurrect the mission. In 1649 the priest, through a lay trustee, filed the claim for the 4,000-acre tract on the Potomac River near Portobacco, which the Jesuits were already occupying at the time of Ingle's invasion. Copley named the manor for St. Thomas. It proved to be his final claim. In 1652 he died at the age of fifty-seven. Despite his chronic poor health, Copley had outlived all of the Jesuits who had come to Maryland with the exception of Andrew White. The country continued to take a steep toll on the missionaries. Of the five Jesuits sent to Maryland between 1648 and 1660, three died, two within three years of their arrival. Another was there a relatively short time before his shortcomings in discretion led to his recall. Unfortunately, the Jesuit who served there the longest during the period also suffered from a lack of discretion. A former military chaplain in Flanders, Francis Fitzherbert, as one historian put it, "brought with him from the soldiers' camp... a mailed fist into civil life, instead of a gloved hand."[6] In 1658, for instance, he was brought before the provincial court for disturbing the peace by haranguing Thomas Gerrard for not bringing the Protestant members of his family to church. In short, the precarious, unstable condition of the Jesuit mission reflected the troubled times that the colony continued to experience through the 1650s.

5. Hughes, *History of the Society of Jesus in North America; Text*, vol. 2, *From 1645 till 1773* (New York: Longmans, Green, 1917), 24.
6. Hughes, *History of the Society of Jesus; Text*, 2:52–53.

REACHING OUT

Two months after restoring proprietary rule in Maryland Leonard Calvert died suddenly, the victim, perhaps, of a venomous snake bite. The
thirty-seven-year-old governor's death was an enormous loss for the colony, as the missteps of his successor, Thomas Greene, all too soon underscored. To Greene and Margaret Brent, whom Calvert had made the
executrix of his estate, fell the burden of fulfilling the government's responsibilities in a society recovering from two years of anarchy. Because
Governor Calvert had made no effort to distinguish between personal
and provincial resources in meeting the needs of the colony, Brent found
herself functioning more as colony treasurer than as private executor.
When the Virginians whom Calvert had hired to help him win back the
colony began demanding the money that the governor had promised
them for their service, Brent deftly used some of the assets of Calvert's
estate, as well as those of the proprietor, to meet their demands. Her
swift action defused the explosive situation but angered Lord Baltimore,
who did not appreciate her appropriation of family property to meet
a government obligation. The assembly, in response to the proprietor's
complaint, supported Margaret Brent. They had not done the same previously when Brent asserted her right as a property holder to participate
in the assembly. For good measure she argued that as Lord Baltimore's
attorney she deserved a second vote in that body. The governor, however,
refused to recognize any such rights, her property or position notwithstanding.

As governor Thomas Greene was a competent manager but tone-
deaf to complaints and thin-skinned to criticism. He initially angered the
assembly by the extravagant salary and perquisites he sought. A Catholic, he gave the impression of favoring his coreligionists in his decisions
and of not being above using his office for personal gain. He even alienated Lord Baltimore when he rashly recognized the son of the recently
executed king as England's lawful sovereign in 1649, a declaration that
Lord Baltimore was quick to renounce, since he was doing everything in
his power at the time to gain the good will of Parliament.

Greene's imprudent behavior aside, Lord Baltimore had already concluded that he needed to radically change the composition of his government if his colony was to survive in an England now ruled by Puritans. His Maryland government could no longer be confined to family and gentry Catholics. In the summer of 1648 he named a new council that had a Protestant majority and no manorial lords. Two of the members had entered Maryland as indentured servants. For governor Calvert went outside the province to the Eastern Shore of Virginia to name William Stone, a Protestant tobacco merchant with an uncle in Parliament (Calvert's likely source of his knowledge of Stone). Calvert was boldly putting his government in the hands of Protestants, with a Virginian at its head who had worked with William Claiborne and Richard Ingle.

Nor was Stone the only Virginian Calvert pinned his hopes on to transform the province. Indeed, one factor that likely led Calvert to choose Stone as his next governor was his promise to bring five hundred of his fellow Virginians with him to Maryland. The proprietor desperately needed people to repopulate his colony. Even before the "Plundering Time," Baltimore, having substantially failed to attract emigrants from England or Ireland, had been attempting to recruit settlers from other regions of British America. In 1643 he had sent Cuthbert Fenwick to New England to extend invitations to Puritan communities there to migrate to Maryland; the Puritans rejected the offers. Five years later Virginia presented an extraordinary opportunity for Calvert to solve his population problem by coming to the aid of a dissident minority. That community of Puritans living south of the James in the Norfolk-Nansemond area was struggling to resist Governor Berkeley's imposition of the worship and laws of the Church of England upon all Virginians. It had been from this very community that Leonard Calvert had found the mercenaries that enabled him to retake Maryland. Now his brother was inviting these settlers, who were well experienced in the tobacco economy of the Chesapeake, into his colony with the promise that they could practice their religion there as freely as they could raise their tobacco. The response was the migration of a Puritan minority that soon constituted a majority of the Maryland settlement.

The first group of Virginia Puritans entered Maryland in 1648 led by Richard Bennett, who had headed the armed band that Leonard Calvert

Margaret Brent

had hired to assist his retaking power in his brother's colony. Hundreds of Puritans followed over the next few years. The vast majority of them took up residence in the Providence area along the Severn River in the new county of Anne Arundel.

With the transformation of both the government and population,

Lord Baltimore needed a more explicit guarantee of the religious toleration that had been the colony's practice since its founding. First, the
proprietor instituted a series of oaths that all major officeholders were
required to take, in which they swore they would not disturb anyone,
and in particular Catholics, in the exercise of their religion. Second, he
had the assembly, in which Catholics still enjoyed a slight majority, take
up a law that would ensure the toleration of the religious speech and
practice of Christians. Most important was the law's prohibition of the
use of force to achieve religious conformity; no one could be coerced to
practice any "Religion against his or her consent." For the first time in the
English-speaking world the law was recognizing the right of Christians
to worship as they would without the government's interference.

The rub for the Puritan newcomers was the oath of fidelity to Lord
Baltimore that all settlers were now to take. Baltimore had required an
oath of the first settlers after they landed on St. Clement's Island. But
that had been an oath confirming their loyalty to the king, not the proprietor. Many Puritans felt in conscience they could take no such oath
to a papist. Their refusal left them in a precarious position, putting their
landholding at stake.

Meanwhile, William Claiborne continued to plot the destruction of
Baltimore's colony and its integration into a consolidated North American Protestant British empire in which Claiborne's economic interests could realize their full potential. With Parliament's triumph Claiborne enjoyed more powerful connections in London than ever before.
Through them he, along with Richard Bennett, secured a commission
from Parliament in 1651 to "reduce all the plantations" within the Chesapeake "to their due obedience" to the new order in England. Greene's
declaration for Charles II, like Governor Berkeley's similar sentiment in
Virginia, had not gone unnoticed.

When Bennett and Claiborne's armed force arrived at St. Mary's they
replaced Governor Stone with a six-man Protestant commission after
the governor refused to recognize Parliament's ultimate authority. Two
months later they reinstated Stone after he agreed to do so but retained
the commission they had created. By 1654 power was clearly shifting
from Parliament to Oliver Cromwell. Baltimore, sensing this shift, in-

structed Stone to reduce the influence of the Puritans on the council by replacing a number of them. That led the Puritan community to accuse Stone of rebelling against Parliament and petitioned Bennett and Claiborne, then governor and secretary of Virginia respectively, to return to Maryland to remove Stone. When the pair once again appeared at the head of an armed force at St. Mary's, they ousted Stone for a second time. In his place they appointed a ten-man commission to rule the colony. The commission set up an assembly at Patuxent that proceeded to repeal the Toleration Act of 1649 and impose a body of blue laws upon the province.

In London Baltimore was steadily gaining more influence in Oliver Cromwell's ruling circle. With growing confidence in his ability to secure the Protector's support for his colonial investment, Baltimore instructed Stone to use military force to recapture the government. With a couple hundred or so hastily gathered militia, Stone in late March of 1655 embarked in boats and headed for the Severn River. On the feast of the Annunciation, March 25, Stone's forces landed on the banks of the Severn, only to be caught in a withering crossfire from Puritan militia onshore and the guns of an upriver vessel. Stone and his men surrendered after suffering heavy losses. The victorious Protestants executed four of the captives, then headed to St. Mary's City, apparently to deal likewise with the three Jesuits in the area. All they found were abandoned houses to plunder. The priests had fled across the Potomac into Virginia.

Having failed in his military option, Baltimore's chances at redeeming his province were reduced to persuading Cromwell's government to uphold his charter rights. For two years representatives of Baltimore as well as of Bennett and Claiborne argued their cases before the Council of State. Meanwhile a pamphlet war had broken out in London between the two parties. Claiborne himself published one in 1655 that recapitulated the revolutionary events in Maryland and Virginia and the justification for them. His representatives were advancing various reasons that Baltimore's charter should be annulled, including the argument that Maryland's very existence as a colony was a violation of the territorial integrity of Virginia. Baltimore for his part was pleading patriotism, respect for his investment in the enterprise, and the principle of religious toleration to save his charter. He was essentially betting that Cromwell would come down on the side of one promoting religious freedom (the Protector's government had repealed the Act of Uniformity in 1650) and holding better prospects for producing a stable society (despite the turbulence of the last decade in Maryland). Events proved his prescience. Cromwell first ordered the commissioners to return conditions in Maryland to their status *quo antea*, a confusing directive that brought no change but gave Baltimore enough confidence in the ultimate outcome to appoint a new governor and council. The protracted dealings finally led at the end of November 1657 to an agreement between Baltimore and Bennett that essentially recognized the proprietor's authority, granted general amnesty, and restored the Act of Toleration of 1649. In the new government both former Governor William Stone and William Fuller, the Puritan militia leader, were members of the five-man council.

The coalition government produced not the stability Baltimore had anticipated, but the third revolt against his rule. The political turmoil in England that followed Oliver Cromwell's death in the fall of 1658 provided an opportunity for the anti-proprietary element in Calvert's government to assert the primacy of the assembly's authority. In February the assembly declared itself "the highest court of Judicature." To conform the structure of government to this new hierarchy of power, Governor Josiah Fendall agreed that in the future the governor, council, and assembly would sit as a single body, a miniature commonwealth. The speaker of the assembly implicitly assumed the role of prime minister with the power to adjourn the assembly.

The "commonwealth" had a short life. Once apprised of the coup Baltimore named his brother Philip to replace Fendall as governor and appointed new councilors, both Protestant and Catholic, who had proven loyal. Along with the appointments came an order from the new king, Charles II, commanding obedience to Calvert's rule. That ended Fendall's "pygmie rebellion," as Baltimore labeled it. The turbulent era in which traditional or new foes had repeatedly challenged Lord Baltimore's authority had finally, after fifteen years, come to an end.

CONCLUSION

Twice in the course of a decade the colony had suffered the repercussions of the English Civil War. What was unique about the two conflicts that divided Maryland in the 1640s and again in the 1650s was the religious character of the opposing sides. It was not royalist against parliamentarian, as in England, but Catholic royalist against Protestant parliamentarian. In the end Calvert adroitly broke through this constricting identity system to save his colony. He had to experience two failures in ecumenical governance, but he achieved his goal, thanks in part to Baltimore's shrewd political maneuvering in England.

Maryland was a very different place in 1660 than it had been in 1645. The Jesuit mission was a shell of its earlier self. So too was the Native American community, whose evangelization had been the primary reason for the establishment of the mission. Gone was the manorial system at the heart of Maryland society. Gone too were the Catholic manor lords who had controlled that system. Jerome Hawley had died in 1638, while Nicholas Harvey died in the late 1640s and Richard Gardiner and Thomas Copley in 1652. James Neale had left the colony in 1644. Giles Brent moved to Virginia in 1650. Thomas Cornwaleys returned to England in 1659. Only Thomas Gerrard remained, and he would depart in 1662. A new class of leaders, religiously mixed and with more disparate social origins, would shape the province's development over the next thirty years.

CHAPTER 4

"MUCH AS THEY DO AT HOME"

The Irish Diaspora and the West Indies

On their voyage to Maryland in 1633 and 1634 Cecil Calvert's adventurers followed the typical Atlantic course ships took from England to the Chesapeake region. *The Ark* and *The Dove* swung southwest to the Canary Islands, then after a stay there of several days rode the trade winds westward toward the West Indies. At Barbados, the easternmost of the chain of islands constituting the Lesser Antilles, they stopped to resupply, only to find officials and merchants there taking advantage of the voyagers' needs by asking exorbitant prices for their goods. There was an abundance of potatoes, which were a staple of the local inhabitants and could be had for the taking, so wildly did they grow on the island. Potatoes, however, were foreign to the English diet, and the Englishmen heading to Maryland pushed on to Montserrat, one of the Leeward Islands. Their departure from Barbados was a hasty one, spurred by the alarm that the indentured servants on the tobacco plantations were conspiring to kill their masters and escape from the island in the first ship that docked there. Realizing that they were the intended targets of the servants' getaway plans, the soon-to-be Maryland-ers hastily weighed anchor and set sail northwestward for the island first sighted by Christopher Columbus, which bore his name.

On their way to St. Christopher (St. Kitts), they stopped at Mont-serrat, the mountainous, twenty-mile-long mutton-shaped body of land on the inner arc formed by the Leeward Islands. Montserrat, White not-ed, was "inhabited by Irishmen who have been expelled by the English of Virginia, on account of their profession of the Catholic faith."[1] From Montserrat they sailed almost due north to St. Christopher's, the west-ernmost of the four Leeward Islands with English settlements. The En-glish settlement on St. Christopher occupied but half the island, the French holding the other half as part of an agreement that had united the two powers' forces to secure the place against the Caribs, the domi-nant indigenous tribe in the area. The voyagers received such a warm welcome from officials in both divisions of the island—not only were the French officers Catholic, but at least two of the English, as well—that they tarried there for a week and a half before beginning their final leg of the journey to the mainland.

The English began to establish colonies in the Caribbean some for-ty years after their first attempted settlement—Roanoke Island—on the mainland and almost two decades from the planting of the first perma-nent settlement at Jamestown. Once the English had staked a presence in the West Indies in the 1620s, the Caribbean became the destination of nearly 60 percent of the emigrants from the British Isles over the course of the remainder of the seventeenth century. Notable too about the de-mographics of the Caribbean colonies was how substantial a minority Catholics were in the region. In the four Leeward Islands, Catholics con-stituted, by one historian's estimate, nearly one-third of the white pop-ulation in 1677. In the two other major British colonies in the West In-dies—Barbados and Jamaica—Catholics occupied a similar niche. One can say in fact that in the seventeenth century there were more Catholics in the Caribbean portion of the English Empire than there were on the

1. White, *Relatio Itineris in Marylandium*, 17.

North American continent. That that was so was due in large part to the predominance of the Irish within this scattered Catholic community, a majority of whom, male and female, began life in the New World as indentured servants. Irish Catholic males presumably constituted a good portion of the workers accused of plotting against the planters on Barbados, according to Andrew White's narrative. On Montserrat they quickly constituted a majority of the whites, as White inferred in his account, but continued to be treated as an alien minority that needed to be watched and checked. In short, Catholics were a vital part of the English colonial experience in the West Indies in the seventeenth century, a truth that has been largely ignored in the history of the region. That Catholics have had such a low profile in the historiography of the region is surely due in part to the virtual lack of any significant institutional presence of the Church before well into the eighteenth century. Lacking the institutional measurement, Catholics have tended to disappear from the historical memory.

Somewhere between 30,000 and 50,000 Irish emigrated to British colonies in the Caribbean and North America in the 1600s. Unlike the demographic pattern of the following century, the vast majority were Roman Catholics from southern Ireland. Most of them went, at least initially, to the West Indies. Of those who did, a minority of the Catholic Irish became landowners; a relative few, mostly Old English in ethnic origin, actually became planters. The typical Irish immigrant began life in British America working out a term of servitude that ranged from five to seven years that he had agreed to by choice, not force. The push factor for most emigrants was the land revolution, beginning with the Ulster Plantation under James I, that displaced them from or reduced their status on their plantations or farms and brought them to seek better prospects across the Atlantic. The peak decade of emigration to the Caribbean, the 1650s, however, was one driven by sheer force, the consequence of developments set in motion by the Rebellion of 1641.

In late October of that year the Gaelic Irish, assuming (falsely, as it turned out) that they had the support of Spain and (again proved wrong) that a sudden, coordinated uprising would produce a bloodless coup that would put them in a strong enough military position to stare

West Indies (1767)

down the English Parliament, attacked several locations in Ulster and within a day had control of most of the province. What they did not control was their own troops. Vigilantism and atrocities led to at least twelve thousand deaths and bitter resistance to the uprising. The Gaels rode the vortex of violence over much of the island. By November the rebels were within the Pale, besieging the government stronghold at Drogheda, thirty kilometers above Dublin, and threatening the capital itself. Five weeks into the uprising the Old English, that relatively small, but wealthiest and most politically powerful group among the indigenous Irish, decided that their rapidly declining position in the Dublin government (reapportionment and disfranchisement had converted an overwhelming Catholic majority, largely Old English, into a badly outnumbered minority) and lack of support by the king to whom they had always been loyal left them with no choice but to cast their lots and considerable fortunes with their Ulster brothers.

By early 1642 most of the country was in the possession of the rebels. In July the Irish uprising became part of the larger English Civil War. The crown itself kept sending conflicting signals to the rebels, many of whom thought they were advancing the king's true interests by rising up against the Irish government, seen as a surrogate for Parliament. If Charles was reluctant to take action against the rebellion, Parliament was not. In March of 1642, to raise the money needed to procure troops to put down the uprising, Parliament passed the Adventurers' Act, which established the mechanism for auctioning off the land of those in revolt once the war was won. Some two and a half million acres of Ireland, much of it the property of Old English, were thus to be redistributed and made working plantations. A month after Parliament's action a Scottish army landed in Ireland to put down the rebellion. In response the defiant Irish formed a counter government, the Confederation, in Kilkenny.

The war dragged on for three years. In the summer of 1645 the king, whose war against Parliament was going badly, struck a tentative deal with the Irish whereby the latter would receive formal toleration and eligibility to hold public office in exchange for 10,000 Irish troops in Charles's service. That agreement was revoked by the papal nuncio, which proved to be the undoing of the uneasy alliance between the Old English and the Gaelic Irish and the collapse of the Confederation . The Gaelic Irish managed to keep the rebellion alive into the summer of 1649. In June of that year Oliver Cromwell, now commander-in-chief of the English expeditionary forces to Ireland, landed an army near Dublin. In a brutal campaign over the next nine months that featured massacres in several towns that fell to the invaders, Cromwell finally broke the back of the revolt, although some Irish, along with Presbyterian supporters of the Stuarts, fought on until 1652.

The peace that Cromwell imposed could scarcely have been more vindictive; it essentially executed the massive land auction that Parliament had enacted a decade earlier. The Cromwellian settlement result-ed in about 2,000 landowners being forced to relocate on smaller, less arable plots in western counties. Over 30,000 of those who had fought for the Confederation were ordered exiled (without their families) to the Continent. Several thousand other Irish were deported to the West Indies, the first wave of an estimated 10,000 involuntary émigrés, including many children (e.g., 2,000 boys and girls under fourteen were apparently transported to Jamaica in September of 1655 as part of the initial English settlement there). All in all there was a massive loss of land for the Irish that especially affected the middling farmers. In County Galway alone, over 90 percent of Irish-held land was confiscated. Throughout Ulster Province Catholic landowning, which had already suffered major losses during James's plantation period, plummeted. With the exception of Antrim County Catholics retained title to less than 4 percent of the land in the province. Although Catholics recovered some of these lands under a settlement act during the Restoration era (the percentage of Catholic landowners rose to 20 percent by 1665), in the long run the percentage of Catholic landowners and tenants continued on a downward path into the eighteenth century. Waves of Scottish immigrants (nearly 150,000 in the latter half of the seventeenth century) proved decisive in transforming Ulster into a province where the mostly landowning Protestants greatly outnumbered the mostly landless Catholics. For many Catholics the West Indies came to hold more promise than Ireland. It continued to be the major destination of Irish emigrants for another three decades.

EXTENDING THE ENGLISH EMPIRE
IN THE ATLANTIC

Beginning in the third quarter of the sixteenth century the English had been reconnoitering the West Indies as well as coastal areas of Central and South America for possible sites for trading centers, privateering bases, and settlements. Until the first decade of the seventeenth century Spain's hegemony over the region kept the British from establishing a foothold either in the islands or mainland. The Anglo-Spanish War (1585–1604) sufficiently changed the balance of power in the area that the English began to undertake certain colonizing projects there. One of the earliest was the trading base begun by Philip and James Purcell on the Tauregue River in South America in the 1620s. The Purcells, either brothers or cousins, were Irish Catholics of Old English stock who had established a successful trading business in Dartmouth, England, before expanding overseas.

Most of those they brought over to America to work for the company were Irish and English Catholics. Like their home business, the Purcells' Amazon trading post flourished until the Portuguese sacked it in 1625, killing most of the seventy-five defenders. Three years later James Purcell led a joint Anglo-Dutch expedition to revive the settlement, only to have the Portuguese return in early 1631 and destroy the trading base for good.

Such bitter experiences proved that the farther from the Spanish and Portuguese spheres of influence in the Caribbean a colony was, the better its chances for survival, even success. It was no accident, then, that the five successful colonies established in the area in the first half of the seventeenth century were all northern islands of the Lesser Antilles: Barbados, Antigua, Nevis, St. Christopher, and Montserrat. Their colonization formally began in 1627, just seven years before the *Ark* and the *Dove* dropped anchor there, when the crown created the first proprietary lord in British America by granting James Hay, the Earl of Carlisle, the right to colonize Barbados, St. Christopher, Nevis, and Montserrat. Actually the English presence in the West Indies antedated the charter grant by three years. In 1624, on St. Christopher, Thomas Warner, who had been involved in the Amazon colony, established the first permanent settlement on the tadpole-shaped twenty-by-six-mile mountainous island of St. Christopher's (or St. Kitts, as the English later shortened it). To do so he needed to combine with French forces to secure the place from both the Carib Indians and the Spanish. The price of the French alliance was a division of St. Christopher into English and French halves, an agreement that more or less lasted into the eighteenth century. Within the first two years of settlement additional immigrants arrived, many of them Irish, such as the group that Anthony Hilton, a trade agent for some English merchants, brought there for a short time before relocating them to Nevis, which offered better prospects for those seeking land. Even after Hilton relocated his party, colonists on St. Christopher outnumbered those on Barbados by 40 percent in 1629 (3,000 on St. Christopher to between 1,600 and 1,800 on Barbados).[2] Immigrants from Ireland continued to

---

2. Shona Helen Johnston, "Papists in a Protestant World: The Catholic Anglo-Atlantic in the Seventeenth Century" (Ph.D. diss., Georgetown University, 2011), 31.

arrive at St. Kitts, including the contingent of 600 Irish Catholics from Tuam in Munster Province that two priests led to the island in 1637— this in the face of the governor's determination to rid the island of Catholics, whom he considered to be disloyal troublemakers.

By 1640 there were perhaps 30,000 Europeans in the five colonies. About 3,000, or 10 percent, were Catholics. Thirty years later an Irish Jesuit who had ministered for three years in the British Caribbean reported that the size of the Catholic population was now four times what it had been in 1640.[3] Throughout the century Catholics would remain a significant minority in the West Indies.

BARBADOS

Barbados, as the first island in the West Indies that one reached on the voyage from England, was in 1627 the second settlement made in the area by the English (after St. Christopher) but the first English colony in the New World to be an economic success. Its easternmost location in the Lesser Antilles afforded it safety from assaults of both the native Caribs and the Spanish. But not only its location attracted settlers. Its lush terrain promised an abundant agriculture ("an Eden with unlimited opportunity," as one historian put it).[4] Somehow two colonial entrepreneurs, Sir William Courteen and James Hay, the Earl of Carlisle, secured government grants to settle and develop the island. Quickly two settlements emerged with two governments contesting control of the island. Over its first decade and a half Barbados was a Hobbesian jungle. Finally Hay prevailed in the power struggle.

With stability and order established, Barbados's planters could concentrate on fulfilling the economic potential that had initially attracted them to the pristine island. Tobacco had been their first choice for a staple crop. The small-scale acreage and limited labor needed for a profitable output plus tobacco's short production season were the chief factors that led plant-

---

3. According to John Grace, the approximate Catholic figures were Barbados, 8,000, Montserrat, 2,000, St. Christopher, 600, Antigua, 400; Johnston, "Papists in a Protestant World," 39.

4. Larry Dale Gragg, *Englishmen Transplanted: The English Colonization of Barbados, 1627–1660* (New York: Oxford University Press, 2003), 28.

ers to this choice. The market success of the first two harvests confirmed for many the wisdom of their decision. But overproduction in Barbados, Virginia, and other tobacco colonies led to a plummeting drop of 90 percent in its market price over the next several years. Making matters worse, the soil on Barbados produced a tobacco inferior to that grown elsewhere, and the amount of arable acreage was too small to allow for an adequate rotation system that would enable fields exhausted from cultivating tobacco to recover their nutrients. Reluctantly the Barbadian planters switched from tobacco to cotton, a staple much in demand on the European markets. That move provided the capital the larger planters needed to invest in a staple—sugar—that promised far greater returns than cotton.

The labor-intensive nature of sugar production made it imperative for planters to secure the cheapest available labor. In the 1640s the falling price for African slaves made them a much more economical labor source than the indentured servants upon whom the Barbadian planters had previously chiefly depended. Barbados thus became the first English colony to utilize slaves as its chief labor source. Within two decades there were 20,000 Africans working on the sugar plantations; they were the vanguard of the 250,000 Africans whom the six sugar colonies imported as slave labor in the seventeenth century. At the same time, due to political turmoil, Brazil, the chief sugar supplier in the New World, had virtually ceased production. By this set of circumstances Barbados became England's first sugar colony and, by the third quarter of the seventeenth century, its richest settlement in the New World (the "crown jewel" of the empire, as one governor of the island termed it in 1666).[5] Sugar brought fabulous wealth to the relatively few gentry and merchants in Barbados, England, and New England who had sufficient wealth to invest in a nascent industry. Barbados by 1689 was a colony dominated by a planter oligarchy who utilized the gang labor that a slave force could best provide to produce a staple that within four decades became the centerpiece of England's international economy.[6] Preserving their neutrality during

5. The governor was Francis Lord Willoughby; *Calendar of State Papers, Colonial Series, 1661–1668* (London: 1880), 382; Willoughby document included in *Calendar* cited in Gragg, *Englishmen Transplanted*, 1.

6. By 1686 Barbadian sugar accounted for nearly 40 percent of the value of all colonial imports

the English Civil War, the planters rode the cultivation of sugar to a booming economy. A settler wrote home in 1652, "[I] do not think there is in the world a more healthful, pleasant and plentiful place than this."[7] Unprecedented wealth was merely one of the byproducts.

By 1652 the war had at last reached Barbados. Royalists on the island, strengthened by the arrival of Cavalier refugees as well as prisoners dispatched to Barbados as indentured servants, had taken up arms to preserve the island for the crown, now in the person of Charles II, then in exile on the Continent. When the Barbados council declared an embargo on trading with England, the victorious Parliamentarians in London sent an expedition of three thousand troops to secure the island for the new Commonwealth of England. Despite their subsequent military subjugation the planters managed to preserve their virtual autonomy as a colony, a condition that lasted until the centralization policy that the Stuarts introduced for the colonies upon their restoration in 1660.

Barbados's Catholic community had a multiethnic makeup from the first decade of the island's history as an English colony. Besides the English and Irish, there were Portuguese Africans like Mathias de Sousa, whom Andrew White brought to Maryland. Some, such as de Sousa, arrived there as free men. Most came as part of the slave trade. Whether slave or free, these Portuguese Africans were typically Catholics who continued to practice their faith as best as circumstances allowed. Three such Africans who arrived in Barbados in the late 1680s paid a great price for their religious loyalty. Brought into the colony as part of a slave shipment, the three claimed to be free men who had been tricked into coming to the island from Africa by slave traders who later put them in chains to be sold as chattel on the island. The governing council to whom they had appealed for their freedom believed their story and released them, only to have the court revoke their status as free men when the three proceeded to practice their Roman Catholicism openly.

By the late 1660s there were some 20,000 Europeans on the island. A

into London, a proportion that soared to 57 percent by the turn of the century; Gragg, *Englishmen Transplanted*, 107.

7. Gragg, *Englishmen Transplanted*, 107.

priest who worked on the island for several years estimated that the Irish made up two-fifths of the white population of Barbados. The characterization of the populace by the governor of the island, Francis Lord Willoughby, as "a strange composition of blacks, Irish and servants" would seem to substantiate this judgment.[8] Although Andrew White found but a few Irish servants on the island in 1634, twenty years later they made up a substantial minority of the servant class there. The Irish, in fact, began their stay in Barbados predominantly as indentured servants, a substantial portion of the 2,000 or more Europeans who entered the colony as indentured servants in its first thirty years. The Irish servant immigrants were mostly young males of Gaelic ethnic origin, although there was more gender equity among the Irish servants than their English counterparts. Their terms of service typically ranged from five to seven years. Political prisoners, convicts, and deportees tended to be bonded to service for at least ten years.

Barbados quickly acquired notoriety for its brutal, savage treatment of both servants and slaves. What one English colonist reported to the Lords of Trade and Plantations in 1688 ("the poor white servants here... are used with more barbarous cruelty than if in Algiers. Their bodies and souls are used as if hell commenced here and only continued in the world to come") had long before become an endemic element of the way of life in Barbados.[9] Such treatment, along with yellow fever ("Barbados Distemper") were the major contributors to the extremely high mortality rate among workers, both slave and indentured, on Barbados as elsewhere in the Antilles. Only the steady importation of labor from Africa and the British Isles could offset it.

As Catholics within an Atlantic Protestant empire surrounded by colonies of the two leading Catholic powers, the Irish, particularly those serving terms of indenture, were regarded by English authorities as potential subversives. Irish Catholic servants in particular, in common with the African slaves with whom they lived and worked closely, were the ever-present objects of suspicion by the ruling class of Barbados. In

8. Johnston, "Papists in a Protestant World," 40.
9. Hilary Beckles, *White Servitude and Black Slavery in Barbados, 1627–1715* (Knoxville: University of Tennessee Press, 1989), 92.

1644 the council passed an act prohibiting Irish immigration. Sugar's demand for labor quickly rendered this law one that was observed in the
breech. And, as White had recorded, the past behavior of both groups
gave grounds for distrust and vigilance. Brutal treatment led to servant
and slave resistance. One tactic that both groups early resorted to, often
enough together, was the passive resistance of running away and seeking
refuge in caves or thickets, a strategy that a growing number of servants
and slaves embraced in the 1680s. From these "maroon" zones they would
venture out to set fire to sugar cane or to persuade workers on the plantations to join them in their lairs. Combating this threat was one reason
the Barbados government instituted a pass system for servants. A governor in 1687 pleaded with the assembly to adopt laws severely punishing
servant runaways as the only way to deter the practice. The legislature
refused. In fact, the legal punishments for runaways in Barbados were
probably the mildest anywhere in English America. In Maryland runaways were subject to capital punishment; in Barbados they were given
an extra day of service (with a maximum of three years) for every two
hours they were absent without permission. The lenient penalties in Barbados were a result of an effort in the 1660s to improve the notorious
reputation that the island had come to have in the British Isles as a place
for emigrants.[10] The effort apparently worked, since the colony remained
the chief destination for servant émigrés until the turn to African slaves
as the main labor source began to dry up the European servant market
by the 1680s and gradually reduce the size of the servant community
to a negligible one, with servants functioning chiefly as a security force
against the slave majority. With the rapid decline of the servant community in the 1680s the assembly might have felt that the changing demographics would solve the problem soon enough.

Occasionally resistance would turn violent, as with the physical attack by two Irish servants on their master on Barbados in 1657. Much
rarer was organized rebellion. Both in 1634 and 1647 general servant con-

10. In 1686 several Irish servants were accused of plotting a revolt with slaves. Significantly, the
Irish suspects were finally released; twenty slaves were executed. On Barbados, as throughout the
English Caribbean, there was always a double standard for whites, even Irish, and Africans, including
slaves.

spiracies, led by Irish servants, were alleged to have been in the making, only to be thwarted by informers. The supposed plan in both cases was for the servants (who then constituted about 60 percent of the work force), having secured arms, to kill all the planters and seize control of the island. Eighteen servants paid with their lives for being implicated in the 1647 attempt at rebellion. In 1655 the Barbadian Council attempted to deal with their "Irish" problem, first by making it illegal for a priest to live on the island and second by threatening to deport all Irish ex-servants who failed to secure employment with an English landowner. Two years later the governor of the island announced that he was disarming all the Irish and other Catholics on the island as a precaution, given their "[Romish] religion and a natural concern about their loyalty.[11] For good measure, vagrants (the government implied that they were virtually all Catholics), whether men or women, were to be whipped and forced to work as laborers for a year. The fallout from the Titus Oates Plot of 1678 brought a new wave of anti-Catholic measures, the principal one being a test act that effectively barred Catholics from teaching and from all government offices. The governor reported to the home office that "such was the heat here that, if I had not past that law, I should my self have past for as arrant a Papist as any was hang'd at Tiburne."[12] But the accession of the Catholic monarch James II in 1685 effectively disabled the legislation, if only temporarily, as it turned out.

Barbados was also a major destination for Irish dissenters and war prisoners whom Cromwell expelled in the 1650s. In November 1655 thirty-seven persons who had been imprisoned for resisting Cromwell's resettlement policy were sent to Barbados. A majority were women, one over eighty. There were also three priests. Almost from the time of the transplanting there have been wild estimates of the number of Irish sent to the West Indies under Cromwell. The papal nuncio to Ireland, Cardinal Giovanni Battista Rinuccini, considered it close to 50,000 a year. A historian writing in the 1930s thought that number the total for the Cromwellian era. More sober estimates have ranged in the 10,000 to

11. Gragg, *Englishmen Transplanted*, 159.
12. Hughes, *History of the Society of Jesus; Text*, 2:138–39.

12,000 range. We do know that some 3,000 Irish prisoners of war had been exiled to Barbados by 1655. Whatever the actual number of these transplants, Barbadian authorities did not appreciate being the dumping ground for Ireland's refuse. When Cromwell's expedition to seize Jamaica arrived at Barbados in 1655 seeking recruits for the undertaking, the local government saw its own opportunity to unload the Irish jetsam that had inundated Barbadian society over the past several years and aggravated the problem of an Irish servant class habitually derided as "insubordinate, incorrigibly idle and lazy."[13] For planters the government offer of £25 for every servant made available for the Jamaica operation only added a financial incentive to a welcome opportunity. As for the Irish, they were more than happy to escape the harsh conditions of plantation work, even if it meant being part of a military expedition. Armed with half-pikes mounted on cabbage stalks, some 3,000 servants and slaves boarded the ships bound for Jamaica. At further stops in the Leeward Islands nearly 1,200 more were recruited for the expedition. This, as it happened, with land available on a scale unknown in the Eastern Caribbean, marked the beginning of a mass migration to the new English colony, a migration that over the next decade would include planters, freedmen, servants, and slaves.

By 1650 the increasingly large plantations of the incipient sugar barons had claimed most of the arable land on Barbados. No longer could servants who had completed their indenture expect to receive the ten acres that was customarily part of the terms of service. With the emergence of the sugar industry the price of land had risen exponentially, a tenfold increase from the 1640s to the 1650s. Irish ex-servants, given their ethnicity and religion in this English Protestant society, faced particularly bleak economic prospects. The English ruling class had no intention of allowing Irishmen to become landowners or artisans and the citizenship to which property or a craft entitled one if they could prevent it. They were only too successful in their efforts to suppress Irish economic and political mobility. By the latter half of the seventeenth century most Irish on Barbados found themselves in the same landless condition that

13. Sean O'Callaghan, *To Hell or Barbados* (Dingle: Brandon, 2000), 137.

had caused them to flee Ireland. As early as 1647 the lord proprietor of Barbados was advising servants that migration to the Leeward Islands was their only hope of ever becoming a property owner. Many took the advice and took themselves there and beyond—to Jamaica, Virginia, New England. Many others did not. Opting for an urban migration, some found employment in the warehouses and docks of Bridgetown and Speightown. But for growing numbers of Irish unemployment was their lot after leaving service. By the latter half of the seventeenth century, Irish vagrants were a common (and disturbing) sight in the Barbadian countryside. Prospects were scarcely better even for Irish immigrants who were unbonded but of modest means.

In Barbados's first decades as a colony, more than a few of the Irish immigrants became small planters—including Cornelius Bryan, whose plantation of twenty-two acres and thirteen African slaves likely raised the composite crop that small landowners favored: some combination of sugar, indigo, and foodstuffs. The Catholic planters tended to be Old English, as did the elite group of Irish merchants in the towns, like John Blake, who had come to Bridgetown in the late 1660s. John, along with his two brothers, Nicholas and Henry, were part of a very small, affluent minority of merchants and planters who migrated to the West Indies from Ireland. The Blakes, an Old English family, were part of the merchant oligarchy ("the Galway Tribes") that had traditionally ruled Galway (John and Henry's father had been mayor of Galway City and a member of the Irish Parliament), had lost their extensive estates, and were forcibly relocated to a much less valuable tract of land, the price of casting their lot with the Confederation in the 1640s. Migration to the Leeward Islands became the means for recouping the family's wealth. Blake discovered at Bridgetown that the mercantile business was not his path to financial success and finally abandoned Barbados in 1676 to seek a better fate in Montserrat. By that time it was becoming clear that "the crown jewel" of the empire was rapidly becoming the "worst poor man's country" in English America.[14] For most Barbadians the choice was migration or lifelong poverty.[15]

14. Beckles, *White Servitude and Black Slavery*, 167.
15. Gragg, *Englishmen Transplanted*, 151.

MONTSERRAT AND THE
LEEWARD ISLANDS

The West Indies became the choice of a majority of emigrants from the British Isles in the seventeenth century. Even indentured servants, when given a say in the matter, preferred the Atlantic Islands, including Barbados. Indeed, by the 1650s Barbados was the destination of strong majorities of those entering service in the Caribbean: 70 percent of males, 65 percent of females. But as the lot worsened in Barbados's sugar economy for those in service or beyond it, the Leeward Islands were the beneficiary in attracting emigrants, particularly from Ireland. Indeed, from their first decade they enjoyed a highly positive reputation as a good "poor man's country." When one labor supplier tried in 1637 to recruit a group of Irish at Kinsdale for service in Virginia, it quickly became apparent that their preference was St. Christopher due to the encouraging reports they had heard about the favorable prospects that workers on that island enjoyed. The supplier accommodated their wish and changed their destination to St. Christopher.[16]

By 1678, in a population numbering somewhat fewer than 3,700, including nearly 1,000 African slaves, Catholics made up about a quarter of the white population on Nevis, St. Christopher, and Antigua. On Montserrat they were a dominant 70 percent. A more welcoming government, available land (for those freemen with capital), a location beyond the orbit of the Caribs (in the early years), Irish planters better disposed (than the non-Irish ones elsewhere) to having Irish as indentured servants, and the toleration of Catholicism, if discreetly practiced, were all factors in producing the reputation that drew increasing numbers of Irish Catholics to Montserrat.

Montserrat, the very small (39½-square-mile) volcano-steeped island just below Nevis in the upper Lesser Antilles, from its beginning had a heavy Irish character. Exactly when that beginning was is a mystery. His-

16. Gragg, *Englishmen Transplanted*, 145; see also Anthony Wheler, "Present State of the Leeward Islands," National Archives, London, Colonial Office 1/29, no. 61, December 14, 1672, cited in Jenny Shaw, "Island Purgatory: Irish Catholics and the Reconfiguring of the English Caribbean, 1650–1700" (Ph.D. diss., New York University, 2009), 104.

torians' best guess is that it was sometime during the two years preceding Andrew White's visit in late January of 1633 or 1634. Nor is the provenance of the first settlers precisely known. White reported them as being Irish refugees from Virginia. The historian Donald Akenson judges that there were several groups that comprised the initial settlement of Montserrat, White's Irish from Virginia being one of them. A second group consisted of Irish that the Portuguese transported to Montserrat, among other Leeward Islands, after capturing them at their settlement in northeastern Brazil. Anthony Brisket, a New English merchant who intended to develop Montserrat as a tobacco-producing colony, brought with him from Ireland a third group that was mostly Catholic. The final constituent of the founding wave, according to Akenson, was a group that came from nearby St. Christopher. What the groups all had in common was their Irish Catholicity.

Montserrat continued to be the strongest magnet in the West Indies drawing Catholic emigrants from Ireland in the seventeenth century. The more the Irish came to dominate the population, the more attractive it became for potential Irish émigrés. Most came freely as indentured servants. In the fifties the island was also the principal terminus for the prisoners of war and other Irish undesirables that Cromwell exiled. By the 1660s the island's white population had probably exceeded 3,000, the vast majority of them Irish Catholics. Twenty years later Montserrat had the highest concentration of Irish to be found anywhere in British America. Irish Catholics gravitated to the southern half of the island, with Gaelic Irish tending to settle in areas further south than the ones in which the Old English clustered. This settlement pattern was partially the result of governmental discrimination that tended to segregate the Irish Catholic community on the most marginal lands of the extreme south. Montserrat was also the island in the Lesser Antilles with the lowest proportion of Africans.

In its first two decades the colony experienced none of the Carib raids that terrorized the more northerly islands in the chain. That changed in 1651, when the Indians attacked plantations on the island. Over the course of the next thirty years, despite an elaborate network of stone or timber warning towers around Montserrat's perimeter, periodic

Carib attacks brought devastated plantations, the loss of slaves taken as plunder, and death. It was a major cause for Montserrat's lagging behind the other Leeward Islands in developing a sugar industry. Not until the eighteenth century did the island enjoy the sugar-generated prosperity that Barbados and other West Indian colonies realized much earlier.

One colonist gave a description in 1672 of the living condition of the several hundred Irish on the French islands of Martinique and Guadeloupe that could have applied to most Irish throughout the Leeward Islands, particularly Montserrat. They lived "much as they do at home, in little huts, planting potatoes, tobacco and as much indigo as will buy them canvas and brandy… and never advance so far as a sugar plantation."[17] They were replicating the primitive, subsistent agriculture of the peasants of Gaelic Ireland. Most of the Irish Catholics lived on small plots, often in mountainous terrain, generally on poor land they either owned (sometimes in partnership with other poor farmers), or more often leased in exchange for a portion of the harvest in what amounted to sharecropping. Catholics made up the overwhelming proportion of the landless and near-landless classes on the island. As such they lacked the land, capital, and slave labor to compete in the cultivation of sugar, which by the 1680s had become the dominant staple crop on Montserrat.

The unrest that such a constricted economic condition promoted among the majority of Irish on Montserrat finally led a group of these underside Irish Catholics to rebel in 1666 and assist French forces in overthrowing the English government. Irish Catholics on the English sector of St. Christopher did likewise. The English regained control in 1667, but the traitorous actions of the Irish on both islands simply confirmed longstanding suspicions about Irish loyalty and their collaboration with either the French or African slaves to overturn English rule in the Antilles. Catholics on Barbados were implicated in alleged slave conspiracies in the 1670s and 1680s, but (unlike the Africans) went unpunished. Relations between the government and the Irish underclass continued to fester over the next two decades as the latter's situation worsened in a sugar-dominant economy.

Such very limited economic mobility proved not to be the lot of all

17. Anthony Wheeler, in Shaw, "Island Purgatory," 104.

Irishmen in the West Indies, particularly on Montserrat, where Irish Catholics probably had the best opportunity for advancement. Some managed to become small planters, working twenty or so acres with ten or so slaves. A few, usually those who brought considerable capital with them, did a great deal better. One such was John Blake, who failed, as noted earlier, in Barbados to recoup his family's fortunes that had brought him and his brothers to the West Indies. After relocating to Montserrat in 1676, John achieved that and more. The brothers had arrived in the Lesser Antilles in about 1668. Their timing proved fortuitous, coming shortly after the French invasion of 1666 that had devastated the plantations on the island and sent many planters fleeing (without their slaves, most of whom the French carried off) to seek a new beginning in Jamaica. With abandoned land available, John and Henry had sufficient capital to acquire a large plantation on Montserrat, which Henry managed while John operated a mercantile business in Barbados at Bridgetown. Henry, despite several shifts in his staple crop (from tobacco to indigo to sugar), realized enough profit from sugar to return to Ireland in 1676 to rejoin his wife and children and purchase large tracts of land, his wealth more or less restored and his family once again an economic force in Galway. His brother Nicholas had made his own return voyage to Ireland a year earlier. John, who had not known success as a merchant on Barbados, found it as a planter on Montserrat as he rode sugar's rising tide to become one of the wealthiest men on the island and marry his daughter to Nicholas Lynch, an even richer Irish Catholic planter (probably of the Galway Lynches, the foremost mercantile family of the "Galway Tribes") with influential connections throughout the colonial world.[18]

The penal laws afforded Catholics very limited possibilities for political participation. In the 1671 reorganization of the Leeward Isles as a separate political unit Catholics were allowed to vote as well as to hold minor elected or appointed positions, but could sit neither on the council nor in the assembly. Catholics served in the highest offices largely by passing as church-papists—that is, by making a minimal profession of

18. Kerby A. Miller, Arnold Schrier, Bruce D. Boling, and David N. Doyle, *Irish Immigrants in the Land of Canaan: Letters and Memoirs from Colonial and Revolutionary America, 1675–1815* (New York: Oxford University Press, 2003), 121–27.

Anglicanism while remaining at heart Catholic. Such seems to have been the case with David Gallway, an Irish Catholic veteran of the 1641 uprising in Ulster who relocated to Montserrat in the 1660s, where he eventually became one of the wealthiest planters. Gallway became enough of an Anglican to hold several offices in the Montserrat government, including council membership, but his true religious loyalty apparently remained with Rome, if his legacies can be read as indicators. James Cotter from County Cork served in the 1680s as deputy governor and in other major offices before he was exposed as "a papist and a rebel" in 1689, but the exposure and deposing seems to have been the penalty for Cotter's having abused his office of attorney general, not for his religious commitment or lack of it. After all, Cotter's religious priorities had been well known (among those who needed to know) for many years. This religious ambiguity was not confined to ambitious politicians. Many Catholic planters, especially those of Old English origins, had learned the value of flexibility in religious profession when trying to advance one's economic interests in a hostile society. This self-serving pragmatism would eventually bring many of the leading Catholic planting families within the fold of the Anglicans.

Cotter's mentor, William Stapleton, played the same game, apparently in order to become the Leeward Island's first governor in 1671. Stapleton, like Cotter, was from an Old English family in Ireland. Like the Blakes, the Stapletons, as Catholics and Stuart supporters, had lost their estates in Ireland. William Stapleton had followed the path of many exiled Catholic soldiers in becoming a mercenary in the service first of France, then Spain. With the Restoration Stapleton returned to England, where he received an appointment as lieutenant colonel in the English army. Sent to Barbados in 1667, Stapleton so impressed imperial officials by his bravery during the fighting against France that he was named governor of Montserrat in 1668. Three years later, with political reorganization, he became the head administrator of the Leeward Islands. Never above using his position to advance his own interests (as was commonplace at the time), he acquired immense wealth in land and slaves. No one ever challenged him on the issue of his Catholic faith, even though his Catholic faith was fairly obvious to all. He was "left in place," one historian has observed, "because he was unswervingly loyal to the Crown, a very able governor, smart enough not to make an issue of his Roman Catholicism and, when necessary—to adopt and support the forms of the Established Church."[19] Holding such top offices, crypto-Catholics like Stapleton could effectively disable much of the set of penal laws, which were real enough on paper but largely ignored.

JAMAICA

Part of the Greater Antilles chain in the Western Caribbean, Jamaica was by far the largest as well as the last of the West Indies islands to become part of England's Atlantic empire in the seventeenth century, the Spanish having ceded the island to the English in 1670 in the Treaty of Madrid. By that time Jamaica had actually been under English control for nearly fifteen years, the chief result of Oliver Cromwell's "Western Design" to achieve English hegemony in the Caribbean and Central America and access to the wealth that the precious metals of the region constituted, financial resources that Cromwell was in dire need of by the 1650s. Thomas Gage's *A New Survey of the West Indies* convinced Cromwell that the Spanish West Indies was an easy target for the taking. The day after Christmas in 1654, a thirty-ship fleet under the command of Admiral William Penn set sail from Portsmouth, England, and headed for the Caribbean. Gage, himself aboard officially as chaplain, was in fact the chief designer of the English plan, which involved the capture of Hispaniola, Cuba, Jamaica, Mexico, Central America, and Peru, in that order. Peru, as nature's Fort Knox in South America, was not only the last objective of the expedition but the greatest prize as well. At Barbados 4,000 indentured servants, many of them Irish, either volunteered or were forced to join the invasion force in return for the promise of land and freedom if the expedition should prove a success. At St. Christopher an additional one thousand servants signed on. This brought the military force of the fleet to 9,000 or so. More than three months after

---

19. Donald Harman Akenson, *If the Irish Ran the World: Montserrat, 1630–1730* (Montreal and Kingston: McGill-Queen's University Press, 1997), 102.

departing England nearly all the troops disembarked at two spots west of Santo Domingo. The two-pronged assault was an utter failure. They failed to take Santo Domino and had one thousand fewer soldiers for their efforts.

To raise the spirits of the morale-challenged troops the English commanders changed their military itinerary and headed for Jamaica rather than Cuba, the former's defenses considered far softer than the latter's. Although smaller than either Cuba or Hispaniola, Jamaica held great promise as an area in which to greatly expand England's sugar production. Sugar planters had for some time been lobbying for the acquisition of Jamaica, an island that could potentially produce more sugar than all the other English colonies in the West Indies put together. Another attractive consideration was Jamaica's strategic location in the heart of the Caribbean. If England could not directly seize the mines of Central and South America, its privateers, operating from Jamaica, could reap immeasurable plunder from Spanish ships carrying extracted precious metals through the Caribbean. Whatever factored into England's decision to attack the island, the calculation about the relative ease with which Jamaica could be taken proved to be all too accurate. When the formidable English fleet sailed into Santiago de la Vega in early May of 1655, the Spanish governor of the island was so shaken by the naval behemoth that he quickly agreed to terms of capitulation, only to have his subjects refuse to go along with his surrender. Instead, after dispatching their women and children to Cuba, the Spaniards, mostly cattle ranchers led by Christóbal Arnaldo Ysasi, began a guerilla campaign, together with their African slaves, against their English invaders. For nearly three years Ysasi kept up his harassment of the new occupiers before persistent English pressure, inadequate Spanish reinforcements, and internal dissension, capped by the defection of 200 slaves, forced the Spanish guerillas to abandon their campaign and the island in 1660.

From their initial expedition in 1655 the English had attempted to recruit settlers for Jamaica in a campaign that was renewed after the end of the guerilla opposition. In 1662 the Jamaican government established a land grant program that offered thirty acres of land to all free immigrants and promised religious toleration for all Christians, including Quakers and Catholics. From 1655 on Barbados had been one of the largest, if not the largest, sources of immigration. By all evidence a great many of the servants and freemen who had been part of the 1655 expedition became permanent residents of Jamaica. Most of the population growth, from 2,200 in 1655 to 7,000 in 1683, can be attributed to immigrants from one source: Barbados. Jamaica was an exotic place that had a special Janus-like quality about it that both attracted and repelled. "It was the largest and grandest place… in the Indies," as the historian Richard Dunn summed up Jamaica, "the most fruitful, the most lushly tropical, in every way the most promising land for settlement. But it was also a thoroughly disturbing place: hot, wet, steamy, craggy, jungled, infested with insects and vermin. The colonists found the environment enervating, even corrupting."[20]

By 1670 there were more than 15,000 colonists. Sugar and indigo plantations sprang up, particularly in the southeast part of the island. Even the cattle industry experienced a boom. For all that, buccaneering remained a major occupation; buccaneers were the most powerful force in the initial period of English rule. No doubt there were Irish among those recruits from Barbados and St. Christopher in 1655 who decided to claim their land and remain in Jamaica. There were also the Irish, young and old, forcibly transported to Jamaica from Ireland by Cromwell. However many there were, they could expect to have no part in the government that was set up in 1661. Citizenship in the island was restricted to English natives and their children. Moreover, the laws of England, which included the penal ones, were declared to be in force on the island.

The first large shipment of Irish servants to Jamaica came in the early 1670s, when more than 500 Irish men and women were transported as bond servants for terms of five to seven years. Other such shipments followed from Ireland, as did much larger ones—usually two to three times the size of the Irish contingents—from England itself. No doubt there were more than a few Catholics among the 1,200 to 1,400 emigrants arriving from England each year in the 1670s.

20. Richard S. Dunn, *Sugar and Slaves: The Rise of the Planter Class in the English West Indies, 1624–1713* (Chapel Hill: University of North Carolina Press for the Institute of Early American History and Culture, 1972), 39.

AN AD HOC ISLAND-HOPPING
MINISTRY

English colonization in the West Indies involved the establishment of traditional institutions, including religious ones. Thus, one of the first acts of the first governor of Barbados was to create six parishes. Construction of churches for these parishes soon followed. By 1641 there were 10 clergymen for the island's population of 10,000, and their numbers kept growing. On Barbados, unlike almost everywhere else in English America, there was no shortage of clergy. And most of them made quite a good living from their salaries and stipends. This, of course, was the Church of England, the established church of the empire. For the Catholic Church, the picture was starkly different. Throughout the seventeenth century the church had virtually no institutional presence in the English West Indies—no parishes, public churches, resident priests—this despite a significant presence of Catholics from the beginning on Barbados, St. Christopher, Montserrat, and Jamaica, a presence that grew substantially during the middle and late seventeenth century.

To the extent that the penal laws applied in the English Caribbean, it was a capital offense for priests even to enter a colony, much more to practice his ministry. In that climate the close proximity of French colonies, including the one on St. Christopher, which the French shared with the English, was a distinct asset for the Catholic community. It ensured a body of priests who could provide at least occasional ministry for the Catholic settlers in the English colonies by offering, on St. Christopher's, a haven where English or Irish Catholics could openly practice their religion and from which priests could make semi-secret visits to Montserrat and the other English settlements.

St. Christopher's unique division between Catholic and Protestant powers apparently explains why it became the base for the first priest sent specifically to minister to Catholics in the West Indies. In 1637, in response to pleas from Catholics on St. Christopher, the archbishop of Tuam, Malachy O'Queely, sent two diocesan Irish priests to begin the first permanent Catholic mission in the region. With St. Christopher as their base, the two extended their ministry to all the islands where

there were English-speaking Christians. O'Queely reported a joyful welcome by Catholics wherever along the chain of islands they went. Unfortunately, both priests died before 1640, and, despite O'Queely's requests
and *Propaganda Fide's* order to resupply the mission, no replacements
were sent.

A decade went by before an Irish Jesuit, John Stritch, was sent from
Europe to work in the English Atlantic colonies. On St. Christopher he
built the first chapel in the English Caribbean (although the structure
itself was located in the French sector), where Mass was said both by
Stritch and French pères. For three years from his base on St. Christopher the Jesuit periodically made the one-hundred-mile crossing to
Montserrat, where, posing as a wood merchant, he daily said Mass surreptitiously in a wooded place for Catholics in the area. Afterward he
would engage in an extended bout of wood chopping to enhance his cred-
ibility as a wood merchant. There apparently was a good bit of pretense
at play on the part of the governing officials as well as that of Stritch.
The officials knew who Stritch really was, but chose not to act on their
knowledge. And Stritch maintained his persona to uphold his end of the
tacit understanding. He would not be the last priest to visit Montserrat
in disguise over the last half of the century. None was apparently ever
exposed. The government, it would seem, was content to ignore any religious services being provided, so long as they were done, as it were, under cover.

The English government on St. Christopher, as it turned out, proved
not as accommodating. Pressured by Protestant complaints about the
Catholics from the English sector passing into the French one in order
to attend Mass, officials issued an order that placed the French portion
of the island off limits for all English-sector residents. When Catholics
continued to slip cross the border for services at Stritch's chapel, the governor had the most prominent Catholics transported to the uninhabited
Isle of Crabs off the coast of Guyana, where, as his order read, they could
experience "the last degree of poverty."[21] For the rest of the Catholic community on St. Christopher, attendance at Protestant services was now

21. Johnston, "Papists in a Protestant World," 99.

made mandatory, with harsh penalties for those who failed to comply.

For a time Stritch attempted to maintain his "parish," despite its official repression, but he finally moved on with some of his congregants to the friendlier environs of a French island, Guadeloupe. From there he occasionally returned under disguise to his former island circuit to minister as best he could to the priestless Catholics there before his order recalled him to Ireland in 1660. Six years later John Grace arrived in the area. As Sonia Johnston notes, he "attended English and Irish Catholics wherever he could find them," whether the colony be English, French, or even Dutch.[22] In doing so Grace, like Stritch before him, depended on French authorities to provide, when needed, a base for his activities and on French clergy for assistance and support. When Grace left the area after a few years the weight of ministering to Catholics on English colonies in the Leeward Islands and beyond fell upon French clerics who were within the region. Their outreach to the Catholics in the English islands tended to be sporadic, the result, often enough, of peculiar circumstances such as occurred in Barbados in the mid-1550s.

Antoine Biet, a French Jesuit, came to Barbados in 1554 as the chaplain of a group of French colonists who had failed in their attempt to establish a settlement elsewhere in the West Indies. Irish Catholics on the island quickly sought him out, hungry for the celebration of the Mass and the other sacraments that the French priest could provide. Biet discovered that Catholics could practice their religion in Barbados, much as they could on Montserrat, so long as they did so discreetly—under cover, as it were. Like many of the priests confronting this *modus operandi*, Biet adopted a disguise, that of a gentleman, a ploy that apparently deceived no one, including local officials. It was well enough known who Biet was. If authorities had wished to enforce the laws they could have easily done so, but chose not to, as they had similarly done on Montserrat.

The unstable political situation in the region during the 1670s and 1680s effectively prevented the assignment of any priests to the English mission in the West Indies. At best, French Jesuits on Martinique and St. Christopher tried to make periodic sub rosa visits to Catholic com-

22. Johnston, "Papists in a Protestant World," 103.

munities on Montserrat and elsewhere but faced increasing risks in attempting to provide the sacraments to Catholics in colonies whose authorities became more and more determined to apply the penal laws against priests venturing into their jurisdiction. Where English authorities had previously more or less winked at Catholic gatherings for Mass or other occasions, they now regarded such activities as subversive ones that needed to be prosecuted. The crisis was reached in 1678. In the wake of the supposed Popish Plot in England there was a crackdown on priests in the English Caribbean. Within a few years one could scarcely find a priest anywhere within the boundaries of the empire's colonies. An Irish Augustinian in the area found it necessary to seek sanctuary in Spanish America.

The unchurched nature of Catholicism in the West Indies put great responsibility on the laity to provide occasions for worship and to build the networks of mutual support that defined a Catholic community. It fell to the laity, often women, to keep alive, both communally and privately, the distinctive rituals and spiritual practices of the Catholic tradition. Such rituals and practices often were an eclectic mix of Gaelic and Roman Catholic culture. That many of the Catholics in the islands had been forced there from Ireland because of their faith was very likely a strong motivation for many to keep their faith alive, as best they could, in a churchless world. From her study of the Catholic community in Barbados, Jenny Shaw found a strong Irish female presence, as well as extensive kinship networks; both, no doubt, were important factors in sustaining the religious life of the group.[23] In religious community building no one probably surpassed Nicholas and George Rice, uncle and nephew, of Limerick, Ireland, who with their extended family emigrated to Barbados in the 1660s and became the center of a thriving Catholic community on the island.

Still, the lack of a regular ministry most likely forced many ordinary Catholics to avail themselves of vital religious services as best they could. On Montserrat and the other English islands of the Lesser Antilles that meant utilizing the established church for baptisms, marriages, and buri-

23. Shaw, "Island Purgatory," 156–57.

als. Donald Akenson believes that such habitual recourse led many Catholics into an amorphous religious status in which religious identification was at odds with one's religious practice. Over time, practice eventually shaped identification.

The coming to the throne of James II restored hopes of toleration and freedom in the Catholic community in the English Caribbean, just as it did among their brethren in the British Isles. When Catholics of several of the islands appealed to the governor to grant them the liberty to exercise their religion, Nathaniel Johnson acceded. For Catholics this was the official go-ahead to begin the construction of chapels on Montserrat and St. Christopher, the islands where most of the Catholics resided. Three prominent Catholics, including Nicholas Lynch, petitioned the governor of Montserrat that Catholics, in light of James II's proclamation on religious toleration, be no longer required to pay tithes in support of Anglican ministers. That too Johnson granted, although indirectly. In the future, he ordered, the burden of supporting established churchmen would fall upon the vestries of these churches, not the government. In Barbados the attorney general and a prominent planter, both recent Catholic converts, openly invited a French priest to Bridgetown to establish a ministry for the Catholic community on the island.

Nowhere in the West Indies did James's coming to the throne have a larger impact than in Jamaica. Despite the presence of a significant Catholic community from its beginning, no English-speaking priest had been appointed to the island during its first three decades as an English colony. What ministry the Catholics on Jamaica received, Spanish clergy provided on an occasional basis to the few surviving Spanish residents as well as the Irish and English newcomers. Not until 1685, with a Catholic ruler, did the Catholics of Jamaica petition the king to send a priest to minister to their spiritual needs. James apparently had difficulty finding a willing priest, but eventually Thomas Churchill, although on the edge of sixty, volunteered for the mission. James in that same year had appointed

Sir Philip Howard, member of one of the most distinguished English Catholic families, as governor. Howard, however, died before reaching Jamaica, and James named the Duke of Albemarle, a Protestant, to succeed him, with the special charge of protecting the Catholic community on the island, including its new priest. Churchill, enjoying a grant of £300 a year from the government, arrived in the island at the beginning of 1688. He found a surprisingly active group of Catholics, despite the absence of any institutional underpinnings and the law forbidding any open practice of their religion. The morale of the group no doubt was improved by the duke's subsequent relaxing of the penal laws that formerly had been in effect. A former Dominican monastery in Santiago de La Vega that an English Catholic couple made available to Churchill became the center for his ministry to the Catholic community. Within a few months Churchill's authority as the church's representative in Jamaica was being challenged by a Spanish priest who had been brought in by Spanish-born, naturalized English citizen James Castillo, a slave trader. Castillo, with important connections in both the English and Spanish empires, had received from the new governor of Jamaica, the Duke of Albemarle, the right to have the first choice of slaves in any particular shipload brought into Port Royal. Castillo built a chapel in the city in which his personal chaplain said Mass. Not content with having his private church, Castillo used his Cuban ecclesiastical influence to have the chaplain made a vicar general, on the basis of whose title Castillo claimed that Jamaica, no matter what its political status, was ecclesiastically still under the jurisdiction of Cuba. The contention over the competing claims of authority dragged on for some months between Churchill and Castillo. Finally Castillo, fearing that English officials were preparing to act against his privileged position, fled to Cuba, taking with him his "vicar general." With Castillo and his chaplain out of the country, Churchill expanded his ministry to Port Royal, where he regularly performed Catholic services out of the Old King's House.

CHAPTER 5

"THE MIRACLE
OF THIS AGE"

Maryland and New York
under the Restoration

A FINE COUNTRY

He that desires to see the real Platform of a quiet and sober Government extant, Superiority with a meek and yet commanding power sitting at the Helme, steering the actions of State quietly, through the multitude and diversity of... waves that diversely meet, let him look on Maryland... and he'l then judge her, The Miracle of this Age.

Here the Roman Catholick, and the Protestant Episcopal... concur in an unanimous parallel of friendship, and inseparable love intayled unto one another. All Inquisitions, Martyrdom, and Banishments are not so much as named, but unexpressably abhorr'd by each other.[1]

So wrote George Alsop in 1666, just six years after the "pygmie rebellion." Alsop, who had immigrated to Maryland in 1658 as an indentured servant, published, with Lord Baltimore's assistance, *A Character of the Province of Maryland* to promote immigration into the province. If his language was hyperbolic

---

1. George Alsop, *A Character of the Province of Maryland* (London: 1666), in *Narratives of Early Maryland, 1633–1684*, edited by Clayton Colman Hall (New York: Charles Scribner's Sons, 1910), 349.

regarding the abundance of economic opportunity and the equanimity of social relations in Maryland, there was a core of truth to the economic mobility and political serenity he extolled, at least for two decades after the dual restoration of the Calverts and the Stuarts. The policy of religious toleration enacted in 1649 (and restored with the return of the Calverts) promoted peace among the province's increasingly diverse population and concomitant social mobility.

Peopling his province continued to be a major concern for Cecil Calvert. The English Civil War had reduced immigration to a negligible level; what there was continued to be overwhelmingly male, with a high mortality rate from "seasoning." A minor factor in the relative stagnation of the province's population was outmigration, for which the Brents, who in the 1650s had relocated to Virginia because of their differences with Lord Baltimore, were a major responsible party. Giles Brent, who had resettled his extended family on Virginia's northern frontier near Aquia Creek in Stafford County, recruited scores of Marylanders, many of them Catholics, to people the Northern Neck, where he had extensive holdings. Such a settlement service disposed Virginia authorities, despite occasional attempts by Virginia Anglicans to enforce the colony's anti-Catholic laws, to exercise a practical toleration toward the Brents and their fellow Catholics. Brents served as officers in the militia, practiced the law; one (Giles Brent's nephew George) even served the king as Virginia's attorney general. George eventually was elected a delegate to the Virginia House of Burgesses.

In 1660 the Maryland population was about 2,500. Over the next fifteen years it more than quintupled to 13,000, thanks mostly to a sharp upturn of immigrants. By 1688 the population stood at 25,000. Male indentured servants, like George Alsop, constituted about 60 percent of the newcomers, a much smaller majority than before the English Civil War. Among the substantial freemen coming into the province there were fewer landed gentry and many more merchants. Protestants dominated both immigrant groups, but wealthy individuals increasingly represented a minority of the new freemen. Typical of the non-binded persons immigrating into the province during this period were the Quakers, who avidly responded to Lord Baltimore's renewed invitation to dissenters to populate his colony. Many of them abandoned Virginia for the toleration and land that neighboring Maryland offered. Settling largely in Anne Arundel County and on the Eastern Shore, they quickly attracted sizeable numbers of converts. By the 1680s Quakers constituted the largest body of Protestants in Maryland and soon occupied an important place in its economy and government.[2]

The most significant change in the demographics of immigration was the increase of families, which accounted for one-third of those arriving in the province during the 1660s. Most were of middling status, lured by promotional literature like Alsop's and the headright system that promised economic success and security and the resources to raise a staple crop, tobacco, which was enjoying a boom period in which production could barely keep up with demand. For those who came as indentured servants, once they fulfilled their four or five years of service high wages for farm labor enabled them within a few years to acquire land cheaply. By the 1660s most free males were small planters working farms of several hundred acres. It was, as three historians have labeled it, the Age of the Yeoman Planter. "In this ... land-abundant, labor-short economy," they note, "the yeoman planter and his farm building were a dynamic element in the development of a prosperous colony."[3] A fine country for rich, middling, and poor alike.

Among the strong minority of families that were Catholic, the experience of the Cole family embodies the economic opportunities available for those of moderate means. Robert and Rebecca Cole, with four children and two servants, along with a modest capital of some £50, migrated from England to Maryland in 1652. Robert, in his mid-twenties, and the older Rebecca (two of the children were from her earlier marriage), acquired 300 acres of land on St. Clement's Manor, owned by the Catholic Thomas Gerrard. With his freehold constituting an above-average plot size for tobacco farming in the region, Cole, with his four sons and two servants as a work force, cultivated about a third of this land. His entrance into tobacco growing could not have been timelier, given the

2. At least according to Charles Calvert; Krugler, *English and Catholic*, 223.
3. Carr, Menard, and Walsh, *Robert Cole's World*, 17.

boom years for the industry after 1650. He also built up a livestock herd for which the expanding population was providing an ever-growing market in the third quarter of the century. In less than ten years Cole had seen his real and personal estate more than quadruple in value. The only thing that prevented this self-described yeoman from reaching the upper ranks of the gentry was his premature death in 1663. His wife, Rebecca, apparently died shortly before him in the same year. Economic mobility notwithstanding, dysentery, typhoid, malaria, and other local maladies continued to produce an extraordinarily high death rate among both men and women and prevented any natural increase of the province's population. Although some 23,500 persons immigrated to Maryland between 1634 and 1681, its population remained below 19,000 at the beginning of the 1680s.

<h2 style="text-align:center">WOMEN AND THE BUILDING OF COMMUNITY</h2>

Cole was not the only Catholic land seeker to find success at St. Clement's. By 1661 Gerrard had sold nine freeholds on his estate, six of them to Catholics. The Newtown area, of which St. Clement's was a part, was becoming a center of Catholic settlement. Catholic families, reflecting their English experience of banding together as a necessity for survival, tended to create informal networks to meet recurring or special needs, such as assistance in the construction of buildings, in illness, or in death. A comparison of the social life in Maryland of Catholics and Quakers, another persecuted group in England, is instructive. Michael Graham found evidence that the Catholic community, like its Quaker counterpart, was sensitive to the economic well-being of its members, both by coming to the aid of its poor and by advancing the prosperity of the group as a whole.[4] And, in a society where death all too often prematurely claimed one or both parents, Catholics outside the family itself provided for the surviving children, as Luke Gardiner did for the Cole children upon the

4. Michael Graham, "Meetinghouse and Chapel: Religion and Community in Seventeenth-Century Maryland," in *Colonial Chesapeake Society*, edited by Carr, Morgan, and Russo, 253.

death of their parents in 1663. These functional networks also may have been in part responsible for the greater frequency with which Catholics married. As with the Quaker networks, the Catholic ones served as the pool within which the young found marriage partners, which led to dense family interconnections among the Catholic community in the peninsula between the Potomac and Patuxent rivers. As Graham notes, "the lessons [Catholics and Quakers] had learned as dissenters in England... served them well. Their banding together as religious community both ensured the vitality of their faiths and provided them with powerful advantages in a fledgling province where immigration patterns, disease, and death conspired against social development."[5]

As in recusant England, the status of women within both communities was higher than that of women beyond them, a reality that Catholic and Quaker belief (Mary as Mother of God and a gender-inclusive deity respectively) promoted. This status was borne out by women's role in marriage, their engagement in activities beyond the family circle, and inheritance patterns. In marriage women were considered not as docile subordinates but as their husbands' partners, sharing the responsibility and authority for managing farms and plantations as well as for raising children. Mothers indeed were the primary religious educators. In the spiritual realm they were the lynchpins of continuity through their supervision of the family's devotional life and religious observance.

Like Margaret Brent, women acted as executors of wills and lawyers in court; others operated businesses such as taverns. More than four-fifths of Catholic male testators named their wives as executrices of their wills. Fathers often made their daughters heirs of real estate, which afforded such women the independence that allowed some of them to opt not to marry. For their surviving partners most husbands, whether of substantial means or much less so, willed large portions of real and personal estate; in some cases the grant was not just during the lifetime of the widow but in freehold, with the recipient able to dispose of it as she wished. Whether a grant was for the life of the woman or in freehold, typically the will authorized the widow to (continue to) manage most,

5. Graham, "Meetinghouse and Chapel," 274.

if not all, of the property. Such independent economic power enabled Catholic widows to live separately from any grown children. It also gave them the wherewithal to become important benefactors. Henrietta Maria Neale was the daughter of a wealthy Catholic family that had served Charles I before fleeing England in the 1640s and eventually settling in Maryland after Charles's son ascended the throne. Henrietta married Richard Bennett, a Catholic who upon his death was probably the richest man in the province. He made Henrietta his executrix and left her the bulk of his estate. She remarried a prominent Protestant, Philemon Lloyd, and by him had several children. Her two children from her first marriage she raised as Catholics. Henrietta remained in firm control of her two estates, "Henrietta Maria's Discovery" and "Henrietta Maria's Purchase." Throughout her life she was an important figure within the Catholic community, as the frequency with which Catholic couples on the Eastern Shore named their daughters after her attests. On one of her estates she built a chapel that became a regular venue where Mass was celebrated.

INSTITUTIONAL EXPANSION

In 1661 an English provincial of the Society of Jesus contemplated dissolving the Maryland mission for the third time. Twice over the past decade and a half the mission had been violently uprooted, with at least three deaths. Then, too, with the Stuarts again on the throne, the opportunities for expanding Jesuit ministries within England threatened to tax the available manpower. As it was, with no support from Lord Baltimore, maintaining the mission in Maryland was a special financial burden for the province. And the ministry that had most drawn Jesuits to Maryland—evangelizing the Native Americans—no longer existed. When the provincial raised the matter of discontinuing the mission with the superior general in Rome, the latter left the decision to the provincial himself. Fortunately, the latter seemed unable to do that. In 1667 his successor approached the superior general again about the prospect of suppressing the Maryland mission. As he had the previous time, the head of the order left the decision with the province, and once more no resolution followed at the local level. The inertia proved providential, as the Maryland mission experienced over the next twenty years its greatest expansion in its brief history.

Henry Warren, newly ordained at twenty-six, became superior of the mission in 1661. Over the next thirty years there were usually no more than four Jesuits—priests, scholastics, and coadjutors (lay brothers)—in Maryland. The death rate of the missionaries remained high. In 1671 the English provincial reported to Rome that "Of those who were sent [to Maryland] these last years, very few survive, the rest having been carried off by death."[6] This loss forced the province to expedite the training of Jesuits to provide men such as Warren for the mission. Warren proved a particularly able administrator of the society's plantations. Through the labor of indentured servants and tenants, St. Inigoes and St. Thomas Manor both began to produce the revenues to support the mission's ministries. Also, in the more secure political climate, Warren was able to transfer the ownership of the properties from lay trustees into his own name (but not as the head of a religious community, in deference to the statutes of mortmain that prohibited religious bodies from holding property). He also had the capital—40,000 pounds of tobacco—to purchase in 1668 a large tract of land on Britton's Neck that became Newtown Manor. When a French Jesuit from Acadia visited the province in 1673, he was surprised to discover the three English Jesuits on one plantation not in black robes, but the two priests dressed like gentlemen and the brother dressed like "a farmer."[7] Their dress revealed their status, if not their employment: priest planters who typically left the actual management of the plantations to coadjutors (brothers). The main occupation of the priests themselves was serving the proliferating missions throughout southern Maryland. From the plantations they went out on circuits by horse and boat for weekly or less frequent visits to the missions that they established as Catholics spread north- and eastward in the province. On Newtown Neck the Catholic residents, including Robert Cole,

6. Hughes, *History of the Society of Jesus; Text,* 2:76.
7. Claude Dablon to Jean Pinnette, Quebec, October 24, 1674, in *Jesuit Relations and Allied Documents,* edited by Reuben Gold Thwaites (Cleveland: Burrows, 1896–1901), 59:72–74; cited in Hughes, *History of the Society of Jesus; Text,* 2:127–28.

financed and built a church in 1661 to serve the spiritual needs of the local community. From 1661 to the 1680s nine chapels were built, including the "Great Brick Chappelle" in St. Mary's City.

There had been a Catholic presence on the Eastern Shore of the Chesapeake at least since Giles Brent had patented Fort Kent Manor on Kent Island in 1640. Other Catholic gentry followed, including the Clarkes on Kent Island, the Lands at Rich Neck Manor on Eastern Bay, the Sayers and Willsons on the Wye River, the Lowes on the peninsula formed by the Tred Avon River and Town Creek, and the Langfords in Kent County on the upper shore. John Langford had received 1,500 acres from a grateful Cecil Calvert for his defense of Baltimore's proprietary's rights ("Refutation of Babylon's Fall") during the London pamphlet war in the 1650s. In the third quarter of the century nonresident Catholic gentry such as Henry Sewall established plantations on the lower shore around the Wicomico River in Somerset County worked by indentured servants—Irish, English, and Scotch—many of them Catholics. Irish Catholic clustering on the lower Pocomoke River led to the area receiving the appellation of "Irish Grove." Smaller planters such as the Stapleforts and Tubmans dominated the Catholic community that grew up in Dorchester County in the 1670s. The largest Catholic landholder by far on the Eastern Shore was George Talbot, a cousin of Lord Baltimore, to whom in 1680 the proprietor had granted an immense tract spanning more than 70 miles in the northeastern corner of the province, at the head of Chesapeake Bay, an area whose boundaries were being disputed by Charles Calvert and William Penn. Over the next several years Talbot brought in scores of tenants to work the land, most of them Catholics, but eventually sold his holdings when Penn seemed to be getting the upper hand in his territorial claims upon the region.

Catholicism had no institutional presence on the Shore in the seventeenth century. To accommodate the occasional ministry of priests from across the bay, the gentry built chapels on their estates or set aside rooms that became the liturgical centers of "Mass Houses," as these dwellings came to be known. Around mid-century Philip Land at Rich Neck constructed a chapel attached to his home where priests from the Western Shore came periodically to celebrate Mass and administer the sacraments.

Other gentry, in the manner of their English counterparts, set aside a room to serve as a liturgical site. One of them, Peter Sayer, built the first freestanding ecclesiastical structure for Catholic worship, the Wye Chapel in Wye Town, across the Wye River from his home on Piney Neck.

As the venues for celebrating word and sacrament increased, so did the outreach to the non-Catholic majority. Unlike England, where the Jesuits had come consciously to eschew proselytizing, in Maryland they deliberately, even aggressively, sought converts. In a society in which the law provided a marketplace for the selling of Catholicism with virtually no competition from the Church of England, there were numerous ones to be made, particularly among the gentry. Our work "is yielding no common harvest," the provincial reported in 1671, "and it would produce more if there were more workmen to till it." In that year alone there had been 50 converts, many "being of the first quality."[8] In a seven-year stretch from 1667 to 1674 there were no fewer than 260, at least 100 of them attributed to Peter Manners, the most noted Catholic controversialist and preacher of the period. Several of the children of Robert Brooke, a Protestant minister who had headed the provincial council in 1652, converted to Catholicism; the converts included Thomas Brooke, three of whose sons became Jesuits.

The Jesuits in Maryland were slow to turn to education, one of their prominent apostolates in Europe. Indeed the first Catholic educator in the province was a former Jesuit scholastic, Ralph Crouch, who began a school in St. Mary's City in the 1640s, then, thanks to an endowment from a Newtown resident, moved it to that settlement in 1653. Crouch maintained the institution until 1659, when he returned to Europe to reenter the Society as a lay brother. Nearly two decades later, in 1677, two Jesuits began a preparatory school of the humanities in the province. Tradition has placed the site of the school at Newtown, but recent archeological discoveries adjacent to the foundation of the Brick Chapel at St. Mary's City present strong evidence that this was the location of the institution that apparently was in operation until nearly the close of the

8. George Gray to Giovanni Paolo Oliva, Annual Letter, 1671, in Hughes, *History of the Society of Jesus in North America*, Vol. I, Part I, "Documents" (London: Longmans, Green, 1908), 134.

century. Some students went on to continue their education at the Jesuit college of St. Omer's in Flanders. One of them, Robert Brooke, in 1684 became the first Maryland native to enter the Jesuits. Two other Marylanders followed Brooke into the Society over the next five years.

Such native vocations offered a long-term solution to the mission's manpower shortage. For the present, the problem caused by Maryland's growing Catholic population (Lord Baltimore estimated the number of Catholics to be 2,000 in 1669) caused the proprietor to seek additional priests outside the Society for his province. The Sacred Congregation of the Propagation of the Faith secured a commitment from the Franciscans to supplement the Jesuit presence in Maryland with their own missionaries. In 1672 Thomas Massey and Henry Carew became the first Franciscans to work in Maryland, at Matappany and St. Mary's respectively. Over the next twenty-seven years as many as nine Franciscans were active in Maryland.

CHARLES CALVERT AND A
BAROQUE CAPITAL

In September 1661 Cecil Calvert named his son, Charles, to succeed his uncle, Philip, as governor. The latter became chancellor of the province. Together the two Calverts provided an effective administration during a time of rapid expansion in which the responsibilities of government were accordingly multiplying. They organized new counties to accommodate the spreading population. They made the bureaucracy more efficient, essentially through its decentralization as judicial and administrative powers devolved upon the counties. The counties now assumed responsibility for building and maintaining roads, licensing inns, raising taxes, building jails, and other matters. It also represented a de-Catholicization of authority, since there were fewer than one in ten Catholics among local officials, many of whom, in particular the justices of the peace, whose duties significantly increased in the 1660s and 1670s, were recent Protestant immigrants of means.

In 1667 Lord Baltimore incorporated St. Mary's as the first official city in the colony. It marked the formal beginning of what Cecil Calvert

Great Brick Chapel, St. Mary's City

intended to be a grand Baroque capital. The proprietor, from Maryland's inception, had had a particular interest in urban development. As indicated by the town dimension of his initial "Conditions of Plantation," St. Mary's figured prominently in Lord Baltimore's vision for the colony. With stability restored in 1660, Calvert was finally able to pursue a bold plan for his capital. In shaping that plan the London-based Cecil Calvert may well have been influenced by the designs that Christopher Wren and John Evelyn developed for the rebuilding of London after the Great Fire of 1666. The actual design of St. Mary's was apparently the work of Jerome White, the proprietor's surveyor general. His city plan centered on a large, open square some 100 feet wide by 150 feet long. Marking the corners of the town's periphery were four monumental brick structures (a chapel, state house, school, and jail), which, in classical Baroque design, formed two symmetrical triangles with the square and were approx-

State House, St. Mary's City

imately a half mile from each other. The distance from the chapel and the state house to the town center was approximately 1,400 feet. The primary streets radiated from the town square, framed by four wooden buildings (the governor's house, two ordinaries, and a lawyer's office), each 125 feet distant from its neighbors. Symmetry and proportion reigned.

The positions of the chapel and assembly house at the opposite ends of the city symbolized the separation of church and state in Maryland in stark contrast to the design of the succeeding capital, Annapolis, three decades later, in which the seats of church and government would be located in adjoining circles reflecting the union of the two realms. Notable too was the fact that the construction and maintenance of the St. Mary's chapel, unlike the church in Annapolis, were funded privately. Still, the prominence of the "Great Brick Chappelle" was a bold statement of Catholicism's public presence in Maryland, a presence it had not known in any English domain since Elizabeth I had ascended the throne more than a century earlier. Situated as it was on the highest point in the area, the three-foot-thick walls of the cruciform building rose some twenty-three feet, topped by a peaked tile roof fifty feet above the churchyard. Nothing remains of the superstructure to indicate its architectural style, but logic as well as the basic shape of the building (a nave nearly twenty yards in length, as well as an even broader apse, spanning the arms of the cross) strongly suggest that the chapel reflected baroque, Jesuit church architecture in Flanders and France. Its cost may have been as high as £650, an unheard-of sum for a colonial seventeenth-century building. This was grandeur hitherto unseen in the British American world.

The chapel, the first of the four brick structures to be built, was completed around 1666 or 1667. The statehouse, constructed a decade later, utilized the same cruciform design and scale as its ecclesiastical counterpart. By the end of the 1670s the public face of the capital was complete; in all, the town now boasted thirty private dwellings. It was an impressive start toward making St. Mary's a fully functioning political and social center.

ANTI-CATHOLICISM, UNREST, AND REBELLION

The restoration of the Stuarts, with their Catholic connections, including the king's mother, the dowager queen Henrietta Maria; his wife, Catherine of Braganza, who had twenty-eight priests among her retinue and, like her mother-in-law, maintained a public chapel at which hundreds attended Mass; and the king's convert brother, the Duke of York, revived in the 1670s a virulent, conspiracy-obsessed anti-Catholicism. The revival produced new test acts in England beginning in 1673 aimed at preventing "the Growth of Popery." By 1678, one historian notes, "the language of conspiracy dominated political discourse in the English Atlantic world."[9] Much of that dominance was due to the legs that one preposterous charge acquired in that very year, the so-called "Popish Plot" to kill the king, burn London, and seat the Catholic Duke of York on the throne. This outrageous story, concocted by Titus Oates and exploited by those intent on foiling any possible Catholic succession to the throne (the Duke being next in line, with Charles II heirless), fell upon ears ready to

9. Owen Charles Stanwood, "Creating the Common Enemy: Catholics, Indians, and the Politics of Fear in Imperial North America, 1678–1700" (Ph.D. diss., Northwestern University, 2005), 27.

have their worst fears confirmed. At least twenty-two persons paid with their lives for this national mix of cynicism and credulity.[10] The narrative predictably spread throughout England and across the Atlantic to British America. The major carriers of such alarming tales were Protestant emigrants going into Maryland, Virginia, and other British colonies who reflected the increasing anti-Catholicism sweeping England in the 1670s and 1680s. They found the inhabitants of no colony more disposed to heed their alarms than the Protestant residents of Maryland, a colony with a Catholic ruler and a significant portion of its population adherents of Rome. Such immigrants were able to exploit economic, religious, and political issues, particularly after Charles Calvert succeeded his father as proprietor in 1675, to build up unrest and opposition to the proprietor and his associates as autocratic papists endangering the liberties and rights of Protestant Englishmen.

Tobacco had been the springboard for the economic mobility that distinguished Maryland in the third quarter of the century. A one-staple economy, however, is a precarious one by its very nature, as Marylanders began painfully to discover in the 1660s when overproduction, falling prices, and rising land and labor costs produced economic ills that steadily worsened over the next two decades. The imposition of the Navigation Acts by the crown, beginning in 1660, aggravated the problems of the growers, who tended to blame the proprietor, along with the Committee for Trade and Plantations, for the restrictive laws. Lord Baltimore did not improve his standing with Maryland planters, especially large ones, when in 1667 he vetoed a bill mandating a moratorium on tobacco growing in an attempt to control prices. Nor did his son, Charles, as his successor, endear himself to his subjects when in 1683 he ended the headright system that had been in place for a half century and substituted a grant of tobacco, a currency worth but half of what its value had been twenty years earlier, for persons brought into the province. Those affected worst by this declining economy were the poor, particularly those completing their period of service who were finding it increasingly diffi-

10. Frances E. Dolan, *Whores of Babylon: Catholicism, Gender, and Seventeenth-Century Print Culture* (Ithaca and London: Cornell University Press, 1999), 158.

cult to join the ranks of independent farmers that had been the traditional outcome for former servants in Maryland. The age of the yeoman
farmer was coming to an end.

By the 1670s immigration had made religious pluralism a prominent
characteristic of Maryland's population. The province was now comprised
of Anglicans, Catholics, and Protestant dissenters (Presbyterians, Inde-
pendents, Anabaptists, and Quakers), the latter constituting the majority
of Christians. Like Catholics, these dissenting groups had not depended
on the government to supply and support their ministers in England and
were fully prepared to continue that tradition in Maryland. Not so the
Church of England. Its ministers expected the proprietor of Maryland
to provide the same support in Maryland that the crown provided for
the church in England. As it was, there had been no Anglican minister
in Maryland before 1650. By the mid- 1670s there were but three. This
occasioned a letter from an Anglican priest in Maryland, John Yeo, to the
Archbishop of Canterbury, in which he complained that there were more
Jesuits (five) in Maryland ministering to the 1 percent of the population
that Catholics constituted than there were Anglican priests (three) for the
rest of the 20,000 Marylanders (most of whom, he failed to point out,
were dissenters—Puritans or Quakers—not Anglicans, even nominally).
Eventually Yeo's misleading complaint made its way to the king's privy
council, who urged Charles Calvert to devise some means to support a
sufficient number of priests of the established church. In reply, Lord Baltimore pointed out that Anglicans, like Catholics, made up but a small
minority of the province's population. From the beginning Maryland had
promised freedom of religion to those who immigrated, with its implication that they would not be taxed to support any religious establishment.
Given this tradition, Calvert concluded, it would be virtually impossible
to reach a consensus as to what particular religious group should be officially funded. The proprietor's argument prevailed. Neither the Privy
Council nor the Board of Trade took any further action to address Maryland Anglicans' complaints. The issue itself continued to fester in the
province, especially kept alive by recent immigrants who tended, unlike
earlier ones, to be practicing Anglicans and expected their religion to be
the established one in Maryland, as it was in England. They especially

resented the options that the province afforded most committed Anglicans: to cease their practice of religion or to convert to a religion widely
available to settlers: Roman Catholicism and Quakerism.

But it was the perception of the Calverts' rule as arbitrary and Catholic-dominated that most fed the criticism of a growing number of Marylanders. There was great opposition to the proprietor's actions restricting
the size of the electorate and the assembly. In 1670 Cecil Calvert exercised
his prerogative to limit the suffrage to freemen with personal estates of
forty pounds sterling or more. Six years later his son reduced the number
of delegates that each county could elect to the assembly from four to
two. When an act of the assembly in 1678 reinstated the original number
of representatives for each county, Charles Calvert disallowed that act.
And no element of the Calverts's rule alienated Marylanders' more than
the bias toward Catholics and Quakers they displayed in appointments
to the provincial council, whose members monopolized the most lucrative provincial fee-paying positions, such as the probation of estates and
the distribution of land as well as the highest military offices. In the period between 1660 and 1689, of the thirty-two who sat on the governor's
council, close to twenty-one, or two-thirds, were Catholics. Fifteen of the
councilors were related to the Calverts by blood or marriage. Among the
eleven Protestants there were a disproportionate number of Quakers. By
the 1680s there was a major struggle between the Protestant-dominated
assembly and the largely Catholic provincial council over taxes, particularly for military expenditures, and over which body should determine
what English laws should apply to Maryland. The assembly increasingly
reflected the frustration of its Protestant gentry and merchant members
at not being able to exercise the political power that their wealth and
status warranted and that they saw as being suppressed by the effectively
autocratic rule of the proprietary family.

When Charles Calvert found it necessary in 1676 to return to England
to defend his territorial boundaries against the conflicting charter that the
king had recently granted the Penn family, disgruntled planters, inspired
in part by Nathaniel Bacon's rebellion in neighboring Virginia, seized
the occasion to take up arms to force a change in government. In Calvert
County sixty or so men assembled at a plantation to march on the capital.

The provincial council twice attempted in vain to quell the uprising, first by ordering the rebels to lay down their arms, then by promising pardons for all but the leaders. Having failed through persuasion, the council sent a militia company to deal with the revolt. One skirmish later it ended in the dispersal of the insurgents and the capture of their head, William Davis, who was subsequently executed. That, as it developed, was not the last to be heard from them. In a formal letter to royal authorities, under the title "A Complaint to heaven with a Huy and Crye... out of Virginia and Maryland," the planters aired their grievances against the proprietor: that he was systematically corrupting government by bribing officials and stacking elections in his favor to make himself "an absolute prince over the King's freeborn Subjects of England." Not only had he fostered the growth of popery through his neglect of the Church of England, but his "popish" council, directed by "the secret Councell of priests," was concocting plots against the Protestant inhabitants of the province.[11]

In London Calvert vigorously defended his rule, and the king's government pursued the dissidents' complaints no further. Calvert County, if not placated, ceased to be a source of stirrings against the proprietor. Not so the adjoining Charles County, where Josias Fendall and John Coode continued to host meetings at which the participants aired their displeasure with the government and circulated the latest rumors of Catholic conspiracies, often involving the Susquehannocks, who still made occasional raids on the colony's northern frontier. Coode, a Protestant immigrant who had made himself a wealthy man through his marriage to a daughter of Thomas Gerrard, had initially been a beneficiary of Lord Baltimore's patronage upon his arrival in the province in 1672. When that bounty dried up Coode became one of the most virulent critics of the proprietor's rule. He found a congenial ally in the former governor, Fendall, who had his own serious issues with Baltimore.

In 1681 all the issues fomenting unrest seemed to come together for the pair, who produced the second uprising in five years. Through the spring of that year rumors of Catholic designs to wreak destruction upon Protestants, either through Indian raiders or imported Irish servants, had

11. *Archives of Maryland* 5:137–47, in "Popish Plots: Protestant Fears in Early Colonial Maryland, 1676–1689," by Michael Graham, *Catholic Historical Review* 79 (April 1993): 207.

been criss-crossing the county. When Indians (or, as some thought, Anglos dressed as natives) murdered several persons in St. Mary's County, it seemed to confirm the worst fears. The provincial council, having good reason to believe that Coode and Fendall were behind the rumors, arrested them on the charge of spreading falsehoods in the cause of insurrection and ordered them to stand trial later in the summer. That preemptive action only gave new life to the rumors that now saw the executions of Coode and Fendall as part of the Catholic plan against Protestants. George Godfrey, a justice of the peace and leader of a troop of cavalry in the country, decided to rescue the pair from the jail in St. Mary's City. On a Sunday in mid-July he set off for the capital with between thirty and forty members of a militia he had organized. The provincial council, having been alerted about the march, had a larger armed group waiting for the insurgents. Like the uprising of 1676, the rebels were dispersed and their leader captured, to be tried along with Coode and Fendall. In the subsequent trial Fendall and Godfrey were convicted for "seditious words" and insurrection. The former was banished from the province and the latter sentenced to be hanged (the sentence was eventually changed to banishment). Coode was acquitted.

Three years later a sensational crime involving a government official and relative of the Calverts provided powerful new evidence of the proprietary government's malfeasance. When an argument broke out aboard a ship anchored in the Patuxent River between George Talbot, a councilman and cousin of Charles Calvert, and Christopher Rousby, a customs collector for the crown, Talbot, "in the height of passion," mortally stabbed Rousby. The ship's captain immediately had Talbot put in irons and confined to the ship. Pleas of the council that Talbot be released into their hands to stand trial went unheeded. Talbot was subsequently taken to Virginia, whose governor refused to extradite him to Maryland, but rather awaited orders from London on how to proceed. Before they could arrive Talbot escaped, apparently having bribed his jailer. Three months later he surrendered to the sheriff in Anne Arundel County. It became Maryland's turn to plead an inability to extradite Talbot, now to Virginia, until they heard London's pleasure. That turned out to be a Virginia trial, where Talbot, unsurprisingly, was sentenced to death in April 1686. A year later the king issued a pardon on condition that Talbot not be allowed to return to Maryland. He didn't, but his crime had provided new substance to the worst suspicions about Catholic power in the province.

A SECOND "CATHOLIC" COLONY

Even before the English seized New Netherland from the Dutch in 1664, Charles II had designated the immense body of land controlled by the Dutch between the Connecticut and the Delaware rivers as a personal colony for his brother, James, Duke of York. New York thus became the second proprietary settlement in British America. When James converted to Roman Catholicism a decade later, the province became the second one to be headed by a Catholic. Like Maryland in its earliest stage, the fur trade dominated the economy. Like Maryland, too, many of the chief officials of New York, from governor to customs collector, were Catholic. And like Maryland under the Calverts, New York under the duke enjoyed religious toleration. Catholics themselves were virtually a non-presence in the heterogeneous general population (approximately 10,000 in 1665), which included Flemings, Walloons, French, Germans, Scandinavians, English, Scotch, and Africans. The province was heavily Dutch in the Hudson River Valley from New York City to Albany, mostly English in the smaller settlements on Long Island, Staten Island, Nantucket, and Martha's Vineyard. What Catholics there were in the province could be found among provincial officials and in the garrisons in the major cities; in the ranks of both, Catholics were disproportionately represented. That disproportionate presence fed the anti-Catholic paranoia that, as in Maryland, increasingly plagued New York from the latter 1670s through the 1680s.

The structure of government at the provincial level included only the governor and his council; there was no assembly, which the Dutch would have inevitably dominated. Local government existed only for the areas with an English majority, as on Long Island and Staten Island. The result was a highly centralized government that set laws and imposed taxes without popular representation, a situation especially resented by the English minority. That the leading officials in the province, from the proprietor to the governor and his council, tended to be Catholics fed

the religious phobias among both the Dutch and the English about arbitrary and autocratic papist governance.

The Duke of York's conversion to Catholicism coincided with the
Second Anglo-Dutch War of 1672–74, during which the Dutch briefly
regained their former colony. When the English reconquered New York
in 1674 James introduced a policy of religious toleration for the inhabitants of the province. As in Maryland, that policy ill-served the majority
of residents in New York: the Dutch, whose Reformed Church had previously been the established religion for New Netherland. Without government support the Reformed Church lost half of its six ministers to
repatriation within six years of the English takeover. Nor did James help
matters by imposing anglicizing Dutch ministers upon the church communities in Albany and New York City, which only served to alienate the
mass of Dutch church members all the more. Jacob Leisler, a clergyman's
son and successful merchant, challenged in court the orthodoxy of the
first such minister, a Dutchman ordained in the Church of England, but
failed in his suit. The duke was more successful with the Dutch mercantile elite in his anglicization campaign by appointing Stephanus Van
Cortland, Nicholas Bayard, and Frederick Philpse to a majority of seats
on the supreme governing body, the provincial council. James's other attempt toward anglicization of the province—recruiting immigrants from
the British Isles—was a failure. The only significant influx of newcomers
to New York proved to be French Huguenots, who took advantage of an
offer of citizenship for settling in the colony. Ironically, the English conquest of New Netherland was responsible for the initiation, or at least
the quickening, of ethnic consciousness among the Dutch.

THE BEGINNINGS
OF CATHOLICISM IN
THE JERSEYS

In the wake of England's conquest of New Netherland in 1664, the Duke
of York ceded to a group headed by two English noblemen a portion of
the newly acquired territory, named New Jersey, roughly the area bound-
ed by Long Island Sound on the north, the Hudson and Atlantic on the

east, the Delaware on the west, and the mouth of Delaware Bay on the south. A dozen years later differences among the proprietors led to a division of the province into East Jersey and West Jersey, an arrangement that lasted until the two were reunited as a royal colony in 1702. Like New York's royal proprietor, New Jersey's rulers early adopted a policy of religious toleration that attracted not only Protestant dissenters but Catholics as well, including Irish masons and French saltmakers seeking to exploit the area's natural resources. So too Catholics in the Jerseys, as in New York, quickly rose to hold provincial offices; among them were Robert Vanquellen, who became surveyor general, and John Tatham, who served in several public capacities. William Douglass was elected to the General Assembly of East Jersey from Bergen County, only to be barred by his peers from serving when he owned that he was a Catholic. As in the West Indies, discretion was the price Catholics were expected to pay to practice their religion, and even more, to participate in public life. Catholicism had only the most ephemeral institutional presence, mainly occasional visits from Jesuit priests during the short period in the 1680s when the Society maintained a house in New York City.

THOMAS DONGAN, CATHOLIC PLOTS, AND THE DOMINION OF NEW ENGLAND

As did Maryland, New York experienced a steady decline in the economy from the mid-1670s onward. Low prices increasingly depressed the fur, wheat, and other exporting industries. The situation for the Dutch merchants in the province deteriorated further from the incursion of London merchants into the local field. When Governor Edmund Andros attempted to protect the interests of the Dutch merchants, the powerful English mercantile bloc had him recalled to London in 1681. Andros's permanent replacement, Thomas Dongan, managed through patronage to appease the English merchants while enabling the Dutch to retain their privileged position within his ruling circle. He also furthered the centralization of authority in the province through the establishment of provincial courts and through the control of the appointment of officials to the county structure of government that he inaugurated.

Thomas Dongan was Irish-born of a Catholic family whose loyalty to the Stuarts had won it both land and titles in Ireland. A career army officer, Dongan had served as lieutenant governor of Tangier before his appointment to New York to succeed another Catholic, Anthony Brockholls, whom James had made acting governor after Andros's recall. Dongan proceeded to fill the leading political and military posts in New York with fellow Catholics: Brockholls and Gervais Baxter to the council, Bartholomew Russell as head of the garrison at Fort James, Matthew Plowman as collector of customs for the port of New York. This at a time when anti-Catholicism had so boiled over in England following the supposed revelations of Titus Oates about a Catholic plot against king and capital city in 1678 that King Charles had ordered his Catholic brother out of the country in a vain effort to lower the temperature. Hundreds of prominent Catholics, both lay and clerical, in England and Ireland were arrested, including eleven of the forty Catholic English peers. More than two score of them were executed or died in prison, the most notable being the primate of Ireland, Archbishop Oliver Plunkett, hanged, drawn, and quartered at Tyburn in 1681.

It was no surprise, then, that upon Dongan's appointment as governor rumors swirled about a supposed charge the new governor had received from his Catholic lord to impose a "papist" church upon the province. His subsequent appointment of Catholics to key positions did nothing to quiet the talk of a Catholic conspiracy to take over the province, including its religious institutions. The fantasizing was only fanned when a group of five Jesuits (Thomas Harvey, Henry Harrison, Charles Gage, and two lay brothers) arrived in New York at the pressing invitation of the duke. Actually Dongan had sought English Jesuit assistance in countering the evangelization efforts among the Iroquois of their French brethren along the Canadian border of upstate New York. When their mission to the Iroquois proved unneeded, Dongan, unlike the proprietary rulers in Maryland, awarded the missionaries glebe land as a permanent endowment and allotted them an annual stipend. In 1684 the Jesuits used the glebe land to open an elementary school in New York

City that attracted the sons of both English Protestants and Catholics. Meanwhile, James, in response to popular pressure and in an attempt to compete with Pennsylvania and the Jerseys in attracting immigrants, agreed in 1683 to establish a general assembly with freeholders electing seventeen deputies from the various regions. The subsequent legislation enacted at the initial meeting of the body, including a Charter of Liberties and Privileges (which guaranteed freedom of religion for all Christians, explicitly even Catholics), was in part an effort to effect a social contract between proprietor and subjects in which the fundamental rights of individuals and the basic responsibilities of government would be stated. Unfortunately, the charter and legislation never went into effect. New York became a royal colony after James succeeded his brother as king in 1685. The assembly itself was dissolved in 1687.

In that year renewed war between France and England sent the already stagnant economy of the province into recession, largely due to the drastic shrinkage of the supply of furs from the upper region contested by the two imperial powers. A threatened French invasion was the occasion for Governor Dongan to impose upon all the inhabitants of the province a new loyalty oath, now to a Catholic monarch. Dongan also led a military expedition to defend Albany, whose prohibitive costs forced provincial authorities to raise new taxes, now upon an unrepresented population. To spread out the tax burden Dongan appealed to London to enlarge the boundaries of New York by annexing Connecticut, Rhode Island, and the Jerseys to it. Instead, in 1688, as part of the crown's centralizing of colonial authority, New York itself became part of the Dominion of New England. Edmund Andros was again head of its government. This combination of events was more than enough to stir up the anti-Catholicism always bubbling beneath the surface and to conjure up a grand Catholic conspiracy at the root of New Yorkers' political, military, and economic miseries. As was so often the case, events in England would have a ripple effect that would bring about profound change in the two "Catholic" colonies.

CHAPTER 6

"AGAINST A COMMON ENEMY"

*The Glorious Revolution and
Its Consequences in the
Atlantic World*

In late July of 1688 Charles Carroll boarded a ship at London bound for Maryland. From a once-titled Irish midlands family that had lost most of its vast landholding and wealth in Cromwell's settlement of the 1650s, the twenty-five-year-old Carroll had been in London for three years studying law at the Inner Temple and clerking for William Herbert, Lord Powis. Powis had been one of two Catholic peers (the other was Lord Baltimore's kin, Henry, Lord Arundell of Wardour), whom King James II had named to his Privy Council in 1686. Their appointments were part of what many within England quickly came to suspect was the openly Catholic king's campaign to restore Catholicism as the religion of the kingdom. At the outset of his reign, in May of 1685, as a sign of his intentions, he had avenged the terrible persecution of Catholics that Titus Oates had set in motion seven years earlier with his Popish Plot tale by having

126

him brought to trial and convicted for perjury. When Parliament met the following fall the king requested that the Test Act and other penal legislation be repealed. When the house refused to go along, James dismissed them. For the rest of his reign he ruled without his legislature. Then followed a wave of appointments of Catholics to high and middle civil and military positions within his government: university rectors, generals, judges, justices of the peace, sheriffs. To evade the Test Act, which effectively barred Catholics from holding office, James pressured judges to dispense his Catholic appointees from it. By 1688 Catholics, who made up about 1 percent of the English population, accounted for a quarter of the justices of the peace and deputy lieutenants in the country. Six Catholics, including a Jesuit, became members of the Privy Council. He named four Catholic bishops to govern the Roman Catholic Church in England and granted them, as though they were prelates of an established church, annual pensions of £1,000. Exercising the crown's presumed prerogative to overrule acts of Parliament, James twice issued Declarations of Indulgence that in effect rendered the anti-Catholic penal legislation null and void. When seventeen Anglican bishops refused to promulgate his declaration, James had them put in the Tower of London.

Some leading Catholics, including Lord Powis, thought the king was pursuing a reckless course that would end in disaster for himself and the Catholic community. When Powis and Arundell urged James in effect to drop his campaign, he rejected their counsel. According to Carroll family tradition Powis confided to his clerk his ominous feelings about the peril Catholics were facing in the light of James's radical actions and urged him to seek his future in Maryland. He could recommend him to his friend Lord Baltimore as a highly promising young man, well qualified to hold a high office in the proprietor's province.[1] Whatever the reason, Carroll left London in a hurry, carrying an appointment from the third Lord Baltimore to be his attorney general in Maryland.

Even as Carroll attempted to put an ocean between himself and the looming troubles in Great Britain, events were in motion that would

1. Ronald Hoffman, *Princes of Ireland, Planters of Maryland: A Carroll Saga, 1500–1782* (Chapel Hill: University of North Carolina Press, 2000), 40.

all too quickly overtake him in his new land. Already in the spring some Protestant lords had begun a series of meetings with James's son-in-law William of Orange, whose wife, Mary, as the king's oldest child (by his first wife), was heir to the English throne and a Protestant, as was her husband. When James's second wife, Queen Mary, a Catholic like the king, gave birth to a son in early June 1688, Protestant England no longer had the assurance of Mary's restoring the established religion of the country to its rightful place, but faced the unnerving prospect of a Catholic succeeding James as monarch and perpetuating the counter-revolution that he was waging. In this crisis negotiations quickened between the claque of Protestant nobles and William. In September William accepted their invitation to rescue England from its "Catholic captivity." On November 5, the anniversary of the Gunpowder Plot, the most infamous exhibit of Catholic perfidy in the nation's history, the Dutch ruler and his expeditionary force landed at Torbay on the southwestern coast of Devon. Six weeks later, after an uncontested march on London that increasingly became a victory parade as more and more of the king's army defected to the invaders, a triumphant William entered the capital. Three days later James fled across the channel to seek refuge in France, where his wife and son had preceded him. Parliament formally declared the throne vacant, made clear that no one but a Protestant could in the future be anointed king, and asserted its newly claimed supreme authority by formally offering the crown jointly to William and Mary. With their subsequent coronation the nexus between Protestantism and the English nation was once again firmly established.

THE REVOLUTION CROSSES
THE ATLANTIC

News of the "Glorious Revolution" began to reach British America by the late winter of 1689. Like a match striking wood so dry that combustion seemed almost instant, the rumors of regime change in England fed the paranoia about a transatlantic Catholic conspiracy threatening local rights and liberties. The failure of provincial governments to acknowledge the new Protestant monarchs of the empire seemed to confirm suspicions about their papist loyalties. From New England to the Chesapeake unrest erupted into local uprisings against papist governance, either real or suspected. That some of the instigators of revolt were exploiting these fears for purposes of self-interest only underscored the damage done: arrests, exile, stripping of rights, and persecution, all in the name of saving the colonies from "popery and slavery."[2]

The first American ripple from the Glorious Revolution across the Atlantic occurred in April in Boston, the seat of the recently imposed super-province, the Dominion of New England, embracing all of British America from the Merrimack to the Delaware. For Massachusetts citizens the greatest price this imperial creation had cost them was the charter that had been the bulwark of their rights and liberties. In its stead they now had the autocratic, papist-centric Andros administration, whose unproductive management of the latest war against French-allied Indians only increased their suspicions of his true Romish leanings. The news of the Prince of Orange's triumph in England was all the Bostonians needed as a rationale for deposing Andros, the creature of the papist king. A mob promptly stormed his residence and hauled him off to jail. The Glorious Revolution had now spread to America.

Word of the Boston uprising quickly carried southward to New York, where the governor, Francis Nicholson, had known of the revolution in England for more than a month but had considered it prudent to keep the knowledge secret, particularly given the swirl of rumors in the province about a French-Indian invasion from the north that Nicholson and other Catholicphiles in the government were supposedly abetting. The Catholics connected with the government, including ex-governor Thomas Dongan, collector Matthew Plowman, and the head of the garrison, fled the city for their own protection. Still, the rumors of an imminent invasion coordinated by internal subversives persisted. The local council, in a desperate move to quiet the populace, issued an order that Dongan return to the city. At May's end Nicholson tipped the scale from agitation to open rebellion when he not only refused to dispatch troops to guard against

2. Owen Charles Stanwood, "Creating the Common Enemy: Catholics, Indians, and the Politics of Fear in Imperial North America, 1678–1700" (Ph.D. diss., Northwestern University, 2005), 91.

the feared French-Indian invasion supposedly advancing on New York City, but threatened to turn the guns of the fort on those pressing him to defend them from the Catholic menace to their north. To a critical mass of the townspeople, including the militia, this was the decisive indicator of the governor's implication in the papist plot to seize control of the province. Militia and people stormed the fort, overwhelmed Nicholson and the six or so soldiers he had brought with him into the compound, and forced from the governor the key to the place that served as the seat of government. Its transfer marked the passage of power from the Stuarts' representative in New York to the Anglo-Dutch coalition that mirrored the one that had just put William and Mary on the throne in the mother country. Indeed, the Dutch majority in the city had been the key to the success of the revolution in New York. That majority shared with English residents the anti-Catholicism that was the catalyst for uprisings throughout British America, from Boston to St. Mary's City. In addition, there was an ethnic factor that drove the Dutch to revolt. Most of them had resented the English conquest of New Netherland; they had welcomed with open arms the Dutch forces that had briefly regained control of the province from 1673 to 1674. Now a Dutchman was actually on the throne of England, a development that, they became convinced, local authorities refused to acknowledge, perhaps in the hope that it could somehow be undone. For the New York Dutch, having the Prince of Orange, the personification of the Protestant cause against Catholics, as monarch of England was almost as good as being under the Dutch flag again. In New York nostalgia played an important part in the wave of revolutions that swept through the colonies in the spring and summer of 1689.

In late June orders finally arrived in New York from England to proclaim William and Mary officially as the country's sovereigns and to maintain all officials in their offices until the ruling pair made their intentions clear. The first order the rebels eagerly complied with. The second brought a much different reaction. When members of the council attempted to resume their duties, they met violent resistance and were soon driven into hiding. The refusal to abide in government anyone who had been connected with the old order reflected the worldview of the military man who had risen to command the uprising on the strength of his charismatic framing of the struggle as an apocalyptic one between a corrupt Catholicism and a redemptive Protestantism. Jacob Leisler had been one of six militia captains who had jointly commanded the forces that had secured the overthrow of the local government in 1689. A German-born soldier and merchant, Leisler, the son of a French Reformed minister, inherited his father's radical religious views, which provided a rigid lens for his Manichean worldview. In July he claimed English support for his leadership and proceeded to form a government of "good Protestants."[3] By the end of the year Leisler, as commander-in-chief, had autocratic control of the revolution.

THE PROTESTANT ASSOCIATION

In Maryland the same consuming fears about conspiracies involving the French, Indians, and local Catholics laid the groundwork for revolution. As elsewhere the rumors about James's ouster by a Protestant usurper (the first such reports began appearing in mid-December of 1688) gave much greater significance to the stories of Catholic intrigue and conspiracy that continued to spiral as winter gave way to spring in 1689. The behavior of Lord Baltimore's newly appointed president of the assembly, the Catholic William Joseph, blatantly demonstrated to many in Maryland the autocratic bent of proprietary governance. In his initial address to the assembly in mid-November 1688, Joseph lectured on the ordained line of authority that ran from God to king to proprietor to assembly, declared a day of thanksgiving for the king's Catholic prince, prohibited the exportation of bulk tobacco (a form of transport particularly favored by small planters), and finally ordered the members of the assembly to swear an oath of fidelity to the proprietor. When administration officials issued a call in January for all people possessing arms to deliver them to the sheriffs for inspection and repair, Protestants interpreted it as a universal disarming, the precursor to an Indian invasion designed to pre-

3. Robert C. Ritchie, *The Duke's Province: A Study of New York Politics and Society, 1664–1690* (Chapel Hill: University of North Carolina Press, 1977), 109–10.

serve the colony for the absent proprietor and King James. Two months later, in March, rumors swirled about Charles County of the imminent attack of as many as 10,000 Senecas and Nanticokes gathering at the head of the Patuxent River and led by the French (one report had Lord Baltimore himself in command). A county militia officer frantically demanded that the government return the arms they had collected; anything less would constitute the officials' admission of betraying the people "to the Common Enemy" (by which he meant the Indians, French, Maryland Catholics, and their local collaborators, all working together).[4] To lay the rumors to rest Maryland officials organized a scouting expedition to the area supposedly swarming with Indians and invited along some of the conveyers of the rumors. When the expedition found no evidence of an Indian invasion in the making, this seemed to satisfy at least some of the alarmists. To ease minds further about the government's integrity, all the sequestered arms were returned to their owners. By April the crisis seemed to have passed.

It had not. Longstanding grievances against proprietary government —its autocratic style of governance and bias toward Catholics and other heterodox Christians (e.g., Quakers) in its appointments; the economic policies that were worsening the depression of the tobacco industry; the government's taking refuge behind the principle of religious toleration to avoid providing for the religious needs of the majority of its citizens—fed the prejudice in popular opinion that men on the political make could exploit by manufacturing scenarios that revealed the sinister intents of Lord Baltimore's government. These men were on the whole recent immigrants who had ironically done well economically but suffered from a sort of political lag—that is, their political positions (overwhelmingly at the county, not provincial level) failed to match their economic and social ones. In July these arrivistes began to organize in the lower western counties: St. Mary's, Charles, and Calvert. The catalyst seems to have been the failure of the provincial council or other administrative officials to proclaim the accession of William and Mary, something the neighboring colony of Virginia had done in April. Maryland officials apparently felt compelled

4. Stanwood, "Creating the Common Enemy," 105.

AGAINST A COMMON ENEMY

to await official instructions from Lord Baltimore before saying anything about the change in government in England. Charles Calvert later claimed that the messenger he had sent with that information died at Plymouth before he could sail for the colony. To those who gathered to form what became known as the Protestant Association, the official silence was a welcome pretext for reviving the tales of a Calvert-Indian conspiracy that represented an imminent threat to the people of Maryland.

In the latter part of July these organizers—John Coode, Kenylm Cheseldyne, Nehemiah Blakiston, Henry Jowles, and Ninian Beale, among others—gathered in Charles County to plot a plan of action. On the twenty-fifth they issued a declaration explaining why they were taking up arms against the government—primarily to save Protestantism from being uprooted in Maryland by an arbitrary papist government in league with a foreign Catholic power. As they made their march southward toward the capital, the revolutionary "associators" grew from the 250 or so troops they had set out with to nearly 700 when they arrived at St. Mary's City. The government, they discovered, had abandoned the capital after the large majority of the militia, as during the Ingle invasion, had refused to fight for the Calverts. So the officials of the government, including William Joseph, Henry Darnall, and Nicholas Sewall, along with about 160 loyal militia, had taken refuge at Mattapany to ride out the storm, as the associators had hoped. After a short siege of that compound by the forces of the association the proprietary leaders realized that they had lost all popular support and surrendered on August 1. Maryland joined New England and New York in undergoing bloodless revolutions paralleling that of the mother country.

A few Calvert officials or prominent supporters were briefly put in prison or kept under surveillance. Most Catholics who had held political positions fled the province; those fleeing included Nicholas Sewall, Lord Baltimore's stepson, who crossed the bay to join his sister's family on Virginia's Eastern Shore. The seven Jesuits in the province once again sought refuge in Virginia, as did two Franciscans. At least two Catholic gentry on the Eastern Shore of Maryland thought it prudent to move down the Delmarva Peninsula to the Virginia portion. In November 1689 John Coode, who had taken command of the interim government, attempted to secure the assistance of Virginia officials in returning to Maryland certain "professed enemyes" of William and Mary who had sought sanctuary in Virginia.[5] Coode's appeal apparently received no co-operation from Virginia officials.

The Coode administration took several steps to ensure that government in Maryland in the future would be properly Protestant. In the official surrender document the Calvert officials, themselves all Catholics, had acknowledged that Catholics would no longer hold any civil or military offices. Subsequent orders forbade Catholic lawyers from practicing in Maryland courts and Catholics from serving as jurors.

Unsurprisingly, supporters of the proprietor in Maryland, Catholic and Protestant alike, were confident that this latest overthrow of Lord Baltimore's government would not stand, just as the earlier revolts of 1645 and 1652 had not. Charles Carroll, who had been attorney general for scarcely ten months before the association's coup, was sure that Lord Baltimore could regain control through recourse to the same legal appeals that his father had so artfully deployed in the 1650s. "[C]ertainly your Lordship's charter is not such a trifle," he wrote his patron two months after Coode's coup, "as to be annulled by the bare allegations of such profligate wretches."[6] As Peter Sayer, a prominent Catholic on the Eastern Shore assured Calvert, "the best men & best Protestants...(men of the best Estates, & real professors of the Protestant Religion), stand... up for your Lordship's interests."[7] James Heath, the husband of Sayer's niece, did just that some months later in a protest to the new monarchs about the scandalous behavior of the Coode ruling circle in ransacking the houses of Baltimore's supporters, whether Catholic or Protestant, and in appropriating the proprietor's revenues for their private use. Lord Baltimore himself had been pleading for a restoration of his palatinate out of respect for the charter, which was still in force. The same month

5. Bruce E. Steiner, "The Catholic Brents of Virginia: An Instance of Political Toleration," *Virginia Magazine of History and Biography* 70 (1962): 407.

6. Charles Carroll to Lord Baltimore, September 25, 1689, *Archives of Maryland* 8:125–26; cited in Beatriz Betancourt Hardy, "Roman Catholics, Not Papists: Catholic Identity in Maryland, 1689–1776," *Maryland Historical Magazine* 92 (Summer 1997): 140.

7. Peter Sayer to Lord Baltimore, December 31, 1689, in *Archives of Maryland* 8:161; cited in Hardy, "Roman Catholics," 140.

Charles Calvert, Third Lord Baltimore

that Sayer had written Lord Baltimore (September 1689), a delegation of Catholics and Protestants had made the voyage to England to make a formal protest to the crown about the illegal overthrow of the Maryland proprietor. Their reception was a chilly one. William and Mary were not about to condemn a seizure of power in Maryland that was so much like the one that had made them sovereigns of England. What the revolution in Maryland provided, as did the ones in Massachusetts and New York, was the opportunity to advance the centralization of the empire by creating royal governments in these colonies. On February 1, 1690, despite all the lobbying in Baltimore's behalf, King William basically upheld the revolution that Coode and his associates had made. Although Calvert would retain his property rights in Maryland, the crown, "out of a case of necessity," would henceforth control the province's governance.[8] Maryland became a royal colony or, perhaps more precisely, a semi-royal one. The ruling itself left room for hope that this was no permanent resolution; that the Calverts might still regain their colony.

THE REVOLUTION IN
THE WEST INDIES

Unlike the governments of the mainland colonies in English America, the government of Barbados welcomed the accession of a Protestant to the throne. In February 1689 authorities resumed an anti-Catholic campaign that James's coming to power had halted four years earlier. They ordered the arrest of certain Catholics, including the recent converts Willoughby Chamberlaine, the son of a prominent planter, and Thomas Montgomery, the attorney general, whom they accused of plotting to join with the French in overthrowing the Protestant government. On St. Christopher Edwyn Stede, the governor of Barbados, learned that "bloody Papists and Irish" had come together to declare their allegiance for King James and to resolve to "kill burn, and destroy all that belongs to the Protestant interest."[9] This tended to confirm the governor's suspicion that there was a cabal among the French, Irish, and black inhabitants of the islands to overthrow English rule. Nor were authorities on Barbados acting in isolation. Stede was in ongoing communication with the leaders of the uprisings in New York and Maryland, Jacob Leisler and John Coode. The experience of two of the Irish Catholics for whom arrest warrants were issued, Patrick Henly and Nicholas Welsh, show clearly enough the intercolonial nature of the Glorious Revolution. Henly and Welsh both fled from Barbados to New York. There Leisler, having found suspicious letters in their luggage, sent the pair back to Barbados. On their return voyage they managed to escape again, this time getting to Maryland., where John Coode put them in custody, only to have them

8. Tricia T. Pyne, "The Maryland Catholic Community, 1690–1775: A Study in Culture, Region, and Church" (Ph.D. diss., The Catholic University of America, 1995), 148.
9. Johnston, "Papists in a Protestant World," 210.

get free once more and make their way to Pennsylvania, finally beyond the reach of the revolution.

The Irish on Barbados paid a heavy price for their alleged involvement in the plot to seize the island. Many went to prison. By and large Irish were excluded from the militia regiments that began to be formed as a security force against the slaves on the island. The English turned to Scots and even slaves themselves for the recruitment of militia. Those Catholics who did manage to become part of the militia were in time replaced by black members. That trend meant even less opportunity for employment for Irish ex-servants and led to a sharp increase in Irish emigration. Those Irish who remained became part of an isolated, impoverished underclass known as "Redlegs," the poster children for the "worst poor man's country" that Barbados had become by the early eighteenth century.

On Montserrat the Jacobite governor, Nathaniel Johnson, defiantly declared that he could not recognize William as the rightful monarch of the kingdom. That encouraged the Irish on neighboring St. Christopher to join with the French to seize control of the entire island. Johnson's opposition to the new monarchs, however, did not sit well with the leading planters on the Leeward Islands. Under pressure from the planters, Johnson resigned. His replacement, Christopher Codrington, immediately took the preemptive measure of disarming all the Irish below the planting class on Montserrat and Antigua and of arresting certain Catholics charged with plotting rebellion. The situation remained tense for months, but Codrington maintained the peace and began the enactment as well as the enforcement of penal laws that would increasingly define the lot of most of the Irish in the Leeward Islands and effectively end their political involvement. A law was also passed that banned any Irish immigration, but that, as it happened, had a brief history. By the early eighteenth century there was no longer any need for laws to keep the Irish out. Socioeconomic developments were not only discouraging the Irish from coming to Montserrat and the other islands; they were increasingly producing an outmigration that rapidly thinned the ranks of the Irish Catholic community. The triumph, late as it was, of sugar cultivation as the dominant industry on the island produced enormous wealth for a small number of planters who increasingly monopolized the land. Most of them turned out to be Irish, but most of the latter seemed to have made the ascent to the plantocracy by foreswearing their Catholic religion. For most Irish Catholics the choices were reduced to eking out a living on Montserrat as a small farmer-worker or seeking a better future on the mainland. Most, especially the smallholders who had some capital with which to make a move, chose the latter. A series of natural disasters and destructive military invasions provided an additional push factor for emigrants. By 1730 whites made up but 15 percent of the population on Montserrat, a pattern that the other Leeward Islands replicated.

A NEW PENAL AGE

With the staunch Protestants William and Mary on the throne, a new era began for Catholics, both in Great Britain and America. In England the penal laws were revived and extended in such a way as to render public life virtually off limits for Catholics. The Disabling Act of 1695 made it impossible for Catholics to practice most kinds of law. Catholics who refused to take the oaths of allegiance and supremacy would have their personal possessions and real estate doubly taxed. The punishment was more severe for those failing to swear the mandated oaths upon coming of age. For these recusants the penalty was loss of their inheritance. Exercising any religious ministry or teaching children were grounds for imprisonment for life. As for property, the 1699 "Act for the further preventing the Growth of Popery" prohibited Catholics from purchasing property. Those who sent their children abroad to recusant schools on the Continent could expect to be fined £100 sterling. Over the ensuing decades of the eighteenth century the punitive legislation shredded the ranks of Catholic nobility and gentry through mass defections from the faith.

For a brief interval it seemed as though James's rule would survive in one part of his kingdom—that of Ireland. The king himself had arrived there from France in March of 1689, assured that he had the firm support of Louis XIV of France. James summoned the Irish Parliament, now dominated by Catholics. That body repealed the land settlement that Cromwell had forced upon the country and set in motion a restoration of the lands that Catholics had lost since 1641. A year later King William landed in Ireland to complete the revolution he had begun at Torbay. On June 30, 1690, at the river Boyne, William's force of 36,000 routed James's 25,000 men. James once more fled to France. William sailed back to England after signing a treaty that assured the Irish that they would have the same rights they had enjoyed under Charles II, including religious liberty, the right to bear arms, and the practice of their professions. Within a few years the treaty was a dead letter. New penal legislation ended any form of Catholic toleration and completed the landstripping that had begun for Catholics centuries before. By 1703 Catholics held only a small portion of the country's land. In a little more than six decades their landholdings had plummeted from nearly 60 percent to 14 percent, a percentage that continued to drop as the century wore on.

New York's revolution had brought a radical anti-Catholic to power. Jacob Leisler, during his tumultuous reign of a baker's dozen of months as lieutenant governor, fanatically pursued a campaign of stamping out any Catholic presence or influence within the city and province, with the definition of "Catholic" or "papist" becoming ever more expansive. Even more of a minuscule element in New York than they were in England, Catholics had come to have grossly disproportionate power within New York's political society. All those Catholics who had held power in the previous government had to go, including the collector of revenues, Matthew Plowman, for the simple reason that "he was no protestant."[10] The government issued arrest warrants for Thomas Dongan and Anthony Brockholls, the top Catholic officeholders in the former administration. What few Catholics there were in the province were to be stripped of any arms they might have. Nor could they hereafter vote in any elections. The Catholic institutional presence in New York had virtually vanished with the flight of the two Jesuits assigned to the province. For good measure Leisler closed the chapel in the fort and the school that the Jesuits had conducted.

10. Jason K. Duncan, *Citizens or Papists? The Politics of Anti-Catholicism in New York, 1685–1821* (New York: Fordham University Press, 2005), 6–7.

All too soon Leisler turned the colony into a papist hunting ground; anyone who had supported the previous regime or was perceived to be opposing the current one was fair game. A climate of paranoia set in during the summer of 1689. Anyone coming into the city was brought to the fort for examination to determine whether he was Catholic or an agent of France or both. An official investigation was begun into the criminal liabilities or Catholic leanings of former officials. This dragnet inevitably caught up people of wealth and high standing in New York, including the Dutch and English merchants who had been members of Dongan's council. Reformed clergymen were arrested for making re-marks construed as critical of the government. All this finally produced a protest to London in May of 1690 from several dozen merchants, both Dutch and English, and Dutch Reformed clergy; the protest detailed the arbitrary jailing, ransacking of homes, and ruination of the economy for which the Leisler government was responsible.

In February of 1690 the fears of Leisler and the revolutionaries about a French-Indian attack upon New York had been realized in the most terrifying way. Just west of Albany a force of French and Indians vicious-ly assaulted Schenectady, a small trading post, and killed or took cap-tive most of its residents. Leisler's immediate response was ordering the arrest of all Catholics in the province as well as all those who had held commissions from Governor Dongan. But that was only the beginning of his revenge against the "common enemy." He invited all the English colonies from Maryland to New England to a conference to plan a coun-terattack on New France. The colonies promised over 1,000 troops and financing for the joint expedition, one part by land skirting Lake Cham-plain, the other up the St. Lawrence River. When the land expedition finally got underway from Albany on the last day of July, far fewer troops and supplies were there than had been promised. Three weeks later the expedition was back in Albany never having encountered the enemy, but victimized by a shortage of supplies as well as by smallpox, which had spread through the ranks. The sea force actually reached Quebec where, after a brief siege, they abandoned it due to the foul weather, more small-pox, and dwindling ammunition—all in all an ignominious ending for Leisler's grand campaign of revenge.

In England Leisler was losing his struggle to shape New York's political future. His misfortune was the far greater influence that his wealthy and prominent opponents had at Whitehall, which in the end brought a reconstruction of government highly favorable to them. A new military officer, Colonel Henry Sloughter, was appointed governor of the province. Most of the council members whom Leisler had removed were returned to their positions. When the major representing the new governor finally arrived in New York at the end of January in 1691, Leisler refused to surrender to him the fort, the symbol of power. Negotiations dragged on in escalating tension for over a month before it erupted in Leisler's firing upon the royal troops in mid-March, initiating an exchange that resulted in deadly casualties on both sides. At this point Sloughter finally arrived with his royal commission and renewed the demand that Leisler hand over the fort. Again he refused. By now Leisler's men within the fort had had enough and began to desert him. Reality penetrated sufficiently within Leisler's warped world that he finally handed over the fort to Sloughter on March 20. A foreordained trial followed in which Leisler and his chief assistant were convicted of murder and treason. As he prepared to be hanged in mid-May, Leisler insisted that everything he had done had been done in the interest of the reigning Protestant monarchs "against popery." He urged his listeners to overcome their differences so they could act in unison "against a Common enemy" to advance "the Glory of the Protestant interest."[11] Three days earlier the newly reconstituted provincial government had put in place the legal framework of this policy by passing laws that extended religious freedom and other civil rights to all except "persons of the Romish religion."[12]

Precious few Catholics remained in the province by the time Leisler mounted the gallows. A 1696 survey found but ten males who were "reputed" to be "Papists." Five years later another resident judged that there were not "twenty papists or Jacobins in the whole province."[13] The lack of Catholics, however, did not mean an end of the anti-Catholic animus that had spurred the revolution. King Williams' War, overshadowing

11. Duncan, *Citizens or Papists*, 2.   12. Duncan, *Citizens or Papists*, 2.
13. Duncan, *Citizens or Papists*, 15.

the province from 1689 to 1696, was in itself enough to keep that spirit alive. Richard Coote, the Earl of Bellemont, appointed governor of New York, Massachusetts, and New Hampshire in 1698, presented the empire as the great bulwark of Protestant liberties. The anti-Catholic legislation Bellamonte sponsored was an integral part of the imperial legal infrastructure that protected Protestant Americans from their common Catholic enemy. The laws that New York enacted in 1701 ranged from the lifelong imprisonment of any priest found within the colony's borders to a £200 fine, as well as three days in the stocks for those who were caught harboring priests. A dozen years later a new law limited naturalization to those willing to take the Test Act. Catholics in New York had been effectively outlawed as the price of maintaining freedom and true Christianity in America.

MARYLAND AS A
SEMI-ROYAL COLONY

The first royal governor, Lionel Copley, arrived in St. Mary's in April 1692. He carried with him the official charge to administer the colony according to its existing laws and statutes. In addition he had with him a private instruction to respect the religious conscience of Catholics within the province. That directive may well have been at least in part the result of a petition that the crown had received the previous December from Don Manuel Coloma, the Spanish ambassador to the English court. In the petition the ambassador had decried the persecution that Maryland Catholics and their allies had suffered from the Protestant Association once it had attained power. King William himself, the head of the established Church of England, was at the same time committed to a policy of religious toleration for dissident groups, including Catholics. Parliament prevented him from implementing this in law, but William was bent on protecting local practices throughout the empire, whether sanctioned by law or custom. For English Catholics that meant respecting their tradition of practicing their religion privately—within the manor, as it were. For Maryland Catholics, however, practice was much more public. William was telling Copley to honor Lord Baltimore's experiment as it had evolved over the past sixty years. The monarch was very sensitive to Spain's concern for the welfare of England's Catholic community. Even before he left Europe to stake his claim to the English crown, William had in person assured Spanish officials that he intended to extend toleration to Catholics as well as Protestant dissenters. Coloma's petition served as a reminder of that promise, and William's instruction to Copley was his reiteration of his intentions.

The king's unofficial policy of toleration hardly became apparent to Maryland Catholics during Copley's two years in office, as the irascible governor became all too thick with the associators. At best Copley sent out very conflicting signals about the place of Catholics in society. Things improved measurably when Francis Nicholson succeeded Copley in 1694. Nicholson reopened the Great Brick Chapel in St. Mary's City as an indication of the government's willingness to tolerate Catholics worshiping publicly. He also returned to Catholics the arms that had been taken from them after the association took power. Catholic lawyers were allowed to practice in certain judicial venues, such as Chancery Court. Although no longer eligible to stand for election to provincial offices, Catholics continued to dominate the proprietary offices, which they used to great effect (or so critics charged) to gain the favor of political officials. In many ways by the mid-1690s Catholics in Maryland seemed to be enjoying a kind of *status quo antea*, a condition Catholics took for granted as a byproduct of Lord Baltimore's charter, which they mistakenly thought was still in effect.

But there *was* a new order in Maryland, symbolized by the transfer of the capital in 1694 from St. Mary's City to "Arundell Towne" (it would be renamed Annapolis the following year). St. Mary's, in the heart of Catholic Maryland, had been the seat of government since the founding of the colony. The first capital had never become anything remotely like the splendid Baroque city that Cecil Calvert had envisioned. Outside of the short periods when the assembly met and the court held sessions, it was a very sleepy hamlet in an isolated part of the province. Arundell Towne was not as developed as St. Mary's City, but it enjoyed a much more central location, and Nicholson had grand plans for its development. It had also, from its beginning in the 1650s, been the hub of Protestant Mary-

land. Two years earlier the assembly had passed an act that established
the Church of England as the official religion of the province. Maryland,
which had been the first colony in which the separation of church and
state had been a hallmark, now made a union of the two parts of its fundamental order. The province was divided into parishes for which the
government committed itself to building churches and to collecting taxes
for the support of the ministers who would serve them.

Despite the privileged position that the Church of England now legally held, the Catholic clergy continued to proselytize; some Catholics
prohibited their servants from attending Anglican services as part of the
pressure put on them to convert. Reports of such aggressive evangelization seemed to peak in 1697 during an epidemic that swept through the
province that provided an occasion for Jesuits and other fervent Catholics to attempt deathbed conversions. This was the tipping point for
Nicholson, who issued a proclamation condemning such "scandalous and
offensive behavior," which went far beyond the boundaries within which
members of tolerated religions ought to remain. He was not-so-subtly
pointing out that, like it or not, England's penal laws applied to Maryland, now that it was a royal colony.

Nor was it just proselytizing by clergy that gave Nicholson concern.
He increasingly regarded the Catholic community (along with their apparent collaborators, the Quakers) as an alien force bent on subverting
the new order that he and the Anglican Church represented. The census
that he ordered sheriffs to take of all dissenters in the province in 1697
was one consequence of his concern, an attempt to exercise some control
over these troublesome minorities. The growing number of Irish Catholic servants being brought into the province gave him more reason to be
disturbed about the Catholic community in his midst. Given their recent history of rebellion against the crown, any significant Irish increase,
Nicholson feared, "may be of very dangerous consequence.... They might
make great disturbances, if not a Rebellion."[14] That Charles Carroll was
responsible for hundreds of them coming to take up land on his estate in

14. Francis Nicholson to the Board of Trade and Plantations, August 20, 1698, *Archives of Maryland* 23:498, in Pyne, "Maryland Catholic Community," 171.

northern Maryland made Nicholson suspect that Lord Baltimore, Carroll's patron, was ultimately behind this Irish planting—part of a grand plot, perhaps, to regain control. So Nicholson urged the assembly to restrict the number of Irish servants coming into Maryland, which it did by imposing an import duty of twenty shillings on every imported Irish servant, the first of five such duties enacted over the next two decades to curb the growth of the Catholic community.

Fortunately for Maryland's leading dissenting groups, Francis Nicholson was recalled in 1698. His successor, Nathaniel Blakiston, had no interest in antagonizing anyone, including dissenters. He was an irenic accommodator who did little, but restored the social tranquility that Nicholson had threatened. King William's death in 1702, however, brought a definite end to the unofficial policy of toleration that Maryland Catholics had enjoyed over the past decade. Ironically, that very year the leading Anglican in Maryland, the Reverend Dr. Thomas Bray, sought to explain to home authorities why a new policy—one that would keep the Catholic community under the strict control that only penal laws could achieve—was vitally important:

It may prove of fatal Consequences to his Ma$^{ty's}$ Interest to have y^t country in [the] *Center of all his Provinces on y^e* Continent of America expos'd to y^e Perversions of y^e Popish Priests at a Juncture when y^e French from Canada are so notoriously Diligent in sending their Emisaries amongst y^e Indians lying on the back of this & th' other Colonies to draw [them] into their Sup'stition & Alliance.[15]

Maryland, the clergyman was arguing, was the keystone of a Protestant British America. The whole edifice would crumble if Catholics in the province were not controlled. That flew in the face of Catholics' own self-perception, seeing themselves at the very center of Maryland's experience whose contributions to the founding and development of the colony had ensured them full participation in its civic life. Experience shaped identity for Maryland's Catholics. They were not about to submit docilely to being reined in—to be subjected to a panoply of penal laws that would cast them to the edge of society.

15. Mathias D. Bergmann, "Being the Other: Catholicism, Anglicanism, and Constructs of Britishness in Colonial Maryland, 1689–1763" (Ph.D. diss., Washington State University, 2004), 79.

JOHN SEYMOUR
AND THE BEGINNING OF THE
PENAL AGE FOR CATHOLICS

Like Francis Nicholson, John Seymour was a military governor (he had
been serving with the Coldstream Guards in Flanders at the time of
his appointment at the beginning of 1703). The contentious, somewhat
reckless Seymour brought with him to Annapolis in 1704 not only his
governor's commission but an anti-Catholic mindset bent on extending
to his new jurisdiction, apparently with Queen Anne's support, the penal legislation that governed Catholics in England. In his new domain
he discovered a rapidly growing Catholic population, in particular the
Irish Catholic servants whom Charles Carroll was settling on the northern borders of the province at the head of Chesapeake Bay. This was an
area most vulnerable to Indian attacks, and Irish Catholics were seen as
perhaps the least trustworthy buffers between the province and its traditional enemy. All this compelled Seymour to take action about Maryland's "Catholic problem." Penal legislation had become one instrument
that English authorities had been employing for over a century in order
to shape a homogenous culture within the nation, essentially by casting
Catholics to its edges, by defining one's authentic members through a legal process that excluded an alien group from fully sharing in the society.
As Seymour explained his mission to the Council of Trade and Plantations, "My Instructions... are different from what other Governors
here have had, their being to admitt of liberty of conscience to all who
behaved themselves... but mine to all such but Papists."[16] Under Seymour's governorship there would be no further public practice of Roman
Catholicism. Catholics in Maryland would have to adjust their religious
way of life to that of Catholics in Great Britain, restricting their worship
and devotions to the private sphere of their homes.

  To promulgate this new policy in the most dramatic way the governor issued summons to the two most important Jesuits in the province,

---

16. Seymour to Council of Trade and Plantations, September 29, 1704, Colonial State Papers,
1704–1705, vol. 22, nos. 585, 264, in "A Plea for Maryland Catholics Reconsidered," by Tricia T. Pyne,
Maryland Historical Magazine 92 (Summer 1997): 173.

William Hunter, the mission superior, and Robert Brooke, a native Mary-lander of a prominent family, to appear before the provincial council charged with carrying out the priestly ministries of consecrating a chapel and saying a public Mass, respectively, actions that the English penal laws prohibited. When the two appeared for the hearing they requested that Charles Carroll serve as their counsel, but the council refused their request. They did well enough without counsel. Hunter pointed out that they could hardly charge him with blessing a chapel, since a bishop alone could do that, and he was no bishop. Brooke owned that he had indeed said Mass in the Great Brick Chapel in St. Mary's, but he was but doing what many others had done before him with no consequences. In what was obviously an orchestrated event (the actions in question had occurred a year earlier, in fact), the council determined that since each offense had been their first, their punishment be restricted to a reprimand by the governor. Seymour more than accommodated the council. "It is the unhappy Temper of you and all your Tribe," he berated the two, "to grow insolent upon Civility and never know how to use it.... You might methinks be Content to live quietly as you may and let the Exercise of your Superstitious Vanities be confined to yourselves without proclaiming them at publick times and in public places." He pretended that they somehow should have known that the old dispensation had passed—that there were new rules that they had willfully chosen to ignore and that they should keep the private place that Queen Anne had allowed them. That being so, Seymour threatened deportation to England for any further offense, where they would suffer the full consequences of the penal laws. "Gentlemen," he concluded, "if you intend to live here let me hear no more of these things...."[17] Seymour was laying down the boundaries within which Catholics hitherto were to operate. After finally dismissing them, he ordered the sheriff to lock the Great Brick Chapel to make sure that there would be no more public Mass saying.

The penal legislation encoding this new policy followed during the fall session of the assembly. In the lower house a bill evolved from one

17. Public Record Office, British Territories, Maryland, 17, Journal of the Council, September 11, 1704, in Hughes, *History of the Society of Jesus; Text*, 2:456.

that initially was restricted to a ban on proselytizing by Catholics to a much more comprehensive, indeed contradictory piece of legislation that included a total ban on priestly ministry, including the saying of Mass, as well as on the conducting of schools by Catholics and the imposition of a tax on all Irish servants brought into the province. Seymour, fearing the influence that prominent Catholics such as Carroll had with members of the lower house because of the power they held in the proprietary offices, rushed the bill through that body; the bill was appropriately entitled, "A Bill for Restraining the Growth of Popery." It passed the house at the end of the session in early October.

When the assembly reconvened two months later the delegates found a petition awaiting them that called for the repeal of the recently passed act. The petition argued that the act violated the clear intent of the charter as well as the Toleration Act of 1649, both of which sanctioned religious liberty as a fundamental, enduring right within the province. The "covenant" between government and people that these foundational documents represented "ought," the petitioners pleaded, "to continue to posterity."[18] The appeal persuaded the lower body of the assembly to suspend that part of the bill that imposed penalties on priests for performing their ministry in private Catholic homes until such time as Queen Anne would rule on the matter. That in fact left the matter up to the Council of Trade and Plantations, the crown's body responsible for the administration of the colonies. The council decided to uphold the suspension out of fear that, should they not do so, there would be a mass exodus of Catholics from Maryland, including a significant portion of its major planters and much of its labor force, which would have a devastating impact on the province's economy. With the monarch's subsequent ratification of the lower house's suspension of that section of the bill, the toleration of private Catholic religious activity became official.

Still, Governor Seymour's complaints about the evils of Catholic proselytizing moved the Council of Trade to summon Lord Baltimore

18. "Remonstrance of the Roman Catholicks of Maryland to the House of Delegates," December 21, 1704, in *Colonial State Papers*, 1704–1705, VII, no. 1530, 735, in Pyne, "Maryland Catholic Community," 185.

and pressure him to send a warning to the superior of the Jesuits in Maryland about the unacceptability of their behavior. Given his family's tradition of promoting an unobtrusive Catholic presence in the colony, Calvert probably was happy to carry out the council's directive. "[You have] given great offense," he wrote William Hunter in December of 1705, "and if you are not very careful to avoyd the like for the future, you will give just occasion for your removal out of that Province."[19]

We do not know the names of the successful petitioners, but can assume that they included the most prominent and successful Catholic planter-merchants, among them Henry Darnall, his son-in-law, Charles Carroll, and Richard Bennett. It marked the first time that a group of Catholics had identified themselves as such in a political process. It represented the beginning of an organized Catholic opposition to the imposition in Maryland of the penal legislation that they or their ancestors had left England to escape. Although they could hardly realize it at the time, it was but the opening campaign of a long struggle for full citizenship that would carry them through most of the remainder of the century. For now the religious life of Maryland Catholics would parallel that of Catholics in England. But, unlike the Catholic community in England, they would not settle docilely into living as a sect consigned to the margins of society.

19. Charles Calvert to William Hunter, December 14, 1705, in *Colonial State Papers*, no. 1508, 728–20, in Pyne, "Maryland Catholic Community," 188–89.

CHAPTER 7

"RELIGION, LIBERTY, AND PROPERTY"

*Maryland Catholics in the
Early Penal Era*

At the dawn of the eighteenth century Maryland was undergoing major changes, not only in the political and religious spheres, but in its demographic and economic ones, as well. First of all, there was an unprecedented rate of growth in the population, from 32,258 in 1701 to 43,000 a decade later and 62,000 by 1720. Immigration, including the importation of Africans as slaves, accounted for some of this population rise, but native births accounted for much more. For the first time the majority of Marylanders were native-born, not immigrants. Several factors were at play in this development; among them were the better health of inhabitants, particularly among the native-born, who had greater immunity to the diseases that typically afflicted immigrants, which translated into longer life expectancy, and the fact that young people, largely free of the indentured service that prevented persons from marrying, were able to wed and start families at an earlier age and thus have more children than the previous generation had (the average age of brides in the early eighteenth century may have been as young as sixteen). As the population became more Creole and three-generation extended families became common, geographic mobility increased, as well. Marylanders expanded the areas of settlement to the north and east. But if they were moving more in the physical sphere and causing a wider distribution of people throughout the province, there was a corresponding decline in social mobility and a consolidation of wealth among the mostly Creole upper- tier merchant-planter families that emerged at this time. One marker of this change was land ownership. From the late seventeenth century to the early eighteenth there was a serious drop in the proportion of household heads who owned the property they lived on— from 90 percent to 70 percent.[1] Renting, sharecropping, or wage labor became the permanent lot, rather than the way stations to land ownership that they had previously tended to be, for more and more residents. Economic mobility for the province's unprivileged young gave way to persistent poverty or migration as the only options.

Stagnation in the tobacco industry was at the root of these developments. After decades of rapid growth, tobacco cultivation plateaued due to falling demand and European wars. To better cope with the economic depression brought on by a stagnant tobacco industry, the great planters began to diversify: to grow other staples, such as wheat or other grains, or to branch into the refinement of iron ore or other metals. The downturn in the Maryland tobacco economy also contributed to a labor shortage as the colony became much less of a magnet for the shrinking pool of English workers, who found much better opportunities at home or in other British colonies. Those who did come to Maryland were much more likely to be those on the edges of English society—orphans, convicts, Irish—than the sons of middling families. The drying up of this traditional source of labor was a major factor in Maryland planters turning to Africa to secure a work force that would have no time limits on its service—indeed, one that would be bound to planters from gener-

1. Robert J. Brugger, *Maryland: A Middle Temperament, 1634–1980* (Baltimore: Johns Hopkins University Press, 1988), 59.

ation to generation. Nor did it hurt that, with Parliament's abrogation in 1698 of the monopoly that the Royal African Company had on the international slave trade, the price of slaves on the international market dropped, making that form of labor a better investment than indentured servitude was.

By the first decade of the eighteenth century about 4,000 slaves were being imported annually into Maryland, at least four times the number of indentured servants arriving. By 1720 the nearly 8,000 slaves in Maryland constituted about a fifth of the total population. Only about a quarter of planters had slaves; of that group only 2 percent held 20 or more, but this small segment came to dominate the economy during this period, thanks in no small part to this new labor supply, which enabled them to expand their landholdings and operate on a larger agricultural scale than ever before.

THE CATHOLIC
PLANTER-MERCHANT
COHORT

Although less than 10 percent of the population, Catholics counted in their ranks some of the richest planters in the province, most notably Charles Carroll and Richard Bennett. Carroll had arrived in Maryland in the fall of 1688, an ambitious young man holding a commission as the province's attorney general. Bitter about the terrible injustices that had stripped his family of the immense landed wealth that had made it a powerful dynasty in Ireland, he was determined to reconstitute the family's fortune in a new land that promised Catholics economic and religious freedom (upon emigrating Carroll had conspicuously changed the motto on the family crest to "Ubicumque cum libertate" ["anywhere so long as I am free"]). Ten months later he had no office, a victim of the Protestant Association's uprising against the proprietor. The revolution left Carroll potentially in the same powerless, marginalized position that had become the lot of his ancestors in Ireland. He did not accept the new order with meekness. Twice in the early 1690s he was jailed for his scathing criticism of the government, the second time by Governor Lionel Copley for "mutinous & seditious speeches."[2]

When the crown upheld the results of the revolution in 1691 and took political control of Maryland, it left intact Charles Calvert's property rights in Maryland along with the offices the Calverts had created to administer this property. Charles Carroll, although no longer the chief law enforcement officer of the province, remained Lord Baltimore's legal advisor for Maryland, as well as the legal counsel to Colonel Henry Darnall, who was Calvert's chief representative in the province. What became Carroll's initial springboard to wealth and power, however, was the traditional one of marriage to a rich widow. In Carroll's case it was Martha Ridgely Underwood, several years Carroll's senior and the inheritor of two hefty estates left her by deceased husbands, whom he married a year after his arrival in Maryland. The following year he began his first mercantile establishment on one of Martha's plantations in lower St. Mary's County. That same year she died in childbirth. Two years later, in February 1693/1694, Carroll married Mary Darnall, the fifteen-year-old daughter of Colonel Darnall, thereby consolidating the patronage he had begun to receive from the well-positioned Maryland Catholic planter. As part of Mary's dowry Carroll received two large tracts of land in Prince George's County. Darnall also named Carroll the head of the proprietor's land office, with a salary of approximately £100 a year, a position that held enormously potential political as well as economic influence.

Over the next three decades Carroll became the largest landholder in the province, with nearly 48,000 acres spread over both the Eastern and Western shores, and with the right to acquire an additional 20,000 acres (half of which were eventually patented by his son). Fiercely proud of his Irish heritage, Carroll named the major tracts of land that he acquired in Maryland after family places in Ireland, including Doohoragen (Déuiche Uéi Riagéain) in Baltimore County, which became his principal residence. His wealth significantly increased upon his father-in-law's death in 1711, when Carroll assumed the lucrative proprietary offices Darnall had held, which enabled Carroll to expand his landholdings and mer-

2. Hoffman, *Princes of Ireland, Planters of Maryland*, 46.

Charles Carroll the Settler

cantile operations as well as his banking activities, which he had begun at the turn of the century. In the 1710s he was the most active mortgager in the province. He was also a major player in the slave trade that was booming in that period. All the while he continued to realize considerable income from his law practice in the chancery and prerogative courts still open to Catholic attorneys (unlike the provincial court). By the second decade of the century Carroll, the immigrant and outcast Catholic, had become the wealthiest man in Maryland.

Richard Bennett III (166?–1749), unlike Carroll, was native-born, the offspring of two distinguished Maryland families. Bennett's paternal grandfather was the Virginia Puritan who had helped Leonard Calvert

regain the colony after Ingle's invasion in 1644, then himself led the revolt against Lord Baltimore's government a decade later. His maternal
grandfather, a Neale, had left Maryland in the 1650s to serve as Charles
II's ambassador to the Iberian countries while the Stuart heir to the
throne was in exile. Shortly after the death of her husband, Henrietta
Maria Neale Bennett, a devout Catholic, had married Philemon Lloyd,
an Anglican politician from Talbot County on the Eastern Shore, and
continued to raise her two children by Bennett in her faith (by Lloyd
she had ten additional children, all of whom were raised as Anglicans).
It was a mixed religious household that was not uncommon among the
Maryland gentry, particularly in the seventeenth century.

A substantial legacy from his paternal grandfather was the gateway
to Richard Bennett's highly successful career as a merchant-planter. Like
Charles Carroll, he invested and speculated in land, if anything on a
larger scale than Carroll, accumulating tens of thousands of acres and
thousands of pounds in sterling in the process. By 1744 he owned nearly
52,000 acres within the province, at least four times the size of Carroll's
holdings. He also became a prolific money lender and supplier of credit, a crucial necessity in the colonial economy. In addition, he operated
two mills in Talbot County. And finally, he profited greatly from acquiring the right to collect quitrents for the proprietor over the course of an
eight-year lease. At his death in 1749, nearly three decades after Charles
Carroll's, Bennett was, like Carroll, the richest man in Maryland.

During the first half of the eighteenth century the richest men in successive generations were Roman Catholics, who for most of that span
had no political voice, being barred from holding office, voting, or serving
on juries. Two political outcasts were the two most powerful figures in
the Maryland economy over those fifty years: Charles Carroll and Richard Bennett represented the epitome of the economic success that the
Maryland Catholic gentry had achieved, despite the penal laws designed
to consign them to the margins of provincial society. On both shores of
the Chesapeake Bay, in St. Mary's, Charles, Prince George's, Baltimore,
and Talbot counties, Catholic families like the Carrolls, Bennetts, Blakes,
Heaths, Sayers, Neales, Darnalls, Diggeses, and Fenwicks flourished economically. How different the experience of the Catholic gentry proved to

be in Ireland and Maryland! In the former place punitive landstripping
and relocation had virtually wiped out the Catholic landowning class.
Those who did manage to hold onto their land (and political voice)—
nearly 1,200 of the Irish upper classes in the first half of the eighteenth
century alone—did so by conforming to the established church. There
was no parallel in conversions among the Maryland Catholic gentry,
who were spared the draconian land expropriation that victimized their
English counterparts. Only a handful, such as Dr. Charles Carroll and
Henry Darnall III, chose to defect, either by total conversion or partial
conformity, to secure the political and economic advancement that usually came with aligning with the established church. The vast majority of
Maryland Catholic gentry, with their estates essentially untouched, were
willing to make the most of their chances, limited as they were largely to
the economic sphere. Their alien status even seems to have served as a
motivator for competing successfully in whatever realms they could.

CATHOLIC SLAVES AND
SLAVEOWNERS

Because of their concentration in the southern Maryland and Eastern
Shore counties that housed most of the colony's slaves, Catholic families
were more likely to be slaveowners than Maryland families in general.
If Tricia Pyne's finding about Catholic slaveholders in upper St. Mary's
County is representative of the cohort in general, then fewer than half of
Catholic slaveowners were property owners, the rest more likely tenant
farmers on property owned by a relative, on the Jesuit plantations at
St. Inigoes and Newtown, or on one of the many proprietary manors in
the county.[3] Slaves indeed became a significant part of the Catholic community, accounting for one-fifth of the colony's Catholics by the late colonial period. Wealthy merchant-planters like Carroll and Bennett had
hundreds of slaves on their plantations; the Society of Jesus, on its three
plantations in St. Mary's and Charles counties, had well over a hundred.
The Catholic Church's record in ministering to slaves was somewhat

3. Pyne, "Maryland Catholic Community," 287–89.

better, Beatriz Hardy has shown, than that of the Anglican Church. At least church records provide grounds for concluding that most slaves of Catholic owners were baptized, and most had church weddings, as well. And, she concludes, Catholic priests had more success than their Anglican counterparts in getting masters to provide for the religious education of their slaves.[4] Some, like Ignatius Digges, were conscientious in fulfilling their responsibilities as stewards of their slaves' spiritual welfare, to the point of securing an agreement from a prospective son-in-law that the latter would allow the slaves a daughter was bringing as part of her dowry to practice their Catholic faith. Slaves themselves might well have found in Catholicism several features that closely resembled those in the traditional religious practices of West Africa, such as devotions to saints and the use of relics and holy water. The abstaining from work that the church mandated in observing the fifteen or so "holy days" throughout the year may have been a special attraction for slaves.

CATHOLIC GROWTH AND
THE GENTRY

The discrimination and exclusion that Catholics began to experience after the 1689 revolution tended to produce among them a greater commitment to their faith. The 1704 bill failed "to prevent the growth of Popery," much less to strip off significant numbers of members of the Catholic community seeking to escape the political ostracism and economic penalties that Catholics now incurred. If anything, the conversion stream, particularly among the gentry, ran toward Catholicism. There were only three notable defections of Catholic gentry—Thomas Brooke, Henry Darnall III, and Dr. Charles Carroll—to the established religion during the eight decades of the penal age. Conversely, a number of prominent Protestant families, such as the Stones, the Coodes, the Halls, the Blakistons, and the Hansons had Catholic branches by the middle of the eighteenth century.

4. Beatriz Betancourt Hardy, "'The Papists... have shewn a laudable Care and concern': Catholics, Anglicanism, and Slave Religion in Colonial Maryland," *Maryland Historical Magazine* (Spring 2003), 9.

The 1708 census revealed slightly fewer than 3,000 Catholics in Maryland, or approximately 7 percent of the population. Given the preponder-
ance of Catholics among servant immigrants of the period (an influx that
occasioned, in 1717, a doubling of the tax on imported Irish servants), as
well as the converts that Anglican clergy continued to complain about,
Catholic growth at least kept pace with that of the population in general. The majority of Catholics were concentrated in the three southern
counties on the Western Shore: St. Mary's, Charles, and Prince George's;
St. Mary's alone, where Catholics made up over 40 percent of the county's population, contained a third of the Catholic population. In her study
of St. Mary's Catholic community, Tricia T. Pyne found that less than a
third of Catholic householders owned property; she concluded that most
were tenant farmers. Outmigration from the traditional hub of Catholicism in southern Maryland—driven by soil exhaustion, very limited
available land, and a one-crop economy that stifled development—was an
option more exercised by the gentry than ordinary, largely landless Catholics. By the early eighteenth century less than 40 percent of the Catholic
gentry were still to be found in the two southernmost counties, St. Mary's
and Charles, in contrast to two-thirds of the general Catholic population.
Nearly 36 percent of the community's gentry were now in Prince George's,
one of the most rapidly growing counties in the province. The rest (23.8
percent) were mostly residing either in or near the capital (Anne Arundel,
Calvert) or on the Eastern Shore counties (Cecil, Queen Anne's); they
accounted for but 8.3 percent of the total Catholic population.

EXPANSION OF THE
MARYLAND MISSION

In 1703 there were eleven Jesuits in the province, the largest number the
Society had ever committed to the province. Besides William Hunter
and Robert Brooke, there were six priests and three brothers, a young
group ranging in age from twenty-eight to thirty-five. Meanwhile Charles
Calvert, although no longer functioning as the proprietor, continued to
support the Jesuit ministry by an annual stipend of 1,000 pounds of tobacco for each Jesuit in the province.

In 1704 the Maryland Jesuits permanently expanded their operations to the Eastern Shore with the founding of a mission in the far northeastern portion of the province, within an area still claimed by both Maryland and Pennsylvania. That choice of location seems to have been a response to the rapid growth of an Irish Catholic community in the region, the result of Charles Carroll's recruitment of hundreds of Irish immigrants in 1701 to work as indentured servants upon land he had acquired in northeastern Baltimore County (by 1705 he had patented more than 15,000 acres in the county), with the promise that each servant would receive 50 acres of land upon the completion of his or her term of indenture. This new influx of Irish immigrants joined an earlier community of Irish Catholics whom George Talbot, Lord Baltimore's cousin, had been responsible for settling in the area in the 1680s. The proximity of the Jesuit site to Pennsylvania, the destination of a rising migration of Maryland Catholics, was probably another incentive for its choice.

Thomas Mansell, the superior of the Maryland mission, acquired in 1706 several hundred acres at Bohemia, close by Bohemia Landing, a port for intercolonial and international trade, and near the Delaware Path, a major north-south link to Pennsylvania. In time the plantation the Jesuits established at Bohemia as part of their mission of St. Xaverius would encompass more than 1,700 acres. Mansell made his residence in a one-room log house that would double as a chapel; in time a frame chapel was added close by the rough-hewn house. As a symbol of the continuity of the Catholic presence in Maryland, the wrought-iron cross that had hung in the Great Brick Chapel in St. Mary's City (that structure now having been demolished) was brought to Bohemia and became the centerpiece in the tiny chapel on this disputed edge of Maryland. Finally, in 1720, a brick structure that served as both chapel and residence replaced the original wooden buildings. Bohemia as a parish served a small congregation of Catholics in the area. More importantly, it became the base for the circuit of missions on the Delmarva Peninsula that priests covered on horseback that allowed Catholics on the Eastern Shore the opportunity to hear Mass and receive the sacraments at least periodically, for some once a month, for others a few times a year.

THE CATHOLIC STRUGGLE AGAINST
ROYAL GOVERNMENT

The political struggle between Governor Seymour and the informal Catholic interest group headed by Charles Carroll continued through the remainder of Seymour's term of office. The proselytizing issue did not die with the 1704 legislation. Complaints continued about aggressively successful evangelizing by Catholics, particularly that which was aimed at their Protestant servants. So a bill was introduced into the assembly in 1706 to prohibit the sale of Protestant servants to Catholics, thus eliminating this relationship, which had traditionally been a propitious one for conversions to Catholicism. But Catholics used their connections by marriage and their influence as proprietary officials to have inserted into the measure a rider that would have prohibited all white women from working in the tobacco fields, an amendment that would have had a devastating impact on planters' ability to secure sufficient labor for seeing their crops through from planting to harvest. Seymour had no choice but to veto the bill.

The following year the governor seized the opportunity to support a complaint brought by a Scotch merchant in Maryland in the expectation that it would undermine the authority and political influence of the top two Catholic officials in the land office, Henry Darnall and Charles Carroll. The Scotsman had accused the pair of prejudice in denying him patents for several tracts of land. To Seymour's chagrin, the lower house declared that the plaintiff had no grounds for his case. This led the governor and the council, in retaliation, to introduce a bill that required a major section of the land office, the surveyors (nine of the dozen were Catholic), to take two of the test oaths. Once passed, Lord Baltimore could only protest in vain to the Board of Trade, which ratified the act. Catholics had lost their hold on an important administrative position and, along with it, more of their dwindling political power.

Until his sudden death of a fever in the summer of 1709, Seymour continued his campaign against the Catholic community, convinced that it was a party to a transatlantic conspiracy aimed at overthrowing the Protestant monarchy now enthroned in England. The census of Catholics and other dissidents that the government ordered in 1708 was but one element of the surveillance that he orchestrated in the hope of bringing to light some plot hidden within the Catholic community. With his death Catholic leaders could take comfort that they had blunted, if not defeated, much of Seymour's anti-Catholic program. True, the assembly had declared that various English penal laws applied to Maryland; but more significantly, they were making no effort to enforce them. Charles Carroll, for one, felt confident that Catholics could win, and win decisively, the next round of their quest to regain their former place in Maryland society.

Catholics were delighted when Edward Lloyd, with close Catholic connections, was named acting governor in 1709. Lloyd, the son of Henrietta Maria Neale Bennett Lloyd and the stepbrother of Richard Bennett, was the perfect executive to restore peace between the government and the Catholic community (Lloyd's wife was also Catholic). "[W]e live very peaceably," a Jesuit wrote a friend a year later. "God send us a good [permanent governor]."⁵ Providence seemed to answer his prayer by extending Lloyd's temporary position for four more years. Then Queen Anne died in the summer of 1714.

Anne's death rekindled hopes of yet another Stuart restoration. Even after Parliament made quick work of assuring a Protestant succession by having Anne's Hanoverian cousin crowned as George I two months later, an uprising of Jacobites in England and Scotland in 1715 ("the Fifteen") secured control of most of the Scottish highlands, which emboldened James Edward Stuart, the pretender, to leave his exile in France and sail to Scotland, where he planned to have his coronation as James III. By the time he landed there in late December the military invasion of England by two Jacobite armies had run aground, with an indecisive outcome at Sheriffmuir and the surrender of James's force at Preston, both in mid-November. A few of the captured leaders were hanged; most of the other Jacobites were shipped to America, including to Maryland, where they were sold as indentured servants.

---

5. Hardy, "Papists in a Protestant World," 130.

THE CALVERTS RESTORED

As James's plans for regaining the throne for the Stuarts were collapsing in Scotland, the Calverts' efforts to win back power were finding greater success. Benedict Calvert, Charles's son and heir, concluding that the restoration of Maryland to the family was more important than remaining a Catholic, publicly declared his allegiance to the established church and withdrew his six children from St. Omer's and convent schools on the Continent. In return, the heir apparent to Baltimore was granted an annual stipend of £300 and the privilege of naming the governor of Maryland. Benedict chose John Hart, who had promised to swell Benedict's income by £500 from the revenue he expected to accrue in the governor's office (Benedict had lost his annual stipend of £450 from his father when he had renounced his religion, but more than redeemed this amount from the promises he received from the crown and Hart). Charles Calvert finally died in February of 1715 at the age of seventy-seven. Seven weeks later Benedict himself was dead, leaving a sixteen-year-old son to whose rule the crown subsequently returned the colony that Benedict had paid so dearly to obtain.

Francis Lord Guilford, whose allegiance to the Stuarts was well known, became essentially the young proprietor's executor. Charles's mother herself had remained Catholic after her husband's pragmatic abandonment of his faith. These circumstances, together with James's then rising fortunes on the tide of "the Fifteen," all fed expectations among prominent Maryland Catholics, including Charles Carroll, that Lord Baltimore's restoration was the gateway for Catholics to regain political power. Indeed, even before Benedict's premature death in the spring of 1715, the Catholics were calculating that the fourth Lord Baltimore's conversion amounted to a church papist's profession—that he would now use the power he was sure to shortly regain to protect and advance the interests of his Catholic subjects in Maryland. Called to England as Charles Calvert's attorney to settle his estate, Charles Carroll carried with him a petition to the new Lord Baltimore from a group of prominent Catholics in which they requested that he make it possible for Catholics to once again "have an equal share in all the public offices of this Province." Just before he sailed for London, Carroll informed Hart about the petition. Furious at this blatant attempt to go over his head, the governor insisted that what Carroll and his fellow Catholics were attempting to do flew in the face of the laws of Great Britain and Maryland. Carroll, according to Hart, promised not to present the address.

Carroll arrived in England only to discover that Benedict Calvert himself had died two months after his father. Benedict's sixteen-year-old son, Charles, was the fifth Lord Baltimore, but until he reached maturity Francis Lord Guilford would serve as his legal guardian and, in effect, as acting proprietor. Carroll presented a memorial in the name of the Maryland Catholic elite to Lord Guilford, calling upon him to overturn the penal laws that prohibited Catholics from holding political office and from publicly practicing their faith. Guilford refused to intervene but did enhance Carroll's position as chief agent for the proprietor.

In doing so, of course, these Maryland Catholics *had* gone over the head of the governor of Maryland, probably because they realized that an appeal to John Hart himself would be useless. Hart, an Irish Protestant, was, like John Seymour, a career military officer. He shared with his predecessor a deep distrust of the loyalty of Catholics, whom he considered secret allies of the pretender. He found particularly vexing the persistent proselytizing by Jesuits and others who took advantage of the scandalous state of the established religion in Maryland to reap converts to their own faith. One of his first acts was to propose to the assembly additional penal acts to deter the growth of the Catholic community, including a new tax of twenty shillings for the importation of "Irish papists" and a bill that authorized the removal of a child from the home of a couple of mixed religion in case of the death of a Protestant father. He also ordered county sheriffs to keep a close watch on "Papists, Non Jurors & others disaffected to the most Sacred Person [the king]."[6]

6. Pyne, "Maryland Catholic Community," 198.

A BIRTHDAY SALUTE AS
CALCULATED PROVOCATION

In December 1715 Carroll had secured three lucrative proprietary offices
from Lord Guilford. The offices included wide powers in collecting revenue, including the right to half the income from fees paid for patent-
ing land, a considerable source of income that had previously gone to
the royal governor, as well as a portion of the money realized from the
collection of fines. It was this latter perquisite that provides a clue to an
odd series of events that touched off a crisis between Hart and Carroll,
with the most serious consequences. On the surface the firing of cannon
on Court House Hill on the occasion of the birthday of James Edward
Stuart seemed a bit of random Irish Jacobite defiance, but it may actually
have been a calculated provocation orchestrated by Carroll to solidify his
newly gained power as multi-office holding agent for the proprietor. On
June 10, 1716, two Irishmen awakened the town with a thunderous salute
from the cannon on Court House Hill in Annapolis. It would seem no
coincidence that both of the perpetrators had connections with Carroll's
nephew, James. William Fitzredmund worked as a clerk for Carroll in the
land office. Edward Coyle regularly did business with the younger Carroll. Two months after the cannon incident James Carroll paid money to
Fitzredmund for "cash lost at hazard," a nebulous phrase perhaps deliberately employed to cover a service performed that better went unmen-
tioned.[7] Hart, furious at this brazen disloyalty, called for the perpetrators (who had taken no efforts to hide their identity) to be punished (as
Carroll probably anticipated), which they subsequently were: committed
to jail until they could pay fines of staggering amounts (£100 sterling assessed to Fitzredmond; £40 to Coyle) imposed on them. Conveniently,
that gave Carroll the opportunity to exercise one of his duties as chief
agent of the proprietor. As he informed Hart, the commissions he had received from the proprietor's guardian empowered him to control both the

7. That is the conclusion Charles M. Flanagan reached, part of the persuasive case he makes for
the cannon incident being a ploy that Charles Carroll devised to provide an occasion for asserting
his authority; Flanagan, "'The Sweets of Independence': A Reading of the 'James Carroll Daybook,'
1714–1721" (Ph.D. diss., University of Maryland, College Park, 2005), 91–92.

proprietor's private revenues and all public revenue raised for the support
of government. The fines assessed for the cannon firing clearly fell into the
latter category, hence it was Carroll's responsibility and his alone to collect
them.

It was a bald power play that obviously blindsided Hart. Unable to
rebut Carroll's claims about the powers of the offices he held from the
proprietor, Hart could only insist that Carroll do what Maryland law required every public officeholder to do: swear oaths of allegiance and abjuration. Carroll replied that in conscience he could not take the latter oath,
which affirmed the Protestant secession to the crown and repudiated all
Stuart claims to the throne. With no oaths taken, Carroll nonetheless
proceeded to collect the fines and order the release of the two prisoners
from their Annapolis jail. Hart brought the matter to his council and convinced it that Carroll had deceived the proprietor and his guardian by getting them to give him commissions to offices that he could not qualify for
by taking the requisite oaths. The council seconded the governor's judgment on the matter, but summoned Carroll to allow him an opportunity
to justify his actions. Carroll explained that, in a quarter of a century of
service to the proprietor, he had never once been required to take an oath;
he saw no reason to do so now. The council was unimpressed.

REAPING THE CONSEQUENCES

Carroll was obviously presuming that his stellar record as an administrator and agent for the Calverts would carry the day for him. That Lord
Baltimore or, more precisely, Lord Guilford would be unwilling to jeopardize the Calverts's tenuous purchase on Maryland, so recently restored
to a family whose real religious allegiance was still questioned by some,
by showing obvious favor to an Irish Catholic Jacobite does not seem to
have occurred to Carroll. So he pressed ahead with his claims, requesting
that the governor forward to him all revenues he received. Hart consult-
ed both houses of the assembly, which advised him to turn over no revenues to Carroll.

When Hart refused to accommodate him, Carroll retaliated by putting a freeze on all patent requests, thereby essentially shutting down the

land office, which action threw real estate dealings in general into chaos. Hart then appealed to Lord Guilford, who shocked Carroll by withdrawing his commissions in 1717.

In the spring of 1716 Maryland held elections for its lower house. The Catholics sought to use the same influence that had served them well in past ones in securing delegates sympathetic to Catholic interests (although the closure of the land office at that time may well have deprived Catholics like Carroll of the chief lobbying pressure that Seymour had accused them of deploying previously). The results this time greatly disappointed Catholic circles. Whether it was the anti-Catholic feelings stirred anew by "the Fifteen" (a boatload of Jacobite prisoners arrived in Annapolis in the summer of 1716), the restoration of a proprietor with dubious religious convictions, or the better relationship, compared to Seymour's, that Hart enjoyed with the assembly, the elected delegates quickly endorsed the governor's penal proposals when they ordered all those holding any office or position of trust in the province, including commissions from the proprietor, to swear oaths of allegiance to King George and to foreswear any loyalty to the pretender. And, to drive home their new "Catholic" position, they greatly increased the tax on the importation of Irish servants from twenty shillings sterling to four pounds currency (reduced to forty shillings after the proprietor vetoed the original increase). But the keystone of the new legislation was the universal oath requirement for holding any office, provincial or proprietary. The revolution of 1689 had brought about the exclusion of Catholics from provincial government, but they still enjoyed the bulk of the proprietor's patronage. Now the door to their having any part in government was totally closed.

Meanwhile the Hart government began enforcing penal laws that had previously largely been observed in the breach. Three of the Jesuits in the province were arrested for alleged violations and jailed for some months. Others went into hiding to avoid being indicted. As the 1717 annual letter from the province reported to the Jesuit provincial in England, "There is at present a terrible persecution in Maryland."[8]

8. Hughes, *History of the Society of Jesus; Text,* 2:480.

The Carroll faction had no intention of accepting this outcome. In the fall of 1716 Henry Darnall II, James Carroll, and Thomas Macnemara (Charles Carroll's lawyer and husband of James Carroll's sister), carried letters in the name of the Catholic community that urged the proprietor's guardian to intervene in their behalf with the provincial government. One warned Guilford that Catholics in Maryland were under the threat of persecution because of their insistence that Lord Baltimore, not the governor, was the chief executive in the province—that ultimate authority rested in his person. What they were saying was that Catholics were the most loyal group that the proprietor had in Maryland. Left unsaid was the conclusion that this being the case, Catholics should have their full place in Maryland's government. This message the trio spent much time spreading among the Catholic gentry during their stay in England in the hope of amplifying the pressure upon Guilford to side with Maryland's Catholics.

This too failed utterly. Guilford affirmed everything the assembly had done regarding Catholics, adding, in his letter to Hart, "none of those laws to which we have assented met with a more ready confirmation than that which makes it penal for men to act in employment without taking the oaths to our dread sovereign King George, whereby Protestants and Papists may clearly perceive that your Lord and Proprietor is not as has been maliciously suggested by some a Papist in masquerade but a true Protestant of the Church of England in which faith he is resolved to live and die."[9] In February of 1717 Carroll's last hope died when Lord Guilford, far from upholding the Settler's claims, revoked his commissions and dismissed him from any further service for Lord Baltimore, ending a relationship that Carroll had had with the Calverts for nearly three decades.

A PYRRHIC PEACE

The denouement for Catholic political participation came a year later, when the assembly effectively disfranchised Catholics for their excessive

9. Flanagan, "'Sweets of Independence,'" 110. That proved indeed to be prophetic about the proprietor, but not about the writer himself. Eleven years later Guilford converted to Catholicism.

politicking since the restoration of Maryland as a proprietary colony in order to regain their traditional privileged political position.[10] In taking this step, the legislators explained, they were simply acting to "Restrain their Power."[11] The alarming growth of the Catholic community through immigration and conversions, together with the alliances they had formed in their aggressive attempts to influence and shape government, had made Catholics too dangerous a bloc to be allowed the vote. At the same time the assembly repealed the 1704 penal act, as well as the 1707 act suspending part of the earlier act, with the understanding that the penal legislation of Parliament (harsher, in general, than the Maryland Assembly's acts) applied to Maryland, hence this separate legislation was unnecessary.

Despite the string of defeats they had suffered, Catholics refused to believe they could not still carry the day with the proprietor and continued to lobby him with accounts of their woeful condition in Maryland and with pleas for relief. In addressing the assembly at their fall session in 1719, Governor Hart issued a public challenge to Maryland Catholics to cite one instance in which any Catholic had been persecuted, "or even prosecuted by Law for Conscience Sake," a challenge he repeated at their spring session.[12] On April 12 the upper house of the assembly, in response to claims that "Papists have Given out in Speeches" of rights being denied them, invited them to appear before the council, by or around April 16, to show "what Privileges of theirs are infringed" by the government, with the promise that they would do them all the justice "that their case requires." Should they fail to appear, it would be their admission that they had no case. They ordered sheriffs to deliver copies of the statement to thirteen "Eminent Papists," including Charles Carroll, William Fitzredmond, and Peter Atwood, the Jesuit superior.[13]

The inclusion of the Jesuit Atwood among the list of prominent Catholic laity at first glance seems odd. The Maryland Jesuits were not

10. Formally the law denied the right to vote to anyone unwilling to take the oaths of supremacy and abjuration.
11. *Archives of Maryland* 33:136.
12. *Archives of Maryland* 33:483, April 6, 1720.
13. *Archives of Maryland* 33:503.

known to be political activists, unlike so many of the Maryland Catholic gentry. Atwood, however, in his eight years in Maryland had garnered a reputation among Maryland Anglicans as a skilled polemicist, more than ready to engage in debates with representatives of the established church. A remark made by Governor Hart in speaking to the assembly in early April 1720 may shed light on Atwood's name being among those Catholics summoned by the council. Hart mentioned that he had been informed that some Catholics had attempted to respond to the challenge he had issued at the fall session by having a paper prepared that they intended to present to the assembly as a defense of their rights that the government was suppressing. In the end they had never presented the paper, because, so Hart speculated, he had made it known that he found the whole matter of their claim to rights offensive, and with this knowledge the Catholics had probably thought it best not to press the matter, particularly since they had reason to believe that Hart would soon be recalled from Maryland.[14] It could well be that Hart had information identifying Atwood as the author of the paper—hence his inclusion on the list.

A paper entitled "Liberty and Property" survives in Attwood's hand that was likely the defense that the Catholic leaders had arranged to be made in their behalf.[15] Atwood had three years earlier prepared a memorial that a delegation of Catholics had presented to Lord Guilford. "Liberty and Property" reveals a man who has studied and thought about Maryland's history and its significance. Its very title suggests Atwood's close following of political happenings in Maryland. In 1717 the Maryland Council had declared that "Religion, Liberty, and Property" were the hallmarks of citizenship, but that only "true English men could claim

14. At least some of the Maryland Catholic gentry were making contingency plans in case Hart continued as governor. They approached the Spanish ambassador to England about securing a land grant in the Spanish West Indies. Although the ambassador seemingly encouraged them to pursue this avenue, events in the spring of 1720 overtook this planning; Hardy, "Papists in a Protestant World," 216.

15. The paper, whose full title is "Liberty and property, or the beauty of Maryland displayed, being a brief & candid inquiry into her charter, fundamental laws and constitution. By a lover of his country," is among the Maryland Province Archives of the Society of Jesus housed in the Special Collections Research Center at Lauinger Library, Georgetown University.

them by right.[16] By implication Catholics could not qualify for citizenship precisely because they were not true Englishmen. Attwood in his paper proceeded to turn that implication on its head.

The triptych of "Religion, Liberty, and Property" was indeed the bedrock of citizenship, Atwood argued, but these were fundamental rights shared by Catholic and Protestant alike, as Maryland's charter recognized and as the province's early history had allowed to flourish. Because they possessed these rights, Maryland Catholics had as much claim to full citizenship as did any Protestant, even one of the established church. Moreover, because of Calvert's charter, Maryland enjoyed an independence from English law. Whatever laws governed Maryland were enactments of her own assembly, not extensions of Parliamentary actions. None was more important than the 1649 law of religious liberty codifying the practice of the colony from its beginning. The promise of religious liberty "had peopled our Province, and made it the most happy and most flourishing of all the British Colonys." To take away that right, of which deprivation had been the sad reality in Maryland for nearly three decades, was to divide the population along religious lines and eventually lead to people voting with their feet over the loss of their religious freedom.

Attwood's paper never became part of the assembly's official record. Nor did any Catholic respond to the council's summons that the sheriffs had delivered to them. When no Catholic appeared by the nineteenth of April, the upper house sent the sheriffs out once more to locate the Catholics. They reported that "the most Eminent of the Papists" were very much in town. Governor and council took this information as conclusive evidence of the Catholics' "tacite Acknowledgment that their Pretensions are groundless and their Exclamations Most unreasonable."[17]

They could not have more badly misread the Catholics' failure to appear. All the circumstantial evidence leads one to conclude that by April 19 the Catholics had decided that they had won the war they had been fighting with Hart over the past five years. Eight days earlier the governor

16. Bergmann, "Being the Other," 83.
17. Archives of Maryland 33:532–33.

had announced that he was reluctantly resigning because of his health. The Catholics knew better—knew that he was stepping down in protest of Lord Guilford's undercutting his authority by reversing the provincial government's revoking of Thomas Macnemara's license to practice law. That was all the Catholic leaders had to know to believe that this represented a fundamental change in their standing with the proprietor and his guardian. What did they have to gain from an appearance before a lame-duck governor and his council? The persons holding ultimate authority over Maryland were now sending a clear signal that they were reactivating their traditional relationship with the Catholic community.

John Hart sailed for England in May of 1720; two months later, Charles Carroll died at the age of fifty-nine. Later that year the proprietor himself, Charles Calvert, wrote a letter to Marylanders that called them to create a new slate, to lay aside the recent antagonism that Carroll and Hart fueled and live in peace, with the Catholic minority submitting to the existing laws. In its turn the assembly announced as a sign of its good will toward Catholics that if Catholics lived quietly there would be no effort made to enforce the penal laws. A rising generation of Catholic gentry was more open to such a message, more willing to heed it, than Charles Carroll and his allies had been. As James Heath, a member of that generation, remarked at the time of the Jacobite uprising in 1715, "I cannot but think that I am in the Right in wishing that Cath[olics] at all times would sit down quiet."[18] Heath eventually got his wish after Charles Carroll's passing from the scene in 1720. Catholics by and large accepted the settlement that had been made informally in the wake of Hart's and Carroll's departures. Certainly conditions improved for Catholics in Maryland under the governors Calvert appointed—some members of his own family, who did not bring the same antagonism toward Catholics as Hart had. After Hart there was no serious attempt for some decades to apply English law to Maryland. On the part of Maryland Catholics there was a gradual acceptance of the legitimacy of a Protestant accession, as a group of Maryland Catholics implicitly acknowledged in 1727 when they sent best wishes to George II upon his coming

18. Bergmann, "Being the Other," 97.

to the throne. But the old relationship between the proprietor and the Catholic community did not really revive. The Carrolls did not regain the proprietary offices that Charles Carroll had had taken away. Nor did Catholics regain the franchise, much less the right to hold office, short of the mortal religious compromise that the test oath represented. The corpus of penal legislation may have gone unenforced, but it was always there, a constant weight on the Catholic community—a living reminder of their outcast, second-class status in the province.

CHAPTER 8

"MANY TO ATTEND, AND FEW TO ATTEND THEM"

The Modes of Being an Outcast Community

In the first four decades of the eighteenth century the Catholic population in Maryland more than tripled, reaching nearly 8,000 by the 1740s. Immigration was a major cause of this growth, just as it accounted for a sharp diversification in the ethnic composition of the Catholic community—in particular Irish, Africans, and Germans. Although there were more priests on the Maryland mission as the century progressed (an average of just over twelve by the 1740s, about fourteen two decades later), their numbers did not keep pace with those of Catholics as a whole. Throughout the colonial period, despite increasing numbers, there was a chronic shortage of priests. As the first half of the century drew to a close, there was one priest for approximately 650 Catholics; four decades earlier the ratio had been one-half of that. Ten years later the ratio had swelled to

1,100 to 1. This was a growing population that was expanding toward the eastern and northern borders of the state and beyond. More than ever the Maryland Catholic community was a dispersed one that could only be reached by a mobile ministry, now primarily by horse rather than by boat, on a regular circuit of chapels and Mass houses.

St. Mary's, the oldest county and the heart of Catholic Maryland, was by the middle of the eighteenth century the backwater of the province, as well—its poorest and least developed region. It did not share in the "golden age" of the province: in the diversification of the economy from a single-staple agriculture to one that included multiple staple crops, mills, ironworks, and shipbuilding and in urbanization and the flowering of a Creole culture in close imitation of English genteel society. In contrast to the architectural flowering that was part of an urban renaissance making life in Annapolis one "much to be envyd by Courts and Cities," as an English visitor judged it in 1746, the Jesuit missionary Joseph Mosley caught the uniform poverty that characterized housing in St. Mary's countryside:

The buildings in this country are very poor and insignificant, all only one storey, commonly all the building made of wood plastered within,—a brick chimney in the better houses.... The poorer people have nothing but a few boards nailed together, without plastering, or any brick about it. Very few houses have glass windows.[1]

The bleak housing for the poor epitomized the economy they were trapped in: an economy in which the consolidation of landownership by the wealthy was reducing the options for the poor to becoming tenant farmers or vagabonds. Mosley found conditions for his parishioners on the Eastern Shore to be even worse: families mired in grinding poverty, abandoned by desperate fathers who were without land or work. Maryland, he concluded, the province that once boasted of being the poor man's best country, was now a shell of its former self, with too many people: "the lands... all secured, and the harvest for [the poor] now over." Slaves occupied the fields once worked by freemen. The consequence:

1. "'Itinerant Observations' of Edward Kimber," London Magazine (1746), 323, quoted in Robert J. Brugger, *Maryland: A Middle Temperament, 1634–1980* (Baltimore: Johns Hopkins University Press, 1988), 70; Joseph Mosley to sister [Helen Dunn], Newtown, September 1, 1759.

"white servants, after their bondage is out, are strolling about the country without bread."[2]

Nowhere did the disfranchisement of Catholics have a more dire impact than in St. Mary's County, where, as a majority of the population (60 percent), they had wielded the greatest political influence. As Tricia T. Pyne notes, "Once resigned to the loss of their political rights, members of this community turned their attention to their families and farms."[3] The physical concentration of more than 70 percent of the county's Catholics in the northwestern corridor, which embraced the Newtown, Lower Resurrection, and St. Clement's Hundreds, facilitated the development of this ghetto mentality. The steady exodus of gentry from the Catholic community in the early eighteenth century due to worsening economic conditions aggravated the homogenization of the community, which became more and more a place of small to middling planters. The circumstances abetted the self-imposed isolation from the larger society and the elaboration of a distinct subculture transplanted from the English Catholic community.

EMERGENCE OF A SEIGNEURIAL CATHOLICISM

The establishment of the Church of England within Maryland and the imposition of penal laws upon the Catholic community had fundamentally altered the religious landscape in the colony. As from the very beginning of Maryland's settlement, the Jesuits found themselves adapting their ministry to the shifting religio-political conditions. Closed off by law from the public ministry that had characterized Jesuit outreach during most of the Maryland mission's history in the seventeenth century, Jesuits adopted, with appropriate variations, the home ministry model that had been so successful for them in England. The penal era required a radical change in the fundamental nature of the locus and form of the practice of Catholicism: from public to domestic, with the home and the laity at the center of Catholic ritual and spirituality.

2. Mosley to sister, Tuckahoe, September 8, 1770.
3. Pyne, "Maryland Catholic Community," 303.

With the enforced closure of the public chapels in St. Mary's City and elsewhere as part of the privatization of Catholic worship, the four Jesuit plantations on the Western Shore (St. Inigoes, Newtown, St. Thomas Manor, and Whitemarsh) assumed a greater importance as centers of religious life for the community—a clerical variation of the estate-centered Catholicism that prevailed in England. Each plantation had its own chapel, where at least twice a month local Catholics, many linked by kinship as well as neighborhood, would gather unobtrusively on Sundays for services. The endogamous pattern of marriages among Catholics of the region tended to reinforce the community's bonds and ensure its survival, even if it tended to strengthen its tribal character, as well.

Beyond the orbit of the Jesuit plantations in southern Maryland, Catholic religious life in the eighteenth century very closely resembled that of its English parent. The dispersion of the Catholic gentry, together with penal legislation that confined the practice of Catholicism to the private sphere, made for the emergence in Maryland of the gentry-centered religion or "Seigneurial Catholicism" (the phrase is Beatriz Hardy's) that characterized English Catholicism. As in England, Catholic religious culture in Maryland took on a pronounced domestic character, one that made the home the center of ritual as well as devotional practice.

The emerging importance of the laity in sustaining Catholicism in Maryland during the penal age is reflected in the sharp increase in the number of bequests to the Church beginning in the 1690s, when half of those making wills included the Church among their beneficiaries. But their major contribution to the development of the community was in their provision of a site for the practice of religion. As Hardy indicates, "If the Catholic gentry outside St. Mary's and Charles Counties wished to attend Mass, they either had to provide their own chapels or provide the Jesuits the wherewithal to build them. The gentry chose the first option,"[4] possibly because in the penal age there was always the threat (made very explicitly in the 1750s) of the government's seizing the property of the Jesuits.

4. Hardy, "Papists in a Protestant Age: The Catholic Gentry and Community in Colonial Maryland, 1689–1776" (Ph.D. diss., University of Maryland, 1993), 93.

And so the chapels on the estates of gentry Catholics proliferated in the first half of the eighteenth century, particularly in Prince George's, Queen Anne's, and Talbot counties, either as distinct appendages of manor houses or as rooms within mansions made available to a priest and ad hoc congregation. At the beginning of the century there had been fourteen Catholic chapels in Maryland. By 1760 there were fifty, situated in counties ranging from the piedmont to the tidewater on the Western Shore to Cecil, Queen Anne's, and Talbot on the upper Eastern Shore. On the Eastern Shore the Bennetts, Blakes, Seths, Heaths, and Knatchbulls were among those who maintained chapels or Mass houses; on the Western Shore, the Carrolls led the way in chapel building, Charles Carroll of Annapolis, Daniel Carroll of Rock Creek, and James Carroll of Anne Arundel County all having chapels on their estates. Charles Carroll was the only planter to have a full-time chaplain, splitting his time between Doohoragen Manor in western Anne Arundel County and Carroll's Annapolis home. Many of the private chapels were quite large, capable of accommodating congregations of a hundred or more. The congregations themselves consisted of the host family, its servants and slaves, and their neighbors, together with the neighbors' indentured or permanently bonded servants. The records show that congregations on the Eastern Shore consisted of many slaves, since the latter outnumbered free persons in the Catholic population. We do know that slaves very much participated in baptisms and church weddings. Black worshippers, in fact, constituted the vast majority of those who were baptized, as well as those married in the church on the Shore. And the vast majority of godparents were black, as well.

The growth of the network of gentry chapels promoted, it would seem, a distinctive communal identity for Catholics that resulted in, if not the ghetto-like condition that the Catholic community in St. Mary's experienced, at least a certain growing isolation from the larger society, as the sharp decline in gentry intermarriage over the course of the third quarter of the century (from 22 percent to 12 percent) would seem to suggest.

Counties devoid of Catholic gentry tended to go without Catholic chapels, the nominal Catholics there essentially unchurched. Indeed, five of Maryland's seventeen counties lacked a Catholic chapel. Somerset County on the Eastern Shore had a large Irish Catholic population. Some of the largest landowners in Somerset were also Catholics. But they were absentee owners, with no home or presence in the county. Where there was no significant presence of the Catholic gentry, there was no significant institutional presence of the church. As a result, the long-range probability of any Catholics in Somerset retaining their faith was virtually nonexistent. Carl Peterman, in his study of the Catholic Church on the Delmarva Peninsula, found that most Catholics in Somerset County eventually joined another church, there being no Catholic church available. The remainder became in time a people of no religious identity.[5] The Catholic experience in Somerset was one, sadly, that was replicated in many places outside of Maryland, particularly in the southern colonies, where Catholics found no institutional resources with which to sustain their faith.

John Mattingly, a Jesuit who grew up in the mid-eighteenth century near one of the "stations" served by the priests on the Newtown plantation, wrote down years later what Sunday was like for these itinerant ministers in St. Mary's County. His description could as easily apply to the circuit of manors that the Jesuits visited, although perhaps not as frequently, on the Eastern Shore or the upper Western Shore.

[O]n Sundays and feast days they go to minister to various stations, called "congregations," at a distance of 10, 15, or even more than 20 miles, all widely scattered. In this manner in each station at least once a month they celebrate mass, administer the sacraments, and preach the word of God; in the main stations they do this two or more times a month, depending on the numbers and… the needs of the faithful.… From very early in the morning until 11 o'clock, they hear confession. Then they celebrate mass, and distribute holy communion. At the end of mass there is a sermon, in which the priest explains Christian doctrine.[6]

Circuit riding made life a very demanding one for the understaffed Jesuits serving a greatly dispersed community. As Joseph Mosley admitted to his sister,

5. Thomas Joseph Peterman, *Catholics in Colonial Delmarva* (Devon, Penn.: Cooke, 1996), 98.
6. John Mattingly, September 1773, *Scritture riferite nei Congressi, America Centrale,* I, fols. 557r–v and 558r, Archives of the Sacred Congregation of the Propagation of the Faith.

Chapel at Rich Neck Manor

I allow our fatigues are very great, our journies very long, our rides constant and extensive. We have many to attend, and few to attend them. I often ride about 300 miles a week, and never a week but I ride 150, or 200: and in our way of living, we ride almost as much by night as by day, in all weathers, in heats, cold, rain frost or snow. Several may think the colds, rains &c, to be the worst to ride in; but, I think to ride in the heats far surpasses all, both for man and horse.[7]

The twenty-eight-year-old Mosley wrote that at the end of his first year on the mission, stationed at Newtown with several other Jesuits in the heart of the Maryland Catholic community. Five years later he was transferred to the Eastern Shore, eventually to establish, by himself, the mission of St. Joseph near the Wye River in Talbot County. The congregations he served there were more dispersed, the distances traveled much greater than those he had known in southern Maryland. The English province, recognizing the hardships intrinsic to the Maryland mission, allowed its Maryland members, beginning in 1712, the option of return-

7. Mosley to sister, Newtown, September 1, 1759.

ing to England after seven years in the mission. Few took it. As Mosley told his sister in 1773,

I've lived entirely alone for these nine years past.... I am thronged sufficiently abroad, but am a true eremite at home.... This last winter, I was riding the whole night to the sick, three or four times, as I remember. One night in particular, in a ride of sixty-four miles, raining from the first jump of my own door till I returned, to a sick person that is as yet alive and little wanted me. It was the third ride I've had to that same man, three successive winters.... I returned through the rain, next day, with no sleep, victuals or drink, except bad water.... I could tell you of a thousand other uncomfortable accidents of this kind.[8]

Despite his brother's prodding to return to England, Mosley remained at his post, enduring the suppression of the Society of Jesus and the events of the American Revolution, until his death in 1786.

As in England, women assumed an important role in the functioning of this home ministry, their responsibilities including the hospitality of the priest and any other guests, the preparation of the chapel for religious services, the catechesis of their children and other household dependents, and, in many instances, the leading of spiritual devotions outside of Mass.

The centerpiece of the priest's visit would be the celebration of the liturgy or Mass. That rite almost certainly began with the recitation of a litany—that of Loreto—followed by the priests aspersing the congregation with consecrated water. The scriptural readings would be in Latin, with the Gospel repeated in the vernacular. Then would follow the central prayer, or canon of the Mass, uttered *sotto voce* in Latin by the priest, his back turned to the kneeling congregation. At the conclusion of the canon the priest recited the Our Father (or *Pater Noster*, the prayer being said in Latin) as a preparation for communion, which few beside the priest likely received on any given Sunday. Despite the Jesuits' conviction that the frequent reception of communion was an essential means of progressing in one's spiritual life, most people, it would seem, took communion but once a year, as canon law required, usually at Easter. Post-communion prayers would follow.

Only then would a sermon be preached, if Mattingly remembered correctly, also in the language of the people. The sermons tended to be cat-

8. Mosley to sister, Tuckahoe, July 5, 1773.

echetical lessons focusing on the distinctive elements of Catholicism that made it the model of authentic Christianity in a largely Protestant world and inculcating the practices that not only constituted the staples of a devout life, but also promoted the common good. There might be appropriate hymns, possibly in the vernacular, since priests were particularly urged to include some songs and prayers in that medium. But the thrust of the Mass was on a double track, with the priest, back turned to those in attendance, making this supreme prayer of the Church on his own, as it were, and the members of the congregation engaged in their own private prayers, either the rosary or those found in recommended manuals. There was little if any sense that the Mass was a prayer of the faithful in which all were participants. It was in essence an individual, almost atomized exercise.

Following Mass there might well be the recitation of vespers, a part of the divine office, concluded by benediction. Then catechetical instructions were given to children and perhaps to those seeking to convert to Catholicism or become members of the church. Special instructions were also required to be given to those wishing to marry. And there might be marriages or baptisms for the priest to perform. Where one of the pair seeking to marry was not Catholic, a dispensation was needed, a rare occurrence in St. Mary's County (mixed marriages made up but 2 to percent of the Catholic weddings), but much more common (affecting as many as 30 percent of the weddings) where the Catholic population was small. On the Eastern Shore there was a tendency toward Catholic-Quaker weddings. As the Catholic population grew there was a decline in mixed marriages, including on the Eastern Shore, even among the gentry.

Geography seems to have been a decisive factor in deciding at what time in the year to marry. Most Catholics (over two-thirds) in southern Maryland married in the fall and early winter. A majority on the Eastern Shore chose to marry in the spring and summer. That may have reflected the different seasons of the two principal staples of the respective regions. Tobacco demanded constant labor from spring through late summer, hence the attraction of the fall for weddings in southern Maryland. The grains of the Eastern Shore were much less demanding, as the nearly two-thirds of Maryland Catholics who married there during the growing season indicates.

SPIRITUALITY AND THE
ASCETICAL LIFE

These manorial visits would be occasions not only for the celebration of Mass and the administration of sacraments, but also for the promotion of family-centered spirituality by instructing the congregation in devotional practices such as the recitation of the rosary or the making of the morning offering to the Sacred Heart. This spirituality was designed for a community in which the laity were primarily responsible for maintaining their active faith by integrating prayer and good works into their everyday lives within their own homes rather than an ecclesiastical institution. One devotion in particular that private domestic chapels made possible was that of the Blessed Sacrament. Following the distribution of the consecrated hosts to the gathered faithful, the priest would place the goblet-shaped ciborium containing the remaining hosts within the tabernacle on the altar for adoration or contemplation by the members of the household or others. The devotion, of course, need not be confined to the purely private sphere. At St. Thomas Manor, the Society for the Perpetual Adoration of the Blessed Sacrament was formed in 1768. Members pledged to spend a half hour twice a month in meditation or vocal prayer before the consecrated host. This devotion proved to be a popular one not merely in Maryland but in Pennsylvania, as well, where both German and English-Irish congregations adopted it.

Reflecting the importance of devotional reading in the development of a vital spiritual life, all of the Jesuit residences maintained libraries. These libraries not only served the spiritual and ministerial needs of the Jesuits themselves but were accessible to the laity, both male and female, who could regularly borrow catechisms, devotional works, lives of the saints, sermon collections, and the like without charge. As Joseph Mosley remarked about the usage of his library at Tuckahoe, "these books are so beneficial to the poor Catholics, &c., who are entirely unprovided of such information."[9]

9. Mosley to sister, July 1786, in "Letters of Fr. Joseph Mosley," edited by Edward I. Devitt, *Records of the American Catholic Historical Society of Philadelphia* 17 (1906): 309, cited in Pyne, "Maryland Catholic Community," 43.

The key instrument that the Jesuits employed to promote communal spirituality was the sodality, a devotional confraternity whose public European format the Maryland Jesuits adapted to a private organization appropriate for a Catholic community bearing the burden of very confining penal laws. Two sodalities that proved popular among Maryland Catholics were those involving the Sacred Heart and the adoration of the Blessed Sacrament. That of the latter can be seen as a kind of glue of the local church or congregation, a communal form of devotion taking place in the domestic or public chapel. The Sodality of the Sacred Heart, on the other hand, symbolized the private nature of Maryland Catholicism, with its centerpiece the morning act of consecration made in the privacy of one's room, of offering up to Jesus all that one did or experienced that day, a modest but profoundly Jesuit way of finding God in all things, even the most mundane. Limited records indicate that these societies transcended class lines, embracing gentry, middling planters, and tenant farmers alike. Such evidence also reveals that women made up the vast majority of the members of these societies, affirming the central place that women had in shaping the spiritual culture of the Maryland Catholic community. Women, in fact, outnumbered men in congregational membership, though not as dominantly as they did in the sodalities, if the congregation at St. Inigoes, for which alone a membership list survives, is representative.[10] And, as in England, mothers were the primary religious educators within the home.

When there was no priest available to say Mass, which was the case at least half the time, families were expected to gather together for prayers, spiritual reading, and catechetical instruction. Where that was not possible individuals needed to develop a private regimen of prayer and devotional reading. Beyond Sundays the laity were encouraged to develop a regular schedule of morning and evening prayers to be recited in common.

The calendar of the English liturgical year was crowded with holy days of obligation, some thirty-six of them, on which persons were expected to attend Mass or, where that was not possible, to participate in

10. There were 163 women to 140 men.

appropriate communal prayers or religious observances. On these special feast days, as on Sundays, there was to be no manual labor for anyone, including servants and slaves. Maryland staple crops, particularly tobacco, could ill afford the neglect that such recurring days of rest would bring. By the early eighteenth century there was widespread violation of the prohibition by Catholic planters and workers. Little wonder, then, that Jesuit superiors in Maryland sought relief from the ban on labor for their fellow Catholics engaged in agriculture. In 1724 they secured a partial release from the regulation. The vicar apostolic of the London district, under whose jurisdiction the Maryland mission fell, dispensed them from observing the regulation during the growing season (May to October), except for the four major feasts of Ascension, Whitmonday, Corpus Christi, and the Assumption.

If there were a formidable number of holy days of obligation during the year, the days on which adult Catholics were required to fast or abstain from meat, eggs, and cheese accounted for more than a third of the annual calendar. Fasting for Catholics meant one meal at midday, with only a warm drink containing water (tea, coffee, thin chocolate) in the morning and a small collation in the evening. That spartan diet was ill suited to the working classes, black and white, who by the eighteenth century made up the large majority of the adult Catholic community in Maryland and who spent their days expending the intense labor that the cultivation of tobacco, grain, and other staples required. Like the prohibition of servile labor on holy days, the regulations regarding fasting and abstinence seem to have been increasingly ignored by the second decade of the eighteenth century. At the same time that Maryland Jesuits requested a waiver of the labor ban on holy days, they sought release from the fast and abstinence obligations, as well. In 1724 London granted a dispensation from fasting and abstinence for those who were involved in the production of tobacco from May to September. Later the superior of the Maryland mission was given the discretion to grant dispensations, from fasting and abstinence as well as from servile labor bans, to the individuals and on the occasions he saw fit. As a result, by the end of the colonial period, the number of fast days had fallen by a third, to sixty-three. Days of abstaining from meats and from servile labor remained virtually intact.

EDUCATION AND VOCATIONS

As the Maryland Catholic gentry prospered in the early eighteenth century, more and more of them sent their sons and daughters abroad to
recusant schools in Europe despite the penalties they risked, including
the students' loss of inheritance, in doing so. Those Catholics seeking a
formal education for their children as a certification of the gentility that
the wealthy increasingly prized had no alternative institutions at home
in which to place their offspring, even for the rudiments of education, for
most of colonial history. There were three short-lived schools begun by
the Jesuits in British America: the school at St. Mary's from 1677 to 1689;
the one in New York from 1683 to 1689; and the one at Bohemia on the
Eastern Shore from 1745 to 1751. The last one, begun by the Jesuit Thomas Poulton, attracted a roster of the children of the Chesapeake Catholic
elite, including Neales, Sayers, Carrolls, and Brents, until it was forced to
close, apparently in part by the virulent anti-Catholic forces at large in
the early 1750s, led in Cecil County by the local Anglican rector, who had
been waging a campaign against the school since it had opened.

Had Catholics even been willing to entrust their children to public
(which is to say Protestant) schools, there was precious little to choose
from in the Chesapeake region beyond a William and Mary College
struggling to survive in Williamsburg and an even more precarious King
William's School in Annapolis. But Anglican education was basically out
of the question, so whatever initial education the children of the Catholic gentry acquired was mostly by way of home tutoring from mothers
or itinerant Irish schoolmasters, a growing presence in Maryland by the
early eighteenth century. For further education they turned, beginning
in the last quarter of the seventeenth century, to St. Omer's in Spanish
Flanders and other schools on the Continent begun by émigré English
religious and clerics. Two alumni of the school at St. Mary's, Robert
Brooke, whose parents were converts, and Thomas Gardiner, son of
Luke Gardiner, in 1681 became the first Americans at St. Omers.

Most of the girls and young women who crossed the Atlantic did so
to enter the convent. Mary Digges, who entered the Convent of the Holy
Sepulchre at Liège in 1721, was the first American to do so; Anna Maria

Parnham, who became prioress in the Liége Carmel, was the second two decades later. In the peak decade of the 1750s the daughters of Brents, Matthewses, Pyes, Boones, Semmeses (seven), Hills, Hagens (four), and Neales all entered European religious communities. Of William and Anne Brooke Neale's thirteen children, six sons went to St. Omer's, of whom four became Jesuits; a daughter became a Poor Clare. In all there were at least twenty-five Marylanders who joined contemplative orders of women in Europe: nine Carmelites, seven Benedictines, five Poor Clares, and four Dominicans.

A Continental education was a costly investment for Maryland's Catholic gentry. To keep a son at St. Omer's for five years cost a family £100 at the minimum. Nicholas Sewall spent £233 in 1772 for his five sons, who were in various recusant schools in Europe. Edward Cole spent over £400 sterling, about a quarter of his personal estate, on the education of his three sons. William Neale, a Charles County planter, found it necessary to exhaust his liquid funds plus the rents from his to-bacco warehouses to finance his sons' education at St. Omer's. The dow-ries that convents expected aspirants to bring could be even more taxing on families. The father of Mary Ann Semmes was willing to provide her with £225, 50 percent more than the usual entrance fee, in order to get the nuns to accept his daughter, whose poor health made her a special risk.[11]

After the initial wave of students to St. Omer's in the 1680s few Maryland Catholics were sent abroad during the next three decades, the period in which the Maryland Catholic community came gradually un-der the penal laws, which included a ban on students attending "foreign seminaries" for their education. Then under the benign neglect that char-acterized the enforcement of the penal laws in Maryland from the 1720s onward, the numbers began a steady increase that peaked in the 1760s. Of the Maryland Catholic gentry who came of age between 1550 and 1775, more than half studied at either St. Omer's or Bruges. From 1759 to 1773 no fewer than eighty-two sons of Maryland Catholics attended one

11. Jean B. Lee, *The Price of Nationhood: The American Revolution in Charles County* (New York and London: W. W. Norton, 1994), 76.

of the two recusant schools. Among the boys in recusant schools in Flanders and Spain in the 1740s to 1750s were three great-grandchildren of Robert Cole. Two became Jesuits. A third died from smallpox on his way to enter the Jesuit novitiate at Watten in 1763. By 1750 there were enough children of the Maryland Catholic gentry going abroad that there was a need to organize the traffic. George Hunter, the superior of the Maryland mission, served as kind of an educational factor, arranging the passage of the students and handling the payment of the fees and dowries required to enter the various institutions. During the Seven Years' War (1756–1763) Hunter had to make provision for his charges being captured by a French privateer. For such an eventuality Hunter provided each youth with two special passes, one in Latin, one in French, which they were to present to their captors to "prevent all bad treatment."[12]

Of those young men who went abroad, forty-nine entered the Society of Jesus, one became a Benedictine, one a Dominican, and three were ordained as secular priests. Ironically, the last two Marylanders to enter the Jesuit novitiate before the suppression of the Society in 1773 were two Brooke brothers, lateral descendants of Robert Brooke, who had been the first vocation from British America nearly nine decades earlier. Twenty-one of the thirty-four who reached ordination returned to America to become part of the Maryland mission. Among these were several generations of Neales, beginning with Henry and Bennet Neale in the 1730s and 1740s and ending with Leonard and Charles Neale in the 1770s. The other thirteen remained in Europe to serve in England and at other posts on the Continent. All in all, by 1773 Americans made up 13 percent of the members of the English province.

Among young women there was an even sharper spike in vocations in the 1750s. Prior to that decade only three Maryland women had entered convents. Now, in that decade alone, there were at least seventeen; in the following one, as many as twenty more took the veil. Unlike their male counterparts, these female religious had no possibility of returning to their homeland, there being no institutional place for them there. That

12. Hughes, "Educational Convoys to Europe in the Olden Time," *American Ecclesiastical Review* 29 (1903): 30–39.

did not prevent some Maryland Catholic women, unable for financial or family reasons to enter a European convent, from functioning informally as religious at home: living under a self-imposed rule, securing a Jesuit director, and finding paracanonical ways of serving the church. Two such vowless religious were Jennie Digges and Elizabeth Carberry, both of St. Mary's County.

The suppression of the Society of Jesus in 1773 disrupted the Atlantic traffic of youth to recusant schools and convents on the Continent. Maryland Jesuits had traditionally, through their international connections, arranged the passage and handled the finances for the aspiring students and novices. Now that network no longer existed. Moreover, the concurrent economic downturn provided no stimulus for the flow of students and postulants from America. It especially made it much more difficult for Maryland families to provide suitable dowries (typically ranging from £100 to £300 sterling) for daughters intent on entering convents. The events of 1775 and 1776 ended permanently this Maryland Catholic tradition of sending the gentry's children abroad for their education.

RIDING THE ECONOMIC WINDS

In the half-century economic boom that Maryland experienced from 1720 to 1770, none benefitted financially more than the planter-merchants. As a result, wealth in the province became much more concentrated. In Talbot County, for instance, the top 2 percent of taxpayers controlled nearly half (45 percent) of all the property in the county.[13] By the 1750s Catholics constituted about 10 percent of Maryland's population, but they had a disproportionate representation among the economic elite. Half of the province's twenty richest people were Catholics, Charles Carroll of Annapolis and Richard Bennett III of Talbot County being at the top of the list. That Carroll and Bennett also happened to be the two largest creditors in the province indicates the linkage between lending and economic success in an expanding economy. For whatever reasons, wealthy Catho-

13. Brugger, *Maryland*, 59.

Eleanor Darnall

lics seemed to be disproportionately involved in providing credit, replicating a role that individuals of another marginalized group, the Jews, were coming to play in many European communities.

The death of his father, Charles Carroll the Settler, in the summer of 1720 had forced Carroll to return home to Annapolis, aborting his law studies at the Inns of Court in London. An older brother's death a year previously had made him, at eighteen, suddenly the unexpected heir to the richest estate in Maryland. Lacking the proprietary, professional, and marriage connections that his father had utilized so deftly as official, lawyer, planter, and merchant to accumulate an unprecedented fortune within the province, Charles Carroll of Annapolis proved to be more than astute in achieving an economic success of the first order through his development of the four plantations he inherited, the moneylending that he took to a new level, the shrewd investment in the real estate of a town that became one of the most important cities in British America, and his partnership in a major industrial undertaking.

His cousin and godfather, James Carroll, managed his estate initially while mentoring him in the intricacies of plantation management and commercial transactions. By the middle of the 1720s Carroll had taken control of his own affairs. He began the slow process of maximizing the cultivation of his plantations on both sides of the bay. He steadily increased the acreage dedicated to the raising of tobacco, grains, and livestock by aggressively recruiting tenant labor, especially from Ireland and Germany. Relying on such self-supporting labor allowed him to develop his vast lands rapidly at minimal expense. By the 1750s he had more than two hundred tenants cultivating more than 19,000 acres. He also added slaves, on a lesser scale, to his work force, particularly at his largest plantation, the 12,500-acre Doohoragen Manor in Maryland's piedmont. With 386 slaves on his four plantations, Charles Carroll of Annapolis was one of the largest slaveowners in the province. He was also one of the largest landowners (but not the largest; that distinction belonged to Richard Bennett III).

Tobacco was the chief staple crop produced on the Carroll plantations. By the 1760s he was exporting about half the annual tobacco yield to no fewer than seven London merchants, whom Carroll adroitly played off against one another to realize the maximum price for his crop. As perhaps the largest tobacco grower in Maryland, Carroll took advantage of the sheer volume of tobacco that he could supply to drive up the demand—and the price—for his tobacco. He who had the most to provide attracted the most buyers who competed to pay the most. Such shrewd marketing was a major factor in the vast real and personal wealth that Carroll accumulated by the 1770s, probably in excess of £100,000 sterling.

Moneylending also proved to be a lucrative investment for Carroll. Although he did not continue the mercantile enterprises of his father (a reflection of the trend toward specialization that was increasingly making planting and trade full-time engagements), Carroll vastly expanded the banking activities that had previously been an integral part of his father's commercial business. He had a great deal of his money in loans (£40,000 sterling in 1776), in most cases mortgages that exceeded £500. He was known as a hard creditor, prone to foreclose without compunction and (as some charged) not above applying compound interest to the debts owed him. Carroll's defense was that he did nothing that the law forbade.

Unlike his father, real estate speculation was not a major economic activity for Charles Carroll of Annapolis. He did, however, play a major role in the most important urban development in the province's history. The diversification of the economy was producing more year-long commercial activity that created a need for everything ranging from merchants to mills to taverns—that is, to a cluster of concentrated enterprises that gave rise to towns, particularly at the fall line of rivers, that marked the navigable terminus for oceangoing vessels as well as a prime location for harnessing water power. So Georgetown on the Potomac was incorporated as a town in 1751. More than two decades earlier an even more significant urban undertaking had had its beginning. In 1729 Charles Carroll was one of the signers of a petition to the provincial assembly that called for the establishment of a settlement to be called "Baltimore Town" on a sixty-acre tract of land in a basin of the northern branch of the Patapsco River, one acre of which property was owned by Carroll. A little more than two years later, a short distance from Baltimore Town on the southern branch of the river, Carroll, along with his brother Daniel and cousin Charles, took advantage of the sustained peace prevailing between Great Britain and the Catholic imperial powers in the 1720s and 1730s to form a rare ecumenical partnership with two of the wealthiest Protestants in the province, Benjamin Tasker Sr. and Daniel Dulany Sr., to capitalize the Baltimore Company, the second ironworks in Maryland. With abundant water power, plentiful hardwoods to be converted into charcoal to heat the furnaces, and rich iron deposits easily extracted, it was a perfect site. The venture quickly proved a very profitable one. Between 1734 and 1737 the company shipped nearly 2,000 tons of pig iron to England. The partners steadily expanded its operations; by the 1740s they were producing iron bar as well as the cruder pig iron. Eventually the giant operation sprawled over 30,000 acres of land, employing a labor force of hundreds, mostly slaves and transported convicts. Within two decades Charles Carroll of Annapolis was earning more than £300 sterling a year, an annual dividend that grew to £400 by the 1760s.

The Carrolls were among a number of Catholic entrepreneurs who were prominent in the development of industry in Maryland. Two generations of Diggeses established ironworks and copperworks in central Maryland. Edward Neale and Ralph Falkner partnered to begin another ironworks in the early 1740s.

Baltimore itself developed much more slowly than its eponymous ironworks. Five years after its incorporation, Carroll purchased twenty-six of the remaining sixty original lots, giving him ownership of nearly half the acreage in the town. No doubt he had his reasons for investing so heavily in Baltimore's future. Over the course of the first decade and a half of the town's life, it seemed a very bad investment; Carroll sold no lots. Not until the middle 1740s did he realize any sales, the first indicator that Baltimore Town could become a significant commercial center. Several converging circumstances, including the climaxing Anglo-French contest for supremacy in North America, a string of harvest failures in Europe, new wheat production in the rapidly expanding backcountry of the Middle Atlantic region, the expansion of sugar production in the West Indies, and new methods of financing and marketing—all these developments combined to make Baltimore an important link in a transformed Atlantic trade basin. By the time of the American Revolution, Baltimore Town had replaced Annapolis as the principal commercial center in the province, a home to some 7,000 people. Carroll himself had sold 220 acres of town land, which brought him a profit that approached £600 sterling.

Remarkably, Richard Bennett III surpassed Carroll in acres owned and commercial activity. When he died in 1749 the *Maryland Gazette* judged him "the greatest Trader in this Province," his ships carrying to-

Baltimore in 1752

bacco, grain, and other products to other mainland colonies, to the West Indies, and to Great Britain. He maintained two stores on the Eastern Shore and owned, in whole or part, a fleet of ships that chiefly plied the waters to New England and the Caribbean. His landholding totaled nearly 50,000 acres. Like Carroll, much of his income accrued from large amounts of money loaned to many people. Like Carroll, too, he was an active player in the lucrative African slave trade. Unlike Carroll, Bennett remained on good terms with Lord Baltimore. He served as an informal consultant to the proprietor and received appointments to proprietary offices, particularly as rent-roll keeper for the province, which provided revenue as well as patronage power. His business and shipping partners tended to be a strong mix of Catholics and Protestants, indicative of the greater inclusion of the Catholic community on the Eastern Shore with the larger society. Bennett's connection with the proprietor was evidently through his Protestant relatives, the Lloyds and the Darnalls, five of whom served at one time or other on the council, the upper house of the assembly. That connection enabled him to avoid the requirement of oath-taking that the assembly had extended in 1717 to proprietary offices, specifically to eliminate the appointment of Catholics. In 1732 the proprietor also appointed Bennett as one of the commissioners to determine (unsuccessfully, as it turned out) the long-running boundary dispute with Pennsylvania.

A GENTEEL PRESENCE

As the eighteenth century unwound, most Maryland Catholic gentry, none more so than Charles Carroll, developed a quite conscious double sense of alienation: growing awareness of being a British provincial along with a persistent consciousness of being a Catholic in an unwelcoming society. The brick residence that Carroll spent more than a decade constructing on the Duke of Gloucester Street, next to the Settler's modest frame dwelling, became a visible symbol of this double identity. By the time of its completion in the 1730s the gambrel-roofed, four-bay dwelling that towered over Annapolis Creek in its rear was the grandest private building in the capital. It was a conspicuous assertion of Charles Carroll's achievement in a hostile society, as well as a defiant reminder that the Carrolls were still an important part of the province, socially and politically discriminated against though they might be.

The exclusion that Carroll and his son Charley experienced in the social world of Annapolis was more partial than that of the political realm, but real enough. Charles Carroll of Carrollton was much more inclined than his resentful, dyspeptic parent to partake in the dinner parties, card games, horse racing, and theatergoing that constituted the Annapolis cultural scene by the third quarter of the century. But he received no invitation to join the Homony Club, the elite social group that in 1770 succeeded the Tuesday Club. Money was obviously not the sole criterion for membership in any organization that defined the smart set. For Catholics, no matter how rich or influential, there were always social limits. That awareness might have been a motivation for the younger Carroll to undertake extensive improvements at the Annapolis mansion, an edifice still imposing, but amid the elegant Georgian residences and gardens that had transformed the town's landscape in the 1760s and 1770s somewhat primitive and unrefined. So he thoroughly renovated the rooms of the mansion, imported elaborate furnishings from England, and created a formal garden that rivaled any in town short of William Paca's. He enlarged the slave staff to eight to be better able to entertain as befit an urban gentleman. Among his dinner guests during the fall racing season of 1772 was Virginia planter George Washington. For Carroll conspicuous display and hosting were means toward commanding respect. By the early seventies Charles Carroll of Carrollton was poised to surpass his father in his standing within society. It would take a bold venture into the hitherto off-limits political realm for the younger Carroll to do that.

MARYLAND MIGRANTS, GERMAN IMMIGRANTS, AND PENN'S COLONY

In 1681 the Duke of York, as a payment on a debt he had incurred, had his brother, Charles II, grant to William Penn the huge tract of territory, previously part of the duke's province of New York, that extended south of the 42nd parallel and the Delaware River to Maryland's northern border. Where precisely that border was had been disputed by provincial authorities in New York and Maryland ever since England had seized the area from the Netherlands in 1664. In the 1670s both proprietary governments resorted to issuing conflicting patents to the same plots as settlers moved into the area from north and south. The Penn grant did nothing to resolve the dispute.

By the early eighteenth century both proprietors, Penn and Baltimore, attempted to lure the rapidly increasing immigration from northern Ireland and the German states into this lush piedmont area southwest of the Susquehanna River. In 1745 Daniel Dulaney founded Frederick Town in the Monocacy Valley forty-five miles northwest of Baltimore as a market center. Holding more than 20,000 acres in the Monocacy River and Antietam Creek valleys, Dulaney offered 100- to 300-acre packets of land to Germans and Irish seeking homesteads in the region to create an ample supply of grain and cattle for his central market. He sold thousands of acres. Frederick Town quickly developed as a town; within five years it was the largest town in the province. In 1762 a Westphalian, Jonathan Hager, repeated Dulaney's strategy by laying out a town that eventually bore his name.

From his earliest days as proprietor William Penn had aggressively recruited settlers for his colony through promotional literature that he distributed throughout Great Britain and the Continent, especially in the German states and the Netherlands. He advertised his colony as one that offered settlers not merely rich, inexpensive land and self-government, but religious liberty. Initially that policy of toleration did not encompass Catholics, whom Penn did not consider to be authentic Christians. Penn never changed his mind about Roman Catholicism but eventually decided that even Catholics possessed the right to practice their religion, as long as they proved to be peaceful citizens. Pennsylvania law itself required all officeholders to renounce Catholicism, which effectively barred Catholics from office. It also prohibited Catholics from holding property and being naturalized. But what the law allowed and what actually became the practice regarding Catholics in Pennsylvania were very different indeed. Catholics came to find Pennsylvania as the most tolerant of all the colonies in the eighteenth century. George W. Nixon, a wealthy Irish Catholic, emigrated from Wexford to Philadelphia in 1686. A few years later Peter Dubuc led a group of French Catholics into Pennsylvania. Both Nixon and Dubuc fully assimilated into Pennsylvania society and even held office. Other Catholics came into the province from New York following Leisler's rebellion. By the late 1680s the Jesuit Thomas Harvey was regularly traveling to Philadelphia to say Mass for the incipient Catholic population. So well were Catholics in Penn's colony treated that rumors resurfaced in England that the Quaker was really a Jesuit in disguise. That toleration was certainly a pull factor for the growing number of German and Irish Catholics who came into the colony from the third decade of the century onward.

Catholics were also settling in the three lower counties of the Pennsylvania tract that eventually formed the colony of Delaware. Priests from Bohemia began including this area within their circuit of missions by the second decade of the eighteenth century. Thomas Wilcox, a former Quaker, John Reynolds, a farmer, and Cornelius Hollahan, an Irish

blacksmith, all maintained chapels. By 1708 that circuit reached as far
north as Philadelphia, where public Mass was being offered on a regular
basis for the few Catholics in the town, including some prominent Anglican converts. A quarter century later the Maryland mission, cognizant
of the Catholic influx into Pennsylvania, established a special mission for
that colony in 1729. Joseph Greaton, the first Jesuit assigned to the mission, made Philadelphia his base, even though there were barely more
than a score of Catholics in a city of 12,000. Four years after arriving
in the city he built a freestanding chapel, St. Joseph's, that became the
gathering site of the first urban parish in British America. The establishment of such a concrete, visible presence in Penn's city by Roman
Catholics proved somewhat off-putting to the Quaker authorities. Anti-
Catholicism, a strong force even in tolerant Pennsylvania, tended to in-
flate greatly the number of Catholics in any particular time or place.[14]
The governor, Penn's son Thomas, notified his council of his "no small
concern" about the building rising on Walnut Street. The council advised him to consult his father about the matter if he thought it serious enough. Either he did not follow through on their suggestion or
was told by London to let it be; in any event the chapel opened with
no action taken by the government.[15] As Philadelphia grew rapidly in
the mid-eighteenth century to become the largest city in the colonies,
St. Joseph's kept pace. By 1757 there were nearly 380 parishioners, the
large majority Germans. The multiethnic congregation, which spanned
the social spectrum from professionals, merchants, and businessmen to
craftsmen, laborers, and servants, provided its own financing through
voluntary contributions, a sharp departure from the traditional funding
of Jesuit ministry in America from farm or plantation revenue.

    Catholics in general found Philadelphia an open, inviting place. One
Jesuit reported from Philadelphia in 1741, "We have at present all liberty
imaginable in the exercise of our business, and are not only esteemed,

14. In 1759, for instance, the Anglican minister William Smith reported with alarm that there
were no fewer than ten thousand Roman Catholics in the state, more than quadruple the actual number. Actually Catholics made up less than 1 percent (0.6 percent) of the general population, hardly a
threatening proportion; Joseph J. Casino, "Anti-Popery in Colonial Pennsylvania," *Pennsylvania Magazine of History and Biography* 105 (1981): 294.

15. Hughes, *History of the Society of Jesus; Text*, 2:182.

but reverenced, as I may say, by the better sort of people."[16] In this tolerant environment Greaton's successor as superior of the mission, Robert
Molyneux, was responsible in 1774 for the first Catholic books published
in British America (*A Manual of Catholic Prayers* and an edition of Bishop Richard Challoner's *The Garden of the Soul*).

The majority of Catholics in Pennsylvania, however, lived outside of
Philadelphia. Greaton knew that, of course, but little about their exact
dispersion throughout the settled portion of the colony. So, shortly after
arriving in Philadelphia, he undertook a proactive course remarkable for
its time: embarking on a reconnaissance journey through the settlements
in southeastern Pennsylvania to identify areas in which Catholics had
congregated and to make appropriate plans to provide ministry for them.
He discovered what he already probably knew: that the large majority
of Catholics to be found in rural Pennsylvania were Germans. His findings apparently induced the Maryland Jesuit superior to appeal to the
Jesuit superior general in Rome to assign some German Jesuits to the
Maryland mission so that they might work among the German-speaking
Catholics in Philadelphia. It represented an unprecedented intention to
broaden the ethnic composition of a mission in order to meet the special
requirements of that mission—in this case, priests who could speak the
language of the people to whom they were called to minister. The general
replied that he could send no German Jesuits unless the English Jesuits
could provide the funds to support their work in the colony. Fortunately
that Jesuit province had recently come into two special legacies: a gift of
£4,000 from an English Catholic peer, Sir John James; and an inheritance that a titled Jesuit, Gilbert Talbot, thirteenth Earl of Shrewsbury,
had brought with him upon entering the order. The James legacy had
specifically designated the money for the "missioners in Pensilvania."[17]
It was most likely no coincidence that James had written his will a few
weeks before the Jesuit Henry Neale had left England for that mission
in 1740. Assured of this timely financial foundation, the general assigned two German Jesuits, Theodore Schneider and William Wappeler,

16. Henry Neale to Charles Shireburn, Philadelphia, April 25, 1741, in Hughes, *History of the Society of Jesus*, Documents, Vol. I, Part I, 342.
17. Hughes, *History of the Society of Jesus; Text*, 2:497.

to Pennsylvania. Seven other German Jesuits followed them to "Penn's woods" in the next three and a half decades, including Ferdinand Farmer (Steinmeyer) and Mathias Manners (Sittensperger).

The endowments proved to be but partial means toward the financial support of their Pennsylvania ministry. As it had been in Maryland from the very beginning of that mission, so in Pennsylvania, outside of Philadelphia, the Jesuits turned to agriculture as the principal generator of revenue to sustain their priestly work. From the 10,000-acre tract of land that John Digges had received from Lord Baltimore in northern Maryland in the Conewago Valley some 125 miles west of Philadelphia (later determined to be in southern Pennsylvania), the Jesuits acquired a farm of 120 acres. Joseph Greaton had begun ministering to the Catholics in the valley as early as 1730. Now ten years later, Theodore Schneider, upon his arrival in America, established St. Francis Regis Mission there. It may have surprised him that his congregation was a mixed one of English and Germans. The English Catholics were Marylanders who had migrated north to settle upon Digges's land, not knowing that they were taking up property outside of Maryland. The Germans were largely Palatines. Both groups were generally poor. From Conewago the Jesuits established several missions, including one in Lancaster, where William Wappeler erected a small stone chapel in 1742. In western Berks County at Goshenhoppen, about forty-five miles northwest of Philadelphia, they acquired 500 acres for another farm, to be worked, like the one at Conewago, by tenants. On this site, which they designated as St. Paul's Mission, Theodore Schneider built a log chapel that they called the Church of the Blessed Sacrament. From Goshenhoppen the Jesuits established further "stations," including one in Reading, where the German congregation was large enough by 1755 to have its own resident priest. The German Jesuits quickly showed their deep commitment to fostering Catholic education as Schneider and Wappeler established schools at Goshenhoppen and Conewago, respectively. Schneider, in fact, who had stepped down as rector of the University of Heidelberg in order to volunteer for the American mission, was responsible for starting several schools in the region during his near quarter of a century's labor.

Schneider was also one of the first Jesuits on the Pennsylvania mission to renew the itinerant ministry to New Jersey that the Glorious Revolution had effectively eliminated. In the guise of a medical doctor, Schneider, as early as 1744, said Mass in northern New Jersey, where proliferating forges had drawn German immigrant ironworkers, including Catholics. In the southern portion of the colony Jesuits from Philadelphia were ministering to German and Irish glassworkers in Salem County. No one was more active in the New Jersey mission than Ferdinand Farmer, who, beginning in the 1760s, became a legendary carrier of Catholicism throughout the colony, from the ironworks in the north to the glassworks in the south. In the northern portion of New Jersey alone, Farmer, in a span of two decades, performed no fewer than 385 baptisms.

The Catholic population in Pennsylvania experienced a rapid growth, from approximately 3,000 in 1757 to more than 6,000 just seven years later, Germans still constituting more than two-thirds of the community. In a population surpassing a half million, Catholics were a minuscule portion, heavily rural and poor. Still, in the span of three decades they had built six churches, two in Philadelphia itself. In the city that in the late colonial period had become *the* metropolis of British America, Catholics, despite their small numbers, had established an important urban presence. As the Catholic gentry in Maryland commanded a disproportionate socioeconomic place within their province, so the Philadelphia Catholic merchants, such as the Irish émigrés Thomas Fitzsimons, Stephen Moylan, and George Meade, did within Philadelphia by the 1770s.

CHAPTER 9

"[CATHOLICS,] BY THE VERY PRINCIPLES OF THAT RELIGION ... CAN NEVER BE FAITHFUL SUBJECTS"

*The Peaking of Anti-Catholicism
and the Seven Years' War*

CULTURAL TRANSPLANTINGS

In 1739 a broadside entitled *Some Thoughts upon America, and upon the Danger from Roman Catholicks There* pleaded the necessity of banning any Catholic settlement in the British colonies because of the potential menace of Catholics there aligning themselves with French Canadians to their north and west. The anonymous broadside appeared in London, not America. But the anti-Catholicism it promoted had long before crossed the Atlantic; indeed, it proved to be among the hardiest cultural dispositions to be transplanted from Great Britain to America. A principal reason for its survival in the New World may well have been the integral element it had become for English identity, even for those in the diaspora. To be English was to be anti-Catholic, since Roman Catholicism stood in stark contrast to every-thing that being English connoted, just as Protestantism was the quint-essential expression of what it meant to be English, as John Foxe had immortalized in his *Book of Martyrs*. To that extent anti-Catholicism proved to be an effective unifying force, both in England and in British America, in defining a society by an "other" that contradicted all that that society stood for and whose very survival the "other," by its very presence, threatened.

In New England, Guy Fawkes Day, which in the seventeenth cen-tury merited only an occasional celebration, by the eighteenth had be-come an annual civic festival of anti-Catholicism, with parades, elaborate effigies of various demons, including the pope, Satan, and Fawkes, and ritual burnings of the figures at the climax of the evening. In New York City the council formally established the day as a holiday in 1700. But it was not until the 1740s that royal officials began to utilize the mum-mery of the day as a reminder to the people of the respective colonies of their need to remain vigilant against Catholic conspiracies. Of course, Catholics were a rare species in New York and New England, the sites of most Guy Fawkes Day celebrations. In both the law banned priests from even being within the boundaries of the colony. But in both places anti-Catholicism served as a powerful bonding force. And so authorities con-tinued to promote Guy Fawkes Day, even when violent clashes between competing groups of paraders became a regular (often lethal) part of the day's observance.

In New York City all kinds of sinister rumors began swirling about in the winter of 1740–1741, ranging from a supposed priest-inspired Iro-quois attack from the north to a Spanish invasion to a revolt by the slaves (one-fifth of the city's population). James Oglethorpe had sent warnings from Georgia to authorities in the other colonies that Spain had had priests in disguise infiltrate the principal cities of English North Amer-ica with the charge to incinerate them. As if on cue, in the late winter fresh rumors circulated about New York that Catholic priests had been sighted casing the city. When a spate of mysterious fires followed shortly afterward in mid-March, it was proof enough to local government that the city had become the target of an international Catholic conspiracy.

Slaves and Catholics (almost all of whom were Irish soldiers stationed in the city's garrison) were immediately under suspicion as the principal marginal groups in the city. That the worst fire had been set on March 17, St. Patrick's feast, seemed the work of the Irish Catholics. In the hysteria that swept the city in the wake of the fires, four Irish soldiers and several black citizens, as well as an Anglican priest, were rounded up for trial. The four soldiers were released when prosecution witnesses failed to appear. The black defendants were all burned at the stake or hanged. The minister, John Ury, who had the misfortune of being a recent arrival in the city, was falsely accused of being a Catholic priest and the instigator of the wave of burnings that were intended as the prelude to a general uprising against the government. Despite his vehement denials Ury was convicted and hanged for the capital crimes of being a priest and of inciting a slave revolt. The executions did not bring assurance to authorities that they had put the conspiracy to rest. More arrests and trials followed in the summer of 1741. An Irish woman, an Afro-Portuguese slave, and an Anglo-American family (father, mother, and daughter) were all convicted of being involved in the plot and hanged. Salem had come to New York.

War with France, a Jacobite uprising, and a religious revival all acted as catalysts in the revival of anti-Catholicism in New England. Anti-Catholicism served as a great motivator of the successful expedition to capture the French fortress at Louisbourg on Nova Scotia in 1745. The Great Awakening, the religious renewal that swept back and forth through much of New England through the first half of the 1740s, seemed to many who were caught up in it the precursor to an imminent apocalypse in North America. These eschatological expectations included an Armageddon-like struggle between the forces of Christ and the anti-Christ that would signal the beginning of the end. The war in which England found itself in the mid-forties against France, the leading Catholic power, seemed providential in setting up the final conflict. That reading of history suffered a serious setback in 1748 when England returned Louisbourg to France as part of the peace settlement. But anti-Catholicism gained a certain institutionalization in 1750 when a distinguished Massachusetts justice, Paul Dudley, endowed a series of lectures, the third of which was

to be devoted to "exposing the Idolatry of the Romish church, their tyranny, usurpations and other crying wickedness, in their high places... the
church of Rome is that mystical Babylon, that man of sin, that Apostate
church spoken of in the New Testament."

ANTI-CATHOLICISM

IN MARYLAND

In Maryland, where there *was* a visible Catholic community, a different
combination of issues ranging from the outbreak of war with France to
the proprietor's tax claims served to promote the same hostile spirit. A
growing suspicion of Catholics led the provincial council in 1744 to order
their disarming and dismissal from the militia. The following year there
were widespread accusations, including the governor's, that Maryland
Catholics were openly manifesting their support of the young pretender's uprising in Scotland, which for several months, before Charles Edward Stuart's invading forces were routed in April at Culloden, England,
seemed destined for success. No doubt many Marylanders shared Benjamin Franklin's conviction that Maryland harbored "a number [of Catho-
lics] ... who of late encouraged the French to invade the Mother-country."[1]
Certainly neighbors of St. Thomas Manor, the Jesuits' plantation near
Port Tobacco, strongly suspected that Richard Molyneux, the superior
of the Maryland Jesuits, had been on a secret mission to the frontier to
conspire with the French. When Molyneux subsequently returned with
several strangers who spoke either French or Dutch (according to those
who had heard them), it confirmed for many their initial suspicions. The
strangers apparently were the German Jesuits Peter Schneider and William Wappeler, visiting from Pennsylvania, but the Protestant observers
in Charles County put the worst possible interpretation upon this evidently innocent event. The arrival of a shipload of Jacobite prisoners in
the area in the summer of 1747, some of whom ended up working Jesuit
fields as indentured servants, only aggravated the public unrest about a

---

1. Cited in Charles H. Metzger, *The Quebec Act: A Primary Cause of the American Revolution*
(New York: U.S. Catholic Historical Society, 1936), 14.

Catholic conspiracy. And frequent gatherings, including black inhabitants, at St. Thomas, ostensibly for Mass (with so many holy days still on the liturgical calendar, that was more than likely the reason for doing so), gave further occasions for suspicion. Indeed, public suspicion was probably the cause of Molyneux's prudently putting all the property of the Society of Jesus in Maryland that he held as superior into the trust of a layman in September 1746.

By that time the pretender's rebellion had been smashed. Two years later the Treaty of Aix-la-Chapelle ended the war England had been waging against France and Spain. Anxiety about Catholic conspiracies in Maryland greatly decreased, if it did not disappear. The lull proved to be a very short one.

THE WAR OF THE CARROLLS

What restirred the anti-Catholic winds in Maryland was a long-running dispute within the Carroll family regarding a legacy that James Carroll had left to two Irish nephews upon his death in 1729. A cousin of Charles Carroll of Annapolis, Dr. Charles Carroll, as co-executor of the will (his cousin being the other), had appropriated to himself much of the monies meant for the nephews who had since become Roman Catholic priests. Charles Carroll of Annapolis had been pressing his kinsman to fulfill his responsibility as executor by paying to the nephews the full value of the legacy, including the interest accrued in the intervening two decades. Dr. Carroll, who since James Carroll's death had apostatized to become an Anglican, was now a member of the lower house of the assembly. He managed to orchestrate a resolution through the Committee of Grievances that urged the assembly to enforce in full the English penal laws in order to prevent the Catholics in the province from becoming "a dangerous, *intestine Enemy*, ready to join [the] French or Indians, who are but too near."[2] Dr. Carroll subsequently argued that he could not release the funds to the nephews, as the penal laws denied Roman Catholic priests the rights to any inheritance.

2. *Archives of Maryland* 28:315, 340.

This brazen ploy was too much for Charles Carroll of Annapolis. Two days after the committee had issued its resolution, he, Luther-like, nailed a petition to the door of the state house while the general assembly was in session. It was a dramatic declaration of Catholic reentry into the public square from which they had agreed to remain apart in the informal pact of 1720. The petition essentially accused Dr. Carroll of attempting to hide his embezzlement of much of the nephews' legacy by claiming that the law kept him from fulfilling his duty as an executor. In response the assembly ordered the Catholic Carroll put under house arrest for the duration of its meeting in order to prevent a duplication of his defiant gesture.

Dr. Carroll later admitted that exploiting anti-Catholic feeling was the only effective weapon he had in contending with Charles Carroll of Annapolis's wealth and influence within the upper ranks of government. Anti-Catholicism, in fact, became a convenient tool for not only Carroll but many members of the lower house in their losing struggle with the proprietor over legislative prerogatives and the control of revenues. Richard Brooke, in their behalf, presented a memorial to the Board of Trade and Plantations that charged the proprietor with being too indulgent of Catholics' public exercise of their religion and of the use of their wealth to corrupt politics. The memorial produced no direct action from the crown's board, but it clearly caused Lord Baltimore to distance himself from Catholic interests. He issued a somewhat enigmatic order to his officials in Maryland to enforce the penal laws to ensure that no one could accuse the Calverts of being pro-Catholic.

The House of Delegates acted positively upon the Committee of Grievances' request that it rescind the suspending act of Queen Anne, thus putting in full force the provisions of the Anti-Popery Act passed by Parliament in 1704. It also sent to the governor, Samuel Ogle, a formal request that he appoint "none but faithful Protestant Subjects" to "Places of Trust and Profit" in Maryland. Aware of the devastating impact these changes would have upon the Catholic community, a group of prominent Catholics, all but one from Prince George's and Anne Arundel counties, composed a petition to the governor in which they argued that the government needed to respect the implicit contract that they had entered

Charles Carroll of Annapolis

into with Catholics in 1720: that in return for Catholics accepting their disbarment from political life, they would not be harassed by attempting to apply the full range of England's penal laws to Maryland. Charles Carroll of Annapolis submitted his own petition, which basically asked for maintenance of the status quo. The rejection of the lower house's bill by the council ensured that this would continue.

Despite this understanding about Catholics abstaining from politics, in the 1751 elections for the lower house they worked, with some success, to defeat those responsible for the anti-Catholic legislation of the previous session. Of the twenty-three delegates who had supported the measures, eight failed to gain reelection.

A year and a half later, in 1753, the province had a new governor, Horatio Sharpe, another military man, but one who came with a reputation as a Catholic sympathizer. The House of Delegates soon found an occasion to test his leanings. In May 1754 they passed "An Act for the security of his Majesty's Dominion, and to prevent the Growth of Popery." The title was an old one, as were the circumstances driving it. As the preamble of the act noted, Catholics were an internal enemy made more dangerous by the Indian-French threat that was growing on Maryland's northwestern frontier. The end of King George's War in 1748 had at best bought a truce between France and England. Under its cover both imperial powers had been strengthening their claims to the Ohio Valley through Indian alliances, the introduction of settlers (British), and the erection of forts (French). The act of the lower house denied priests the right to own land, made it a capital offense for a priest to convert anyone, and disinherited anyone educated in a Catholic school abroad. Sharpe found himself trapped. Realizing that public opinion was heavily in favor of the measure, the governor had no stomach for a veto that would simply inflame the populace. So he signed off on the legislation.

PRELUDE TO WAR: THE OHIO VALLEY AND NOVA SCOTIA

In the spring of 1754 Virginia sent Colonel George Washington and a small body of militia into western Pennsylvania to guard against any invasion by the French and their Indian allies. Washington subsequently erected Fort Necessity just above the Maryland-Pennsylvania boundary, but during the early summer a superior French force caused him to surrender the fort. The defeat sent alarms throughout the Middle Atlantic colonies, including Maryland. Governor Sharpe himself took charge of militia units scrambling to defend possible avenues of invasion through frontier areas at Hagerstown and elsewhere. In London the government authorized an expedition of British and colonial forces to drive out the French from the Ohio Valley. Sharpe spent much of the winter of 1755 reconnoitering the hundreds-miles-long route the force would take to its destination, the French Fort Duquesne. In June General Edward Braddock led westward a 2,000-man force, including some indentured servants from Maryland. They never reached their target. An Indian ambush just short of Fort Duquesne terrorized Braddock's army; the resulting casualties were devastating. A mere 577 men made it back to Virginia. Braddock was not one of them.

As Braddock was heading to his rendezvous with disaster in the Ohio Valley a thousand miles to the northeast, British authorities were poised to take decisive action against what they perceived to be their worst security threat within the North American imperial domains: the 15,000 or so Acadians on Nova Scotia, the peninsula jutting out from eastern Canada that had been under British control since 1713. French settlement of this strategic outcropping of land originated in the first decade of the seventeenth century, a few months before the English arrived in Virginia. After two short-lived attempts, the first permanent community on what became known as l'Acadie was established in 1636. Intermarriage with the indigenous Mikmaq became quite common for the heavily male Acadian population. By the late seventeenth century l'Acadie's people were an ethnic melting pot with their own distinct culture. The area fluctuated between English and French control during the seventeenth century. Neutrality became the *modus vivendi* for Acadians in dealing with the question of a sovereignty that was seemingly ever-shifting. But neutrality did not breed isolation. Acadians were very much involved in the commerce of the Atlantic world, which bred competition, particularly with New England, and fostered ideas about removing the Acadians, for both strategic and economic reasons, from the peninsula. As early as the 1700s Samuel Vetch, a Scotch trader based in New England, was urging Massachusetts officials to invade Nova Scotia and transport "the greatest part of the inhabitants" (he meant the Acadians) to the French island of Martinique in the West Indies. To fill their places Vetch thought that the Scots, who had played a similar role in northern Ireland, were a very good fit. Indeed, the transplanting of peoples was a familiar device in England for getting rid of untrustworthy subjects and for opening up valued lands for developing. Both motives seem to have been at play from the earliest proposal on how to deal with the Acadians.

Samuel Vetch was second in command of the fleet that carried 2,000 men for an invasion of Nova Scotia in September of 1710. The French forces there surrendered after a two-week resistance. The British offered to transport any settler who wished to leave. Few did, to the consternation of the officials who had already promised New Englanders who joined the expedition the property that the Acadians had developed. In the Treaty of Utrecht that followed three years later, the British gained dominion over l'Acadie (as well as Newfoundland); the Acadians were again given the option of leaving or remaining with the assurance of religious freedom should they elect to stay. The French government wanted the Acadians to relocate to Cape Breton Island (Ile Royale) to provide supplies for the garrison of the fortress and military port (Louisbourg) that they intended to erect on the north Atlantic coast of the island. The British, on the other hand, now preferred that the Acadians remain on Nova Scotia to continue to supply their garrison at Annapolis Royal while denying the French a source of supply for Louisbourg. All they required was an unconditional oath of loyalty. Of the 500 Acadian families, only about a tenth of them made the move to Ile Royale, and some of them were back within a short time. The rest remained but resisted taking the oath. The French themselves were by this time happy enough with this outcome, having concluded that it was to their advantage to have a people whose primary allegiance was to France living in a British area, especially since they could be counted on for (illegal) supplies to Ile Royale. Both powers were cynically exploiting the Acadians.

The British continued to vacillate between campaigns to secure an unconditional oath from the Acadians and considerations of ways to remove them. In 1730 the British governor-general finally got them to take the oath with the assurance that they would never have to bear arms, which to them was a guarantee of preserving their neutrality. Over the next quarter century Nova Scotia, thanks to the exceptionally high fertility rate of the Acadians and relatively low mortality rate (a diverse diet and the absence of epidemic diseases were key factors), became the fastest-growing colony in North America. The population more than doubled, from 6,000 to about 15,000. The French government continued, through the bishop of Quebec, to supply priests to minister to the community. Then in 1745 the conquest of Louisbourg by New England forces revived the option of removing all the Acadians from the Maritime region. In the ensuing Treaty of Aix-la-Chapelle Louisbourg was returned to the French and any thoughts of Acadian removal dropped. Instead the British decided to transplant settlers from Great Britain to strategic areas of Nova Scotia to serve as security against adjacent Acadian settlements. In 1749 more than 2,500 British, with a few Irish Catholics among them, were settled on the northwestern portion of the peninsula. At the same time authorities initiated a new campaign to secure a truly unconditional oath from the Acadians; those who refused to take it were to be removed, with no compensation for their property. Token emigration to Ile Royale was the result; the British lacked the specific plan or force to remove the Acadians as a community.

When French forces captured Fort Necessity in the Ohio Valley in the summer of 1754, the British response was to attack a French fort situated at the juncture of Nova Scotia and the mainland. That fort capitulated to the expeditionary force, largely New Englanders, in June of 1755. Some Acadians had been among the fort's defenders. They were allowed to return to their homes. All the Acadians on the peninsula were ordered to surrender their arms, which several hundred did. In the ensuing weeks came reports of the arrival of French reinforcements at Louisbourg, then news of Braddock's disaster on the Ohio. In the midst of these dispiriting developments the British governor ordered the Acadians out of Nova Scotia. When a delegation pleaded that he rescind the order, Governor Charles Lawrence gave them one last chance to take the unconditional oath. When they hesitated, the governor informed them that he intended to send them to France.

On Sunday morning, July 13, 1755, authorities at Annapolis Royal interrupted the Mass that the local Acadians were attending in their chapel to announce that they were to deliver all their weapons to the fort and choose thirty deputies to represent them at a meeting to be held in Halifax. Once the deputies arrived at Halifax, the governor informed them that they had one choice: to take the oath without reserve. They said that they could not. Given the weekend to reconsider, on the following Monday they confirmed their inability to take the oath, whereupon they were arrested, having been told that they would be deported to Louisbourg or France to ensure their cooperation. The reality was that the British had already determined to disperse them throughout North America to minimize any possibility of their ever returning to Nova Scotia. The authorities intended to settle New Englanders on their vacated farms.

"ONE OF THE GREATEST THINGS THAT EVER THE ENGLISH DID IN AMERICA"

An anonymous letter written from Halifax in August 1755 was reprinted in newspapers throughout most of British America in subsequent months. It reported, "We are now upon a great and noble Scheme of sending the neutral french out of this Province, who have always been secret Enemies, and have encouraged our Savages to cut our Throats. If we effect their Expulsion, it will be one of the greatest Things that ever the English did in America."[3] Acadians had heard threats of deportation many times, none of which were acted upon; no doubt many thought the British were bluffing again. They weren't. The Acadians were about to be part of something unprecedented in North American history, a massive relocation marked by deceit, trumped-up charges, intellectual genocide (the destruction of their records), the separation of families, and widespread death.

Over the next three months the fleet of vessels rounded up the Acadians in Annapolis Royal, Minas, Chignecto, and other villages. By ruse or force soldiers separated the males ten years or older from the women and children in most of the communities. At Minas the adult males were summoned to the church, supposedly to renew their former qualified oath. When they arrived troops surrounded the building; the men were then told that they were to be removed from the province, and their land, cattle, and property all now was forfeited to the crown. The shocked Acadians were allowed to send twenty of their number to communicate

---

3. John Mack Faragher, *A Great and Noble Scheme: The Tragic Story of the Expulsion of the French Canadians from Their American Homeland* (New York: Norton, 2006), 333.

this terrible news to the community. The next morning, as 230 men and boys were marched to the waiting ships, weeping women and children formed lines through which the motley procession passed.

Some men, including two-thirds of those at Chignecto and nearly all at Annapolis Royal, managed to escape into the woods. Other communities fared much worse. At Fort Lawrence, as one Acadian remembered a grandfather's account, "Families were seized and thrown pell-mell into the transports. No one was granted any grace. The least resistance meant death. Terror was everywhere."[4] At another village inhabitants awoke to find troops surrounding their homes. When some tried to escape the cordon, they were shot at.

Near the end of October 1755 the convoy of ships, accompanied by four British men-of-war, finally weighed anchor at Minas and headed south with its cargo of more than 4,000 Acadians. Six weeks after that a second caravan carrying 1,664 inhabitants, mostly women and children, sailed out of Annapolis Royal. In all nearly 7,000 Acadians were removed. Somewhere between 5,000 and 6,000 managed, one way or another, to elude the dragnet. As the ships left Annapolis Royal, Acadians on board watched their homes going up in flames, a cautionary measure the British had taken to prevent escapees from finding any shelter in the vacated town. The ships themselves were terribly overcrowded, providing a lethal environment for smallpox, which was the main culprit for the staggering mortality rate of 20 percent on at least two of the vessels. On the *Cornwallis*, carrying 417 Acadians from Chignecto to Charleston, the toll from smallpox was much worse—210. There was one success story: on the *Pembroke*, 226 Acadians overpowered the crew and guards and eventually brought the ship to a safe harbor on the St. John's River, from where they made their way to Quebec.

As planned, the ships deposited their human cargo at various ports along the east coast, with those Acadians considered most dangerous transported to the most distant destinations of Charleston and Savannah. In Massachusetts and Connecticut each town was responsible for the care and control of a certain number of Acadian families. At An-

4. Faragher, *Great and Noble Scheme*, 357.

napolis five vessels carrying 900 Acadians arrived in late November. The Maryland council decided to apportion the exiles to several counties of the province, where they would be at the mercy of the locals' charity. In most places the Acadians were left to shift for their survival, wandering as beggars across the countryside. In response the Maryland assembly passed a law authorizing the imprisonment of indigent Acadians and the binding out of their children. Eventually a majority of the young Acadians were taken from their parents and given as indentured servants to Marylanders. Baltimore was one exception to this treatment. Local Catholics there gave shelter, work, and aid to the Acadians, who settled in an area later known as "Frenchtown." There Jesuits began saying Mass regularly for the exiles. In 1770 the exiles from Nova Scotia founded St. Peter's, which became the first parish in the city.

New York responded in the same way as Maryland for the 200 Acadians they were allotted—with more or less the same pathetic results. Officials attempted to scatter their Acadian consignment to the most remote and least exposed areas in order to minimize any possible subversion on their part. To further ensure Acadian cooperation, their children were taken from them and placed with Protestant families. When a government official found them in a state of near starvation, the assembly's solution was to pass a law binding out the Acadian children.

In Pennsylvania the displaced Acadians became victims of the witch hunt for "subversive" Catholics still sweeping the colony when 454 Acadians (the first of more than 1,200) were unloaded from their transport ships in Philadelphia in November 1755. Regarding them as likely enemies who would, if allowed, speed themselves to the frontier to link up with their French compatriots or at the very least link up with their fellow German and Irish Catholics already in the province, authorities had them kept, under guard, on board the ships. When smallpox inevitably struck, the governor reluctantly allowed the Acadians to disembark in early December and quarantined them on Providence Island. Thanks to the intervention of the Quaker Anthony Benezet, the Pennsylvania Assembly authorized emergency relief. Then, after Acadian protests, in the spring the governor allowed them to move to wretched housing close to St. Joseph's Church in Philadelphia in "neutral huts" within the city, where Benezet and the Jesuit Robert Harding attended them. In time the Acadians were carefully dispersed throughout the province, with one family assigned to each township. By then disease, spread by their close confinement in Philadelphia, had taken a heavy toll. Those who survived were absorbed, largely through intermarriage, into the larger Catholic society.

As bad as was the treatment the Acadians experienced in the middle colonies, it proved even worse in the southern ones. Virginia officials, regarding them as subversives dumped in their midst, had the more than 1,200 Acadians they had been allotted shipped to England to be deposited on docks and in workhouses. In South Carolina the nearly 1,000 Acadians, refused permission to land, were quarantined on Sullivan's Island, where many subsequently died. The 400 Acadians who attempted to land in Savannah likewise found themselves confined to Typee Island. Finally government officials of South Carolina and Georgia allowed the Acadians in their colonies to depart in ships that they had somehow secured. Several hundred eventually made their way back to Nova Scotia. Others got only as far as Long Island and Cape Cod, where the governments ordered them dispersed to the custody of towns in the respective provinces.

When Louisbourg fell to the British in the summer of 1758 they carried out a second round of Acadian deportations. This time the destination was actually France for the 3,100 who were gathered for relocation (about 1,500 had managed to escape). Of those shipped to France, about a half died en route. That fall the British once again sent squads of soldiers to burn whatever Acadian structures remained in the villages as one measure to counter the guerilla resistance the remnants of the population had been mounting over the past three years; the operation produced scores of additional Acadian deaths.

In November 1759 one group of resistant Acadians surrendered to the British after receiving the promise of amnesty and the freedom to return to their homes. It was another deceit. Instead of reclaiming their property, about 1,000 Acadians were put into prison. As for the Acadian property, government authorities were already well along with plans to resettle it with migrants from New England. By 1770 Nova Scotia had become an eastern expansion of New England, with some 10,000 settlers from Massachusetts and Connecticut now constituting two-thirds of the general population. Many Acadians found themselves laboring as prisoners for others on lands they had previously owned. In all, an estimated 10,000 Acadians, mostly children and infants, died in the years-long removal operation. The majority of those who survived, either in Nova Scotia or in the other colonies, eventually chose to settle in Canada or Louisiana. By 1770 there were about 6,000 Acadians to be found from Quebec to the north shore of Nova Scotia. It was Louisiana, however, that became the new l'Acadie. By the end of the eighteenth century there were some 4,000 Acadians there, the beginning of what would become the Cajun people.

WAR AND PARANOIA

Formal war between Great Britain and France was declared in 1756. The Seven Years' War was the last of five trans-Atlantic conflicts involving England and France that spanned nearly three-quarters of a century, from 1689 to 1763. It became the first truly global war in history. As the tragic experience of the Acadians epitomized, the war also produced the high-water mark in the anti-Catholic crusade that was so thick a part of colonial culture.

The war became an occasion for expecting the imminent fulfillment of the direst scriptural apocalyptic prophecies regarding the pope and Catholics (as some Protestants had read them). The evangelist Theodore Frelinghuysen, serving as a chaplain, explained the biblio-political connections: "Antichrist must fall before the end comes.... The French now adhere and belong to Antichrist, whereby it is to be hoped that when Antichrist fall, they shall fall with him."[5] Another Presbyterian evangelist, Samuel Davies in Virginia, saw the war as the fulfillment of Revelation's prophecy of the "grand decisive conflict between the Lamb and the beast."[6] For many, if not most, New Englanders, the stakes in the war could not have been higher. As the Congregational minister Ebenezer

5. Theodore Frelinghuysen, *Wars and Rumors of War* (New York: 1755), 36, quoted in Fred Anderson, *Crucible of War: The Seven Years' War and the Fate of Empire in British North America, 1754–1766* (New York: Alfred A. Knopf, 2000), 17–18.

6. Anderson, *Crucible of War*, 18.

Pemberton told a Boston artillery company, should the French and their Indian allies prevail, they could expect to see "our cities in flames, our inhabitants desolated, our virgins deflowered, our streets deluged with Blood and the Temples of God prostituted in superstition and Idolatry."[7] No wonder that New Englanders volunteered for the war in extraordinarily high numbers.

Wherever there were Catholics in significant numbers (New England not being one such place), alarmists pointed them out as part of the international conspiracy against Protestantism that the French and Indians were waging in America. So thundered the evangelical ministers George Whitfield and Gilbert Tennent, who had spread the Great Awakening across the colonies in the previous decade. So too the Anglican priest William Smith of Philadelphia, who in sermons and pamphlets warned stridently of the grave threat that local Protestants faced from their Irish and German Catholic neighbors, who were poised to join with their French and Indian allies in murderous mayhem. Smith's anti-Catholic campaign moved Robert Harding to meet with the Penn family physician to refute Smith's charges. "I am an Englishman and have an English heart," Harding explained to Dr. Thomas Graeme, "and I . . . assure you that I should be extremely concerned ever to see the French possessed of a foot of English America." As for the size of the Catholic population in Pennsylvania that Smith regarded as a menace to the security of the colony, Harding assured Graeme that in reality there were most likely no more than 1,600 Catholics in the entire province—hardly a threat by any sober calculation.[8]

Unfortunately, the disturbing events of the summer of 1755 did not promote sober assessments. In the wake of Braddock's shocking defeat in July 1755, the justices of Berks County in eastern Pennsylvania reported to the governor that some Catholics in the area had openly rejoiced at the news of Braddock's terrible defeat; further, that at least thirty In-

7. *Sermon to Artillery Company of Boston* (Boston: 1756), 16; cited in Metzger, *Catholics and the American Revolution: A Study in Religious Climate* (Chicago: Loyola University Press, 1962), 9.

8. Thomas Graeme to Thomas Penn, July 1, 1755, *Penn Official Correspondence* 7:67; cited in Helen Heinz, "'We are all as one fish in the sea . . .': Catholicism in Protestant Pennsylvania, 1730–1790" (Ph.D. diss., Temple University, 2008), 212.

dians, armed with guns and swords, had been seen lurking around the Catholic chapel at Goshenhoppen; further still, that the German Jesuits in the country had informed their congregations that they would be absent for more than two months; to the justices, that indicated that the priests were off on a treasonous mission to the frontier to consult with the French. When the governor appointed a special committee to investigate the charges, they came back with the deflating finding that the Indians at Goshenhoppen were six adult males with their families for whom Theodore Schneider was providing food and shelter as charity.

Clearly, in Pennsylvania as elsewhere, conspiracy charges provided a good rationale for making sense of defeats. And in the early years of the war there seemed a steady stream of them for the British. Then, too, Catholic paranoia was a useful tool for exploiting the ethnic concern of many Pennsylvanians, including Benjamin Franklin, about the growing numbers of German aliens in the province, at least one-quarter of whom (as Smith insisted) were Catholics, even though in actuality Catholics represented less than 1 percent of the German population in the colony. Such unfounded accusations eventually led to violence against German Catholics in the form of the destruction of St. Mary's Church in Lancaster by arson in 1760. By that time the Pennsylvania legislature had already taken steps to control its suspect Catholic residents by disarming them and dismissing them from the militia and by requiring them to register as Catholics and to pay double taxes. A law to ban Catholic landholding was enacted, but the governor vetoed it.

In New York all persons of French nationality seeking to enter the province had to prove they were Huguenots or faced detention. Few French Catholics may have entered New York during the war, but many other Catholics did, in particular Irish who were serving in the British army and navy. Of these a significant minority deserted, either remaining in the city or seeking a new life elsewhere in America. Of course, those deserters who were captured faced the prospect of execution, as did anyone who abetted them. Thus Edward Jefferys, an English military deserter, and Patrick Dunn, an Irish priest, were seized in New York, from where they were attempting to escape to Canada. Both were tried and executed. A good many more Irish Catholic soldiers, some of them

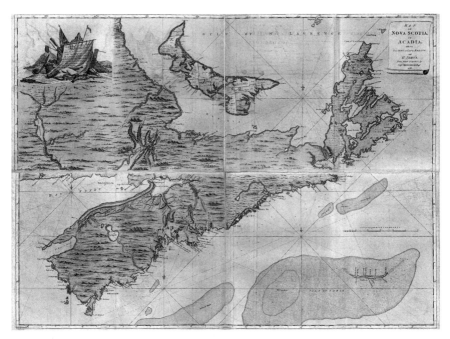

Nova Scotia, or Acadia (1768)

enlistees from the backcountry, were more successful, some even seeking refuge with the Iroquois.

MARYLAND AND THE FRUITS

OF ANTI-CATHOLICISM

In Maryland anti-Catholicism was as much a factor in waging the war as anywhere. In October 1754, three months after George Washington's surrender at Fort Necessity had set in motion the events that inaugurated full-scale conflict between England and France, a letter to the *Maryland Gazette* enumerated the various indicators of Catholicism's troubling growth in Maryland. The writer laid the blame for this disturbing trend squarely at the feet of Maryland's government, which had not been exercising adequate control over its Catholic population, a population

that by the very nature of its religious beliefs had to be controlled for the
well-being of the rest of society. "[Catholics]," the writer reminded, "by
the very Principles of that Religion... *can never be faithful Subjects*."[9] One
particularly effective way to eliminate this Catholic threat, he suggested,
was for Maryland authorities to imitate their counterparts in Ireland by
reducing the ranks of Catholics to those of the landless (and powerless)
poor by stripping the Catholic gentry of their property. And to ensure
the docility of the Catholic community, Maryland should expel the Jesuits to remove their insidious influence.

   Braddock's defeat set off a wildfire of rumors of imminent Indian attacks on towns, like Frederick, near the western frontier, as well as of
internal uprisings of the "aliens" in the province: slaves, convicts, servants,
and Catholics. One recruiting song for a militia company contained the
stanza, "No Popery nor Slavery, No Arbitrary Power for Me." The *Maryland Gazette* dutifully replicated stories about the eschatological consequences of a French victory. It also carried accounts of mysterious ab-
sences of Jesuits living on the edge of the frontier in Frederick that could
only deepen suspicions about their loyalty. In Charles County, the home
of the second largest concentration of Catholics in the province, rumors
were rampant, starting with the outbreak of hostilities, about conspiracies involving Catholics, both slave and free, black and white. In Baltimore the Anglican minister, Thomas Chase, warned his congregation at
St. Paul's that their situation was as perilous as that of Protestants in Ulster on the eve of the Irish massacre of 1641. Indeed, Catholics had come
to be regarded as such a threat to the security of the county that a collective petition from "the Freemen, and the Electors" urged the assembly
to ban the further immigration of Catholics, priests or laity. Within the
assembly itself the lower house seemed obsessed with depositions showing that Catholic parents were not only sending their children abroad to
St. Omer's and other "papist" schools in disturbing numbers, but were
also attempting to persuade Protestants to entrust their children to these
institutions. From this claimed reality it was a short leap to the charge
that the children at these schools were being indoctrinated into becom-

9. *Maryland Gazette*, October 17, 1754.

ing part of an international conspiracy to overthrow Protestant rule in both England and North America. Various charges of disloyalty were raised against Catholics, from Jesuit priests taking to the back country to conspire with the French to dissuading persons from joining the militia, even resorting to force to prevent recruiters from making enlistments, to seeking to stir up slave revolts—all these familiar accusations ranging from the plausible to the fantastic reappeared with the start of the war. The lower house in March 1755 passed a measure that greatly inflated the tax on Catholics attempting to enter the province to unprecedented levels (£200 to £500), but the upper house managed to kill the bill through the continual introduction of amendments that eventually prevented any agreement between the two bodies. Amid the firestorm of stories engulfing the province after Braddock's defeat, the governor and council tried to restore calm by ordering a province-wide investigation into the behavior of Catholics. As governor and council had hoped, the counties unanimously reported that the stories had no foundation. There was no evidence of Catholic disloyalty. At the same time, Catholics attempted to assuage suspicions of their loyalty by contributing heavily to a defense fund that had been set up in the wake of the disaster in western Pennsylvania. Nonetheless, anti-Catholicism maintained its hold on much of Maryland's population.[10]

In 1756 the lower house turned to what amounted to economic warfare to curtail Catholic proselytizing and the education of children in recusant schools on the Continent. They levied steep fines on priests convicted of proselytizing; all priests had to post a £500 bond assuring behavior appropriate for loyal citizens; foreign priests who attempted to preach were subject to a £200 fine. On the other hand, any Catholic who converted to Protestantism would recover all the monies he had previously been fined

10. With Maryland Catholics banned from the militia, there was, of course, little opportunity, if any, for Catholics to serve in the war effort, even if they had wanted to. In fact, few Marylanders at all participated as soldiers aside from a small body of militia assigned to patrol the western frontier, where they skirmished with French troops at Fort Duquesne. Maryland's record as a supplier of the war effort was equally modest. Delaware was a different story, where the militia, unlike the situation in either Pennsylvania or Maryland, was open to Catholics. Limited militia records for 1758 reveal that at least a dozen persons known to be Catholic served in Delaware units during that year and took part in a campaign to capture Fort Duquesne.

as a Catholic. This bill, too, the upper house prevented from becoming law.

Anti-Catholicism in the province was also a pawn in the intensifying struggle between the lower house and the upper reaches of proprietary government. A dispute between the House of Delegates and the rest of the government over what share of the war's expenses the proprietor should be bearing led to the assembly's refusal to provide any further funding for the war until the proprietor assumed his own fair share. At the root of the dispute was the delegates' dismay that proprietary ex-penses (such as salaries of officers and Anglican ministers and export taxes) were nearly twice as high as those of the provincial government, while the proprietary administrators provided much less in services than did their provincial counterparts. The proprietor's resolve to protect his economic interests in the province was being tested by the growing pres-sure he was coming under for his perceived favoritism toward Catho-lics. To counteract that perception Cecilius Calvert ordered Governor Sharpe to dismiss anyone from his government who had his children in Catholic schools abroad. Two months later he was constrained to in-struct Sharpe that he should enforce Parliament's laws against Catholics, a drastic change of position from a proprietor whose predecessors had always insisted that parliamentary legislation did not apply to Maryland.

Wealthy Catholics had come to the painful realization that in times of crisis their extraordinary possession of property, far from being a com-pensating asset in a hostile society, could become a highly vulnerable com-modity. That moment arrived during the spring session of the assembly in 1756. With the war going badly for the British, there was a pressing need to provide ample funding to improve its prosecution. The lower house passed a supply bill, the funding of which was to be defrayed in large part by imposing a heavy tax on the proprietor's extensive landholdings as well as a double tax on the property of Catholics. The upper body proposed its own version of a bill with startling anti-Catholic provisions, including a ban on property holding by priests and a requirement that they post a bond for good behavior, as well as making the conversion of Protestants to Catholicism "punishable as high treason." The two bills appeared to be headed for the usual outcome for anti-Catholic legislation, a stalemate between the upper and lower houses, when suddenly in early May 1756 a conference committee reached a compromise regarding the two measures. Benedict Calvert, the proprietor's half-brother and a member of the council, urgently advised Charles Carroll to assemble a delegation of Catholics to make their case with the governor and council for rejecting this legislation. Carroll, together with three other Catholic leaders—Ignatius Digges, Basil Waring, and Clement Hill—secured an audience with the governor and members of his council. They appealed to them to reject the bill on the grounds that they were unfairly being punished for something they could not legally do (serve in the militia); that, despite being unable to serve in the military, they had financially made substantial contributions to the war effort—that all the accusations of their disloyalty and of their involvement in conspiracies had no basis in fact. Governor Sharpe implausibly informed the quartet of petitioners that he had received no such bill. Shortly after meeting with the Catholic delegation he signed the bill into law. What he apparently could not bring himself to own to Carroll and the others was that if he failed to sign the measure he would be accused of favoring Catholics. That, as he later explained to the proprietor, was something he could simply not afford. Even more so, he could not afford to put the frontier residents of the province at risk by failing to fund the war effort, especially for a tax that imposed a minor burden on Catholics.

The Catholics had one last recourse: direct appeal to the proprietor himself. Once again they chose a Jesuit to make their case. George Hunter, on behalf of Carroll and the others, prepared a petition in which he rehearsed, much as Peter Atwood had nearly four decades earlier, the unique period of Maryland's history during which the religious liberty and property holding of Catholics had been treated as sacred rights. Hunter, like Atwood, reframed the Maryland Catholic experience as one that was central to the province's life. It was a cry for the proprietor to act in the spirit of that early Maryland tradition and do Catholics justice by protecting, once again, their rights. This petition, along with others, Hunter personally carried to England to present to Calvert. Lord Baltimore, like his governor, fearing to have his patriotism impugned should he not approve the supply bill, signed it in the face of Catholic pleas to the contrary.

What alarmed wealthy Catholics, however, was not the actual size of the tax (for all Catholics the cumulative tax of two shillings per hundred acres would have been about £158) but the precedent it set for further attacks on Catholic property that might well lead to dispossession. When the proprietor approved the bill Catholics had even more cause for concern about their future. If they could no longer count upon the upper house and the proprietor to protect them, would the provincial court now reverse its course as well and begin to enforce strictly the English penal laws in Maryland? When the Jesuit James Beadnall was arrested in the following September for celebrating Mass and attempting to convert a Quaker, it seemed an ominous sign of what was in store for Catholics—especially when his bail was set at the ludicrous level of £1,500.

For Charles Carroll of Annapolis, Lord Baltimore's desertion of the Maryland Catholic community was the final straw, a fatal repetition of the rejection that Charles Carroll the Settler had experienced forty years earlier. He solemnly wrote his son, still in studies in Europe, "remember ye ill treatment yr Grandfather met with after so long a series of services, remember ye cruel usage of ye Roman Catholicks by ye late & present Ld Baltimore & let yt so weigh with you as never to sacrifice yr own or yr Country's inter[es]t to promote ye inter[es]t or power of ye Proprietary Family."[11]

In his petition to Lord Baltimore, George Hunter had warned that should the double tax bill become law, it might well lead to a massive exodus of Catholics from the province—that some were already considering emigration as a solution to their predicament. Charles Carroll was one. Less than two weeks after the double tax bill became law, Carroll announced in the *Maryland Gazette* that he intended to sell his Maryland property. He began making plans to move to Louisiana, including a trip to Paris to exchange his Maryland landholding for a comparable tract in the French colony. Indeed, there is some evidence that Carroll went to France not merely for himself but as the representative of a number of Catholic gentry who were ready to quit Maryland. If Carroll's trip to the heart of France had become public knowledge, it would have confirmed the worst suspicions about Catholic loyalty.

11. Charles Carroll of Annapolis to his son, 1759, in Hardy, "Roman Catholics, Not Papists," 152.

Whatever the scope of Carroll's mission to Paris, no Louisiana acquisitions resulted. Still he remained resolved to abandon Maryland; it held no more promise for him now than Ireland had held for *his* father seven decades earlier. "Who would live among men of such dispositions," he wrote his son in 1759, "that could live elsewhere?"[12] That same year London merchants who did a great deal of business with the Maryland Catholic planters petitioned the monarch that he act to provide relief to Maryland Catholics. The merchants feared the economic consequences from the trade they would lose should there be a mass migration of Catholic planters from British to French America.

Relief finally came for Catholics when the war turned in Great Britain's favor. By the time Quebec fell in 1759, they had regained the support of the proprietor. Perhaps under pressure from the king (responding to the merchants' intervention), Lord Baltimore had instructions sent that Catholics were to be spared any *"future* penalties" unless there was "Sufficient Cause" for imposing them.[13] The provincial council had already reached that conclusion. When the lower house voted to continue the double tax on Catholics, the upper chamber accused them of seeking "popular Applause ... by the unhumane Act of wantonly persecuting any Christians." Was the bill, it sarcastically inquired, meant to drive Catholics out of Maryland or make them "more peaceable"? If it was really the latter, the council went on, they could not have been worse informed, for "the Roman Catholics have from the Beginning of the War behaved in a very quiet and inoffensive Manner."[14] In these circumstances it was utterly unjust to pursue policies that would only force Catholics to abandon Maryland. In 1760 the assembly let the double tax on Catholics expire. For Charles Carroll, it all came too late. "I leave you to judge," he wrote his son in that summer, "whether Maryland be a tolerable residence for a Roman Catholic. Were I younger I would certainly quit it."[15]

12. Charles Carroll of Annapolis to his son, February 9, 1759, Carroll-McTavish Papers, quoted in Hoffman, *Princes of Ireland,* 277.

13. Cecilius Calvert to Horatio Sharpe, March 30, 1759, *Archives of Maryland* 56:256; cited in Hoffman, *Princes of Ireland,* 268.

14. Cited in Bergmann, "Being the Other," 224.

15. Charles Carroll of Annapolis to his son, July 14, 1760; cited in Hughes, *History of the Society of Jesus; Text,* 2:529.

CHAPTER 10

"WHO IS THIS MAN THAT CALLS HIMSELF A CITIZEN?"

*Catholics and the Road
to Independence*

A BISHOP FOR AMERICA

In retrospect the outcome of the Seven Years' War accelerated the timetable for American Independence. The Treaty of Paris reshaped in radical fashion the imperial landscape in North America. The ceding of Canada and the Floridas to Great Britain had not only more than doubled the size of British America but tripled its Catholic population, as well. The Treaty of Paris had placed nearly 70,000 French and Huron Catholics in the Quebec Province under British sovereignty. Among them were about 200 priests and 6 communities of religious women (in the older British North American colonies there were 25 and none, respectively). The vicar apostolic of London, Richard Challoner, who had only a few years previously been informed that America was part of his jurisdiction, now confronted the disturbing reality that the distant area for which he was suddenly responsible was this vast continent containing more Catholics than in England itself. Understandably Challoner urged Rome to appoint a bishop for America alone, whose see would be Philadelphia, the largest American city. Rome replied that it was already examining the matter of a resident prelate for British America—that it was in fact considering the possibility of naming two or three vicars apostolic for the area.

When news of this development reached Catholics in America it was nearly the last thing they wanted to hear. After all, it was well known that the Holy See recognized the Stuart pretender, Charles Edward, as king of England. Worse, the pretender's brother, Henry Cardinal York, wielded great influence in the appointment of bishops to the British dominions. And he was no friend of the Jesuits, who *were* the clergy in British America, at least south of Canada. More importantly, such an episcopal appointment would certainly rekindle the anti-Catholicism that had plagued Catholics during the recent war. In a petition sent to the English provincial superior of the Jesuits, 256 Catholics, led by Charles Carroll of Annapolis, laid out the fatal consequences that would flow from appointing an American bishop. "[S]uch a step," they warned, "would give our adversaries, bent on our ruin, a stronger handle than anything they have hitherto been able to lay hold on, and consequently terminate in the utter extirpation of our holy religion."[1] In a separate letter to Bishop Challoner, Carroll pointed out that fierce opposition had caused the Anglicans to back off from their plan to send a bishop to America. If Americans refused to accept an Anglican bishop, what could one expect their reaction to be to a Catholic prelate imposed by Rome? The English provincial dutifully forwarded the other petition to Challoner, as well. The vicar apostolic dismissed them both as the work of Jesuits who feared a potential rival authority in America.

When Rome saw fit to take no action about a resident episcopacy in the colonies, Challoner proposed that the bishop of Quebec be given responsibility for all of British America, including the islands, presumably because Quebec was much closer to the other mainland colonies than London was.

---

1. Charles Carroll et al. to Richard Challoner, July 16, 1765, Maryland Province Archives; cited in Hughes, *History of the Society of Jesus; Text*, 2:591.

A NEW WAVE OF CATHOLIC
EXPANSION

By 1765 there were approximately 16,000 Catholics in Maryland, or about
8 percent of the province's population. The largest portion, a third, was
still in St. Mary's County. The crisis that anti-Catholicism had produced
for the community had in the end been an annealing force. The post-
war period proved to be one of notable religious vitality for the Catholic
community. Its growth over the ensuing decade was greater than that of
the general population in the province. The number of priests also increased, as did the number of chapels, particularly public ones.

Public chapels had been illegal since the overthrow of the Calverts in
1689. After a hiatus of seventy years, the postwar years saw a renewal of
building public chapels. Between 1766 and 1775 construction began on
seven Catholic churches in rural and urban settings on both shores of
the province. The first known addition was St. Francis Xavier at Newtown in 1766, a modest brick building whose interior, with its pew boxes
and nonseparation of sanctuary from nave, reflected Anglican colonial
church design. The chapels went up on rural sites, notably Jesuit plantations, around which Catholics had long clustered, but also on lots in
recently founded towns to which Catholics, along with others, were mi-
grating. Churches were built in the two fastest-growing towns of Maryland, Frederick and Baltimore, the latter structure on a lot purchased
by the Jesuits from Charles Carroll of Annapolis. There was a parallel
between Catholic public chapel construction in England and Maryland
in the post-war period. This dual development reflected the decline of
anti-Catholicism in both places, which encouraged religious superiors
to build publicly without serious fear that they would encounter official
opposition. Tricia Pyne has noted that this revival of public chapels in
Maryland represented a return to the parish-oriented ministry that the
Jesuits had originally tried to organize in the seventeenth century.

There was a more open atmosphere for Catholics by the mid-1760s,
one in which Jesuits, for instance, could proselytize at the Port Tobacco
courthouse in Charles County without fear of their being challenged in
any other way than that of religious polemics. In 1771 George Hunter,

the Jesuit superior, felt enough emboldened by the new climate that he attempted to become a town developer, advertising in the *Maryland Gazette* a large tract of land, part of St. Thomas's Manor, that he planned to name Edenburg, no doubt in honor of Maryland's governor at the time, Robert Eden. Despite this gesture, Hunter's project came to nothing after he was advised that he might be accused of illegally alienating church property by selling lots to potential builders.

CATHOLIC COMMUNITIES
ELSEWHERE ON THE
MAINLAND

In New York, immigrants, displaced victims of war, and imperial military forces had increased the number of Catholics, but, as they were institutionally unorganized, they remained, in Jason Duncan's apt words, "a shadowy population."[2] Individual Catholics were left to devise their own ways to meet their spiritual needs. Some went to near-heroic lengths to practice their religion, as did the merchant John Leary, who regularly traveled to Philadelphia to hear Mass at St. Joseph's or St. Mary's (although his import business may have been a reason for the trips, as well). Many more, not as zealous or well-positioned, joined either the Anglican Church (as did most who converted) or one of the various other Protestant churches that were proliferating in the province between 1750 and 1775 (approximately seventy-five of them) or dropped out of organized religion entirely. A few, such as John Jenkins and Thomas Barry of Albany, returned to the Catholic Church after it established an institutional presence toward the end of the eighteenth century. By the 1770s, despite being illegal, Mass was apparently being said—secretly—at the home of a German immigrant on Wall Street by Ferdinand Farmer, who would, in disguise, make visits from Pennsylvania to the city as well as stops in New Jersey.

John Adams's remark that Catholics in colonial New England were as rare as comets or earthquakes was clearly a stretch, but made its point.

2. Duncan, *Citizens or Papists*, 28.

There were a few Catholics in New England. Some Irish could be found in seaports, like John O'Kelly at Warren, Rhode Island, or the sixty Irish laborers and fishermen who migrated via Newfoundland to Newport in 1774. Aside from them, Catholics indeed were hard to find in New England, which only seemed to intensify the anti-Catholic animus so imbedded in the culture of the region.

CHARLES CARROLL
OF CARROLLTON

On his twenty-seventh birthday, in September 1764, the third-generation Charles Carroll, Charles Carroll of Annapolis's only son, sailed for home from England after a sojourn of sixteen years pursuing his father's master plan for a European education in the humanities and law that had carried him to St. Omer's, Rheims, Paris, and London. Much less consciously Irish, more emotionally detached, and much more broadly educated than his father, Charles Carroll of Carrollton, as he began to sign himself shortly after returning to America, shared his father's single-minded determination not only to survive in an alien world at least partially closed to him, but to know extraordinary success in the spheres in which he could operate. In the end his deftness in navigating the roiling political seas of the 1770s enabled him to lead the Catholic community back into the very center of public life, where he played a principal role in framing the issues that led to war and in shaping the republic born of it.

He returned to an Annapolis that, with the Seven Years' War over, was on the cusp of an architectural boom that would erect elegant Georgian mansions that would make the provincial capital the urban gem of British America, buttressed by a social infrastructure of race track, theater, gentlemen's clubs, and other signposts of the conspicuous wealth that the lawyers, officeholders, and proprietary appointees of Maryland were increasingly enjoying.

Still, as Carroll found, probably not to his surprise, there were social levels to which a Catholic could not aspire, no matter his wealth or education. So Carroll had no invitation to the Forensic Club that prominent

Annapolitans like William Paca had founded five years earlier. And the law and politics were professions closed to him, as well.

From his father Charlie took over management of most of the Carroll estates worked by tenants on the Western Shore. Made a partner in the Baltimore Company by his father, he gave considerable time and attention in trying to improve, with some success, the efficiency of its operations and profits. But developments in the political realm from which he was excluded would soon change the trajectory of his life into a very unexpected direction.

THE STAMP ACT: BEGINNING
OF THE IMPERIAL CRISIS

In the milieu of the Seven Years' War, coming close on the disrupting revivals of the Great Awakening, there was a reworking among American Protestants of the prophetic elements in scripture to make sense of contemporary experience. As Thomas S. Kidd notes, "The Great Awakening and the Seven Years' War forged a visceral bond among Protestantism, anti-Catholicism, and liberty."[3] In this process of revision there was a broadening of the concept of "popery" to denote any kind of oppression, not just that emanating from Rome or its demonic agents.

The Americans and British brought very differing expectations out of the war. For the Americans the elimination of Great Britain's two leading imperial rivals imbued great optimism about a future of geographic and economic mobility. For the mother country, the mountainous costs of administering a North American empire suddenly doubled in size led to legislation in the form of the Sugar Act of 1764 and the Stamp Act of 1765 that raised new alarms about the security of American civil liberties.

Through the apocalyptic filter by which the Great Awakening had conditioned evangelical Americans to frame their understanding of events, the Seven Years' War had been a providential deliverance from a tyrannical Catholic power. Just one year after the successful ending of that

---

3. Thomas S. Kidd, *God of Liberty: A Religious History of the American Revolution* (New York: Basic Books, 2010), 16.

Newtown Church and Manor

conflict, threats to liberty began to appear from an unexpected source that had always, in the minds of most Americans, been synonymous with freedom—the British Parliament. In the course of one year that body enacted two laws—the Sugar and Stamp acts—that generated political protest on a scale not seen since the Glorious Revolution seventy-five years earlier. The catalyst for the legislation had been the staggering debt Great Britain had accrued in the course of prosecuting the war, compounded by the heavy expenses that now came from maintaining an adequate military force in America to guard its greatly expanded borders against potentially hostile Indians. During the war the national debt had exploded from £72 million to more than £123 million. The annual cost of maintaining troops in the newly acquired western territories turned out to be over £400,000, nearly twice as much as had originally been expected. Together with the costs of administering the newly acquired territories of Canada and Florida, the colonial expenses would constitute no less than 6 percent of Great Britain's budget. To British authorities who had to raise a great amount of revenue to offset these expenses, it seemed perfectly reasonable that Americans should pay their fair share, since they were the ones most benefitting from these costs. That the tax burden of the colonists was but a fraction (around 5 percent) of that of the British people made a larger contribution from the colonies seem all the more a matter of equity.

So the Sugar Act passed in 1764 taxed, among other items, molasses and wine entering the colonies. In addition, it stipulated that certain materials, such as iron or lumber, had to travel through Great Britain, no matter what the final destination. The British government hoped to realize at least £100,000 a year, about a fifth of the cost of maintaining troops in North America. What bothered many Americans was not only the unprecedented action by Parliament of imposing a tax on commerce, not to regulate trade, as had been the custom, but to raise revenue. They objected also to the increased costs that came with shipping everything through Great Britain and found the methods that the British adopted to enforce the act—such as transferring cases brought under the law to vice-admiralty courts rather than the normal colonial ones and putting the burden of proof upon the defendant rather than the prosecution—smacking of arbitrary government.

The Sugar Act brought scattered demonstrations from the colonists, widespread smuggling, and concomitant bribing of officials, as well as the formal protests of nine provincial legislatures. Parliament finally resolved the matter, more or less, by lowering the tax to the point that it was less than the amount normally paid to bribe an official. By the time it took this action in 1766, it had already enacted an act that would have much more of an impact on relations between the North American colonies and the British government. Having failed to realize nearly the revenue they had anticipated from the Sugar Act, the Granville administration passed in March 1765 the Stamp Act, which required Americans to purchase watermarked (stamped) paper for the production of newspapers, licenses, and assorted legal documents.

The American reaction was a tsunami of protest that swept through the colonies. The Stamp Act, so Americans found it, was a grave imposition of a tax not on external trade but on the most quotidian internal transactions. To the business community of planters and merchants in Maryland and other colonies that found themselves heavily indebted at the end of the war, the ubiquitous tax was particularly onerous. Little wonder then that prominent merchants like Samuel Chase led protests that, at the least, included ritual hangings of stamp collectors' effigies and the burning of packets of watermarked paper they intended to sell as stamps in order to coerce them to resign. Some of the protests became violent; homes and offices were attacked, and riots ensued when sheriffs attempted to disperse the crowds. Following the lead of Boston, gentry and artisans in the various colonies organized as "Sons of Liberty" to plan and direct the resistance. In Maryland Samuel Chase and William Paca were among the initiators of the "Society for the Maintenance of Order and Protection of American Liberty" that was formed in Baltimore County in February of 1766. Boycotts of imported British goods sprang up, and a pamphlet war developed over the act and its constitutionality. In Maryland the most influential essay came from the pen of Daniel Dulaney, who castigated the notion of virtual representation ("a mere cob-web") of the colonists in Parliament as a justification for the imposition of internal taxes upon them.

The Catholic gentry were wary, perhaps fearful, of getting involved after their experience of the mid-fifties, of making themselves convenient targets for renewed persecution by getting involved in the politics of dissent. A French traveler, in passing through Maryland at the height of the public demonstrations against the Stamp Act, found the Catholic community "very cautious" about the whole issue.[4] Charlie Carroll, who had arrived home just a few months before the onset of the crisis, found the turmoil generated by the Sons of Liberty and their like to be the fruit of "ignorance, prejudice, and passion."[5] Like most of Maryland's gentry he opposed the Stamp Act but condemned the violent resistance that

4. "Journal of a French Traveller in the Colonies, 1765, II," *American Historical Review* 27 (October 1921), 73; cited in Hardy, "Papists," 372.
5. Aubrey C. Land, *Colonial Maryland: A History* (Millwood, N.Y.: KTO Press, 1981), 249.

it had brought into being. If property was the keystone to liberty, then the destruction of the former was to undermine the latter. Carroll felt strongly that the proper avenue of protest should be through boycotts and written polemics, like Dulaney's (which, despite his personal feelings about its author, Carroll admired). Still, he felt there was no place in the polemical marketplace for a Catholic voice like his. When Parliament, facing an increasingly effective American boycott and the resignation of most of the stamp distributors in the colonies, reluctantly repealed the Stamp Act in March 1766, it marked a distinct victory for the American opposition. But the simultaneous Declaratory Act that proclaimed Parliament's unconditional power to legislate for the colonies, including taxation, was an ominous statement that the war was hardly over.

FIRST CITIZEN: REGAINING
A POLITICAL VOICE

The twenty-eight-year-old Robert Eden, the brother-in-law of Lord Baltimore, succeeded Horatio Sharpe as governor in 1769. Within a year and a half of his taking office what became known as the Tobacco Fees Controversy had him at total odds with the House of Delegates. The dispute grew out of the arrest, at the order of the lower house, of the clerk of the land office for collecting fees after the expiration of the Tobacco Inspection Act. At the root of the conflict was the control and size of the fees that had traditionally been the province of the proprietor and his agents. When the governor resorted to proroguing the house as a means of releasing the clerk from custody, the delegates retaliated by issuing a report that showed the extensive income that proprietary officers had been receiving through the plethora of fees they collected throughout the province. In turn the governor dissolved the assembly, which action seemed to opponents of the proprietor the height of arbitrary governance. Lurid scandal (Lord Baltimore had been forced into hiding to escape rape charges in London) only worsened the proprietor's standing in Maryland.

The fees controversy eventually provided the opportunity for Catholics to regain political access by an unlikely forum. In January a long piece submitted by "Antilon" appeared in the *Maryland Gazette* in the form of a dialogue between two "citizens," "First Citizen," an opponent of the fees, and "Second Citizen," a supporter. "Second Citizen" prevailed in the concocted debate, with the trumping argument that Governor Eden was not imposing taxes so much as he was setting a ceiling for fees beyond which collecting officers could not go. Everyone knew who "Antilon" was: Daniel Dulaney, the provincial secretary and the second-most-powerful officeholder in Maryland No doubt the self-confident Dulaney, considered the most outstanding legal mind in Maryland, expected no challenge to his defense of the prerogatives of proprietary government. By 1773 he had a corpus of public pamphlets to his credit that had established him as a staunch defender of British rights and liberties, including the proprietor's.

Several weeks later a rejoinder by someone signing himself "First Citizen" pointed out that such a regulation of fees was really a step toward absolutism, since it meant a transfer of the control of public finances from the legislature, where it should be, to the governor, where it should not. First Citizen's identity soon became public knowledge: Charles Carroll of Carrollton.

Carroll was no stranger to Dulaney. Their fathers were founding partners of the Baltimore Company. Charles Carroll of Annapolis had had his son call upon the younger Dulaney in London, where Carroll was studying law at the Inns of Court and where Dulaney had come on business as secretary of the provincial council of Maryland. The elder Carroll wanted Charlie to make Dulaney's acquaintance as well as seek his advice on a lawsuit Carroll was involved with. Charlie deeply resented the high-handed reception he had received, even more so the rude fashion in which Dulaney had treated the materials of his father that the son had asked him to review. His subsequent dealings with Dulaney when both became partners in the Baltimore Company only confirmed his initial impressions. Carroll's personal contempt for Dulaney trumped any intellectual respect he had for him.

In his response to Dulaney, which ultimately spanned four letters, Carroll, echoing the Jesuits Atwood and Hunter, reflected on the constitution within a historical framework. For them the constitution represented the consolidation of the political experience of the English people.

Charles Carroll of Carrollton

"The wisdom of ages," "First Citizen" judged, and the accumulated acts of political patriotism had been responsible for bringing "the constitution to its present point of perfection."[6] After an exchange of two sets of letters Dulaney, confounded by Carroll's arguments, turned the dialogue *ad hominem*. He clearly knew the identity of "First Citizen":

[W]ho is this man, that calls himself a Citizen.... He had no share in the legislature, as a member of any branch; he is incapable of being a member; he is disabled from giving a vote in the choice of representatives, by the laws and con-

6. Peter Onuf, ed., *Maryland and the Empire, 1773: The Antilon-First Citizen Letters* (Baltimore: The Johns Hopkins University Press, 1974), 17.

stitutions of the country, *on account of his principles,* which are *distrusted* by those laws…. He is not a protestant.

"Antilon" was saying, First citizen, the penal laws of this province are a permanent warning that because of your religion the state cannot trust your loyalty. In its largesse it suffers you to live in this society, so long as you keep the lower place the law assigns you. So I would advise you to cease your agitation. If you persist in your argument, the state may well conclude that your attacks on public officials clearly demonstrate your disloyalty and act accordingly. Watch yourself!

In his third letter "First Citizen" took "Antilon" to task for playing to people's passions by exploiting the anti-Catholicism that had so dogged Maryland's history. His religion, he rejoined, was not the issue; his political principles were. When Dulaney doubled down on his religious attack, that Carroll's religion rendered him unfit to participate in governance, Carroll in his last letter reiterated his political principles, principles of civil and religious liberty upon which the Glorious Revolution had been based. Dulaney, Carroll implied, was turning his back on that revolution by denying Catholics their civil and religious liberties. He was also revealing the self-interest that motivated him to support the governor's right to impose fees, since he and his family, in holding lucrative proprietary positions, had much at stake in the controversy.

The May assembly elections of 1773 proved to be a referendum on the extended debate that Carroll and Dulaney had waged over the past five months. Riding the coattails Carroll had acquired by his besting of Dulaney, the Popular Party, as the coalition of hitherto non- or marginalized participants in Maryland's political sphere became known, took control of the legislature. Improbably Carroll found himself, because of his "First Citizen" success, at the center of the coalition, even though he had not been a candidate for any position. His letters had made a Catholic the voice of the "popular party." With that party now in control in Annapolis, Carroll, though he held no office, was suddenly one of the most politically powerful people in Maryland.

As leaders like Samuel Chase and William Paca attempted at last to put the fees controversy behind them by reaching some compromise with the governor, a much larger controversy, sweeping not just through the province but all the colonies, suddenly made the fees dispute seem insignificant. In May 1774 the British Parliament imposed a series of punitive acts upon Massachusetts for its resistance to the latest British plan to raise revenue: the Tea Act of 1773. "The Intolerable Acts," as the laws quickly were dubbed by outraged colonists because of their abridgement of the economic and political rights of Massachusetts citizens through such despotic measures as the closing of the port of Boston and the limitation of local political meetings to one a year, galvanized opposition from New England to Georgia. In Annapolis some eighty men, mostly "Patriots" (Popular Party members), resolved to form a "nonimportation association" that would promote and enforce the ending of all commercial and financial dealings with Great Britain, including trade and the payment of debts.

Out of that Annapolis meeting came the election of delegates to a convention that gathered in the capital the following month, the first of several such paralegal gatherings that became, by 1775, the de facto provincial government. The ban on Catholic political participation kept Carroll from being one of the delegates, to his frustration. When the convention selected delegates to attend the First Continental Congress in Philadelphia in September, they asked Carroll to be an unofficial member of the delegation, although he could not attend the actual sessions. Carroll agreed "to serve them in a private capacity," even though he found his continuing exclusion from active political life to be an absurdity. In November the religious barrier for Catholics was finally lowered; Carroll was elected from Anne Arundel County to the second provincial convention and became a fixture at the seven remaining ones. Carroll led the way for the Catholic gentry's reentry into Maryland governance. That reentry proved to be an astonishingly rapid and comprehensive one. By 1777, as Beatriz Hardy has found, more than 40 percent of the Maryland Catholic gentry who had come of age between 1750 and 1775 were serving in government.[7] How they came to align themselves with the revolution that produced that government is a longer story covering developments in both Europe and North America that very much affected their decision.

7. Hardy, "Papists," 314.

SUPPRESSION OF THE SOCIETY OF
JESUS AND THE QUEBEC ACT

In June 1773 Pope Clement XIV capitulated to the pressure of Catholic imperial powers and signed the brief *Dominus ac Redemptor* suppressing the Society of Jesus throughout the world. That decree affected every one of the twenty-three priests in Maryland and Pennsylvania, as well as most American priests who were serving abroad, like John Carroll, or those Americans, like Charles Neale, who were in formative studies toward the priesthood. As Joseph Mosley wrote his sister, upon learning of the brief, "To my great sorrow the Society is abolished: with it must die all that zeal that was founded and raised on it.... [T]he Jesuit's metamorphosed into I know not what.... As the Jesuit is judged unfit by his H[ol]iness for a mission, I think that it is high time for me to retire to a private life."[8] John Carroll was even more devastated by the event. "I am not, and perhaps never shall be," he wrote his brother from Bruges, "recovered from the shock of this dreadful intelligence. The greatest blessing which in my estimate I could receive from God, would be immediate death."[9] Mosley did not retire, to England or anywhere, but remained at his post on the Eastern Shore until his death fourteen years later. Carroll, deciding that the expungement of the Society had made him his "own master," returned to Maryland after an absence of a quarter century to become a chaplain for his extended family, which spanned the Maryland and Virginia portions of the Potomac Valley.

The ex-Jesuits in America, as well as the laity, formally were now subject to the vicar apostolic of London, Bishop Challoner; in reality they were headless, as war would soon make clear. The Catholic community in America had always been connected to the international church through the Society of Jesus; now that link had been broken. That breaking perhaps prepared the community for the political severance that was to follow just three years later.

---

8. Mosley to sister, October 3, 1774, Mosley Papers, Georgetown University Special Collections.

9. John Carroll to Daniel Carroll, Bruges, September 11, 1773; cited in *American Jesuit Spirituality: The Maryland Tradition, 1634–1900*, edited by Robert Emmett Curran (Rahway, N.J.: Paulist Press, 1988), 128–29.

In the context of other imperial acts, the Quebec Act of 1774 looked particularly ominous. In the previous decade there had been passionate opposition to Anglican plans to appoint a bishop for the colonies, as the appointment of an Anglican prelate would be, so critics alleged, just the first step toward the establishment of popery in America. Now in the neighboring province of Quebec the British government had confirmed the worst fears about its ultimate design to impose popery on the colonies. It had given Roman Catholicism a privileged position in the Canadian province by honoring the church's traditional status. It allowed Catholics to hold office without taking an oath impugning their religion. And it extended the southern border of Canada from the St. Lawrence River to the Ohio, seemingly bringing a vast area in the west under the control of the government in Quebec and making likely new alliances between Catholics and Indian tribes in the territory. All in all, it was a harbinger, demagogues announced, of things to come in the rest of British America regarding traditional liberties and the place of Protestantism in society.

Particularly in New England, the lesser the Catholic presence, the more prevalent were anti-Catholicism and anti-popery. Anti-popery became an instrument of resistance to Great Britain as British rulers, from the king to Parliament, were made over in the popular discourse of sermons, pamphlets, and newspapers into secular popes who threatened liberty and true religion. Beginning in the November following the implementation of the Stamp Act, New Englanders adapted Pope's Day to become part of the protest against British imperialism. Nine years later the Quebec Act was a lightning rod in the process of delegitimizing British authority. So universal was the opposition to the act that in the observance of Guy Fawkes Day in 1774, the rival Boston gangs who usually paraded separate "popes" joined to burn a "Union Pope," which was much more a surrogate for London tyranny rather than its Roman counterpart. Opinion began to circulate that since Catholicism had evidently captured George III like it had his Stuart predecessor, James II, the only due recourse was to a second Glorious Revolution. Another story had the British using the act as a ploy to recruit Canadians to suppress Americans in a coming war. In South Carolina, no hotbed of evangelical Christianity, the Quebec Act occasioned the revival of Pope's Day in Charleston for which thousands turned out. Even in "Catholic" Maryland, where the act occasioned much less paranoia, it nonetheless made its mark. The *Maryland Gazette* considered the act's implications for American liberty worse than those of the Stamp Act. Another source reported from Maryland that the Quebec Act was as unpopular as the Intolerable Acts that had stunned the province a few months earlier.[10] Thomas Paine would complete the equation of British and Catholic tyranny when, in his *Common Sense*, he would define monarchy as "the Popery of government." For Paine, as for many others, anti-Catholicism became a medium for demonizing Great Britain.

Assemblies at the local and provincial levels passed formal resolutions to express their concern and outrage over the Quebec Act. The Suffolk County Resolves of September 1774 became the model for collective protests that other assemblies throughout the colonies composed. The Massachusetts county's resolution condemned the Quebec Act as a virtual establishment of religion in an adjoining province; it represented a dangerous inroad upon the liberties and civil rights of all Americans. A week later the First Continental Congress unanimously approved the Suffolk Resolves. It then proceeded to issue addresses to two audiences: the inhabitants of the British colonies and the "People of Great Britain." To the former the delegates justified their opposition to the Quebec Act on the grounds that it established Roman Catholicism, not merely tolerated it. To the latter it warned that English Protestants were the ultimate target of the act: once the British government has succeeded in its conspiracy to make America Catholic, it will use these newly created Catholics as a force to cross the ocean to subdue them. Incredibly, five days after penning these letters, which verged on the hysterical, the Congress, without blinking, addressed the Canadian people themselves to persuade them that there was no need for the act, which merely restated what God had already instilled in them—liberty of conscience—while denying them other fundamental rights. Their only hope, so the Congress assured them, lay in the colonies to their south.

10. Metzger, *Quebec Act*, 59.

THE CHOICE FOR CATHOLICS

If the delegates thought that somehow they could segment these contradictory addresses so that no one would make comparisons, they were mistaken. Catholics in Canada as well as in the older British colonies on the North American mainland were dismayed at the sentiments expressed and had to wonder how they would ever fit into such a hostile society.

The road to revolution and the declaration of independence involved, for the Americans who took that road, the emergence of a peculiar consciousness that increasingly set the colonists apart from those in the motherland. Creolization gradually produced an awareness of American distinctiveness—this while the colonies were becoming culturally more Anglican. Indeed, as their culture became more like England's, their social links with those in Great Britain ironically weakened, thus strengthening their sense of being their own people. Catholics certainly shared in this identity shift, yet for them there was a special niche of distinctiveness or separateness into which they had been forced by the larger society as legal and political outcasts. Their colonial history hardly provided any grounds for hoping that home rule throughout the colonies would dramatically improve their status in society. That those who were most in favor of independence from Great Britain were the very people who were most anti-Catholic, as the Maryland minister Jonathan Boucher pointed out, only seemed to reinforce the lessons of history.

Against this background it is perhaps remarkable that the large majority of Catholics chose to cast their lot with the patriots. Even the English-born and -bred Jesuits who constituted most of the priests in Maryland and Pennsylvania supported the Revolution, at least to the extent of taking loyalty oaths. Joseph Mosley, who confessed to his sister that he felt "between hawk and buzzard" when war broke out in 1775, nevertheless joined his Jesuit confreres, if somewhat belatedly, in taking the oath—and urged his congregation to do the same.

Of course, there were Catholic loyalists, such as the Catholic Scotch Highlanders in the Mohawk Valley of New York. Many, if not most of them, like the Catholics in upstate New York and Palatine Germans, were recent immigrants. The German Catholics who had been in the colonies for a half century or more were more evenly divided; a number of those in the Conewago area joined a loyalist German regiment. As for the Catholic minority among the Irish in British America, the majority appears to have favored the rebels. Out of the Catholic Irish gentry in the Philadelphia area came an impressive number of officers in the colonies' armed forces: Joshua Barney and John Barry in the navy, Thomas Fitzsimons, Stephen Moylan, James Mease, and George Meade in the army.

Maryland seems to have produced few loyalists among the Catholic community, John Heffernan, a Baltimore teacher whose school was forced to close, being one of them. Beatriz Hardy argues that the Catholic gentry who came of age during and after the Seven Years' War had no experience of the community's relationship with their traditional protector, Lord Baltimore, who in a way had been their link to the British government before Calvert abandoned them during the 1750s. Lacking that connection, she concludes, the Catholic gentry who became important players in the events leading up to independence had no longer any particular vested interest in remaining part of Great Britain's empire.[11] For Maryland Catholics, as for their fellow Marylanders, the imperial policies and proprietary politics of the 1760s and 1770s predisposed them to challenge the crown's authority.

Charles Metzger, in his study of Catholics and the Revolution, concluded that no other group in the colonies had a harder choice than Catholics did in deciding to be patriots, loyalists, or neutrals. In the end, he thinks, many, particularly those in Maryland, simply chose to forget the painful past and take the risk, despite much contrary evidence, that the future held an equality and freedom that Catholics had never known for most of their colonial history. Also a factor was the double alienation from the proprietor and the international Catholic Church that Maryland Catholics experienced. The disappearing links with Europe that the proprietor's betrayal and the suppression of the Society of Jesus had brought about weighted the scales toward opting for independence. That

11. Hardy, "Papists," 311–12.

alienating experience was, in a sense, a recapitulation of their experience of becoming aliens in Maryland that preconditioned them toward separation from Great Britain. As Gerald Fogarty has written, "when the patriots began arguing for no taxation without representation, no laws passed without the consent of the governed, and no parliamentary jurisdiction over the colonies, they found ready allies in the Maryland Catholics" who had known this condition for more than eight decades—indeed, "had been expressing the same theory since 1634."[12] Also, it was clear by the end of 1774, thanks to Charles Carroll, that the movement toward independence offered Maryland Catholics the chance to be political participants again at all levels and to open the way, they could hope, for the full legitimization of Catholics as citizens of the republic they were creating.

12. Gerald P. Fogarty, "Property and Religious Liberty in Colonial Maryland Catholic Thought," *Catholic Historical Review* 72 (October 1986): 599.

CHAPTER 11

"THE WONDERFUL WORK OF THAT GOD WHO GUARDS YOUR LIBERTIES"

Catholics and the Revolution

THE APPEAL TO OTHER COLONIES IN BRITISH AMERICA

Article XIII of the initial "Articles of Confederation" proposed by Benjamin Franklin in July 1775 invited "every colony from Great Britain upon the Continent of North America and not at present engag'd in our Association may upon application… be receiv'd into this Confederation." Franklin then illustrated how broadly they were drawing the boundaries of this continent by enumerating the potential members of the new union they had formed: Ireland, the West Indies, Quebec, St. John's, Nova Scotia, Bermuda, and the Floridas. The delegates who had formally declared the independence of the thirteen colonies from Great Britain were obviously hoping to enlarge their confederation by attracting fellow colonists throughout the British Empire to join their revolution. For those provinces contiguous to the thirteen in rebellion, the invitation might come in the form of invasion, as Quebec found out shortly afterward.

Quebec, along with Nova Scotia, offered the best possibilities for the united colonies to acquire additional members for their "association" in the war against Britain. Quebec had been a conquered province for barely fifteen years. There was much resentment of British rule. In the maritime province of Nova Scotia, half the population were recent migrants from New England—the thousands who had settled there as replacements for the Acadians. The Continental Congress had first extended an invitation to the Québécois to join their cause against Britain in 1774 in their hypocritical condemnation of the Quebec Act for undermining the rights of the Canadians, particularly in matters of religion (as though the laws in most of the colonies did not deny outright that Catholics had any such rights). Canadians knew the history of American anti-Catholicism too well, a tradition that had just manifested itself anew by the response to the Quebec Act.

As the American expeditionary force set out for Canada in mid-September 1775, George Washington issued an address to the *habitants* in which he urged them, as American citizens, to "unite with us in an indissoluble union." Their choice, he told them, was between liberty and slavery. "The cause of *America* and of liberty is the cause of every virtuous *American* citizen, whatever may be his religion or his descent. The United Colonies know no distinction but such as slavery, corruption, and arbitrary domination, may create." The army that was marching into their province was an army of liberation.[1] In November of 1775 George Washington banned any celebration of Pope's Day in the Continental Army, pointing out to his troops how incongruent the putting of the effigy of the pontiff to the torch was to the American effort to win the Catholic Canadians over to their side. In fact, in the initial stages of the American two-pronged drive on Quebec in the late summer and early fall of 1775, the reception from the *habitants* was a friendly one. Commercial considerations (selling supplies at a good profit to the invading force) were clearly an important factor. Still, economic self-interest did not account for the hundreds who joined the ranks of the invaders as

---

1. Martin I. J. Griffin, *Catholics in the American Revolution* (Philadelphia: Published by the Author, 1907), 1:128–29.

they swept successfully toward the Canadian capital. That support gathered momentum with the capture of Montreal in October. A Canadian ironworks in Trois Rivières began casting mortars and shells for the American army. Two regiments were formed in January 1776 from the French Canadian recruits the invading forces had attracted. One, under Col. James Livingston, failed to survive the following summer when their term of service expired and few cared to reenlist. The other regiment, under Col. Moses Hazen, lost most of its members when they decided that they were not ready to become exiles for the patriots' cause, but it managed to retain a core of 100 or so soldiers as well as their chaplain, Louis Eustace Lotbinière, who retreated with the other American units back to Albany, where they continued to serve in the Continental Army. Notable among Hazen's regiment was Captain Clement Gosselin, who joined Montgomery's army in the fall of 1775 only to be captured later in the campaign. Gosselin was imprisoned in Quebec for two years until his escape in the spring of 1778. Rejoining Washington's army in New York, he was one of four French Canadians to undertake secret missions to Canada to secure or convey information. At the climactic Battle of Yorktown, Gosselin was wounded. By the end of the war in 1783 he had risen to the rank of major.

Other notable American supporters were the priest Pierre Huet de la Valinière and the Marquis de Lotbinière. Valinière, a Sulpician, became such a fervent advocate of the American cause in Quebec that the English governor had him deported to England in 1779. Lotbinière became an agent of the French government in America.

In the late winter of 1776 the Continental Congress decided to send a special mission to Canada to lobby influential habitants, both lay and clerical, to join the American fight for independence. Samuel Chase immediately urged that the Congress make his fellow delegate from Maryland one of the three members to be chosen. Carroll, Chase argued, had two very valuable assets for the delicate negotiations the mission would entail: his religion and his fluency in French. Carroll, along with Benjamin Franklin and Chase himself, were appointed as commissioners to the Canadians. General Charles Lee of Virginia had another idea for shoring up the religious credentials of the mission: Charles Carroll

John Carroll

had a cousin John who, as a Jesuit priest, would in Lee's estimation "be worth battalions," should he be "of liberal sentiments, enlarged mind and a manifest friend to Civil Liberty."[2] John Carroll, despite his conviction that ministers of religion "generally fall into contempt" when they involve themselves in political matters, agreed to join the mission. So the odd quartet headed to Montreal, with John Carroll the least optimistic about their chances of success, particularly in light of the virulent anti-

2. Charles Lee to John Hancock, February 27, 1776, *Researches* 24 (July 1907), in *John Carroll of Baltimore: Founder of the American Catholic Hierarchy*, by Annabelle M. Melville, 44 (New York: Charles Scribner's, 1955).

Catholicism the Quebec Act had recently stirred throughout the American colonies. The experience of the American delegation in Montreal proved only to confirm Carroll's expectations. When Carroll visited his fellow ex-Jesuit, Pierre René Floquet, whom Col. Moses Hazen had reported to be the chaplain of his Canadian regiment, he got a chilly reception. Floquet did allow him to say Mass at his residence, but offered little else. Even this token hospitality infuriated Bishop Briand, who had forbidden his clergy to have anything to do with the Carrolls and the Americans, including the ministering of any sacraments. Floquet had already offended Briand, first by accepting from General Montgomery the Jesuits' pre-suppression house in Montreal, which the Americans had seized upon their arrival (a house that since the suppression belonged by law to the bishop), then by hearing the confessions of and giving communion to American troops. The bishop proceeded to put Floquet's church under an interdict until the former Jesuit issued an apology for his "misdoings" during the American occupation.[3]

The American mission proved a failure, aside from the occasion it provided for John Carroll to impress the hitherto anti-Catholic Franklin by his learning and generosity (Carroll accompanied the elderly Franklin back to Philadelphia when he took ill in Montreal). Charles Carroll and Samuel Chase stayed on for some weeks longer, but eventually concluded that their enterprise was hopeless, so they headed home, as well.

Pro-American opinion proved fleeting, reflecting partly the ultimate failure of the Montgomery and Arnold campaigns to take Quebec, partly the open condemnation of the invasion by Bishop Briand. Chaplain Lotbinière later claimed that he had to dissuade many of the soldiers in his regiment from abandoning the Americans because of Briand's decree denying the sacraments to any Canadian who had joined the American cause. Briand made no attempt to conceal his feelings about the American invasion. When the Americans were forced to retreat from Quebec in 1776, the bishop called for the *Te Deum* to be sung at the cathedral in a solemn Mass of Thanksgiving at year's end. In the American repulse Briand saw the hand of God, in his providence, turning defeat into victory,

3. Archives of Quebec, November 29, 1776; cited in Griffin, *Catholics* 1:108.

a victory that had "restored ... to the whole colony, the blessing of liberty." In the bishop's sacred universe God's providence was as active as it was in that of the most patriotic American evangelical, but its work was the up-holding of the British, not their overthrowing; the British, not the Amer-icans, were the providers of liberty.[4] On the appointed day, as the choir intoned the *Te Deum* in the cathedral, Catholic militia stationed at its doors fired numerous salutes and cannon in the plaza boomed their own hymn of praise. In keeping with the "Year of Jubilee" atmosphere, two Canadians who had taken up arms against the British during the Amer-ican invasion were set free as a gesture toward reconciliation and peace.

BRITISH COLONIES
AND THE WAR

The thirteen colonies in revolt against Great Britain represented less than half of British America. In terms of those that remained loyal to Britain, besides Quebec, in Canada there was Nova Scotia and St. John (Prince Edward Island); in what had formerly been part of Spanish America was East and West Florida; in the West Indies there was Bar-bados and Jamaica, as well as four islands in the Lesser Antilles chain, Granada, Montserrat, St. Vincent, and Dominica. The colonies of Que-bec and Nova Scotia contained about 120,000 Europeans, predominant-ly Catholic (French and Scotch) in Quebec (110,000), mostly Protestant (English and Scotch) on Nova Scotia since the replacement of Acadians by New Englanders during the previous decade. In the New Englandiza-tion of the peninsula British authorities had severely retarded the de-velopment of any political autonomy on the part of the new settlers by strictly controlling the selection of local officials. As a result there was little transfer of the vibrant political culture from the New England colo-nies as a potential source of challenge to British authority. The other co-hort of recent immigrants, the Scots, had a vestigial loyalty to the crown. Thus when the Nova Scotian native Jonathan Eddy attempted to stage a liberating invasion of the Chignecto Isthmus in the fall of 1776, his

4. Griffin, *Catholics* 1:96–97.

small force (180 or so) attracted little support from either New England or Scottish transplants. Only the Acadian minority tended to favor the Americans' revolution, and they lacked the numbers to make a decisive difference. British naval control of the North Atlantic through its base at Halifax, the lack of American support, and the indifference of Nova Scotians in general doomed the invasion.

Two other Canadian provinces, Newfoundland and St. John, had populations that were approximately half Irish and very apolitical. Other major ethnic groups on St. John's were several hundred Catholic Highland Scots, who had migrated to escape pressures to conform to Presbyterianism and British culture, and a like number of Acadians, the survivors of the deportations of the 1750s. On St. John's Captain John MacDonald, a Scotch Catholic laird who had transported more than 200 Highland Catholics to his estate, at the outbreak of the war formed a company to defend the island for the crown.

The British Caribbean colonies had much in common with those on the mainland: a political culture and ideology, trade, and proximity. As Joseph Galloway of Pennsylvania remarked about the West Indian isles in considering the likelihood of their joining the revolution, they were as much "natural appendages of North America as the Isle of Man and the Orkneys" were of Great Britain.[5] Yet when the Americans issued their invitation from Philadelphia in 1776 for their fellow colonists in the Atlantic islands to join them, they received one response. Bermuda sent delegates as observers to the Continental Congress; that proved to be as close as any Caribbean colony came to joining the mainland colonies in their revolt. The sojourning character of much West Indian settlement as well as the slave-dominated demographics on the islands had bred a dependency on the mother country that the mainland colonies did not share. There was a transient quality to gentry life in the Caribbean; the goal was all too often to become a British-based absentee planter, an outcome much more feasible for Caribbean planters because of the potential wealth realizable than it was for their mainland counterparts. The social

5. Andrew Jackson O'Shaughnessy, *An Empire Divided: The American Revolution and the British Caribbean* (Philadelphia: University of Pennsylvania Press, 2000), xi.

ties forged by intermarriage and a common education were much stronger between West Indians and the British than those between North Americans and the British. The dominance of the Anglican Church in Great Britain and in the islands reinforced the sociocultural ties. So, too, the single-staple character of the Caribbean economy locked the islands into the mercantilist system that the mainland colonies were outgrowing. Indeed, the islands' economic importance to Britain, outweighing that of the mainland colonies, had helped shape the imperial policy that had advantaged the Caribbean colonies over those on the mainland and led to the latter's uprising.

In addition, the threat of foreign invasion constantly elevated West Indians' consciousness of how vital was the security that the British military provided for them.

But it was the peculiar demographics of the British West Indies that was the most prominent factor promoting security consciousness among white settlers. The overall numbers of European migrants to the West Indies was quite comparable to those who went to North America (around 500,000), but there was a vast difference in the survival and growth rates in the two regions. By 1776 the white population in the British Caribbean was barely 50,000; in North America it was 40 times that number, at 2 million. At the same time, those 50,000 whites in the West Indies found themselves outnumbered by 416,000 black inhabitants, almost all slaves. A society in which slaves constituted more than 85 percent of the population spawned a garrison mentality among whites. Realizing the growing prospects for a successful slave uprising, West Indian whites looked increasingly to Great Britain for security. At the same time the hyper-provincial character of the islands tended to thwart any movement toward union or confederation. It was not surprising, then, that there was no significant resistance to the Stamp Act, even though it impacted the islands' more adversely than it did the mainland colonies. The threat of a boycott by the latter did cause the British West Indians reluctantly to use their influence to adopt a more conciliatory policy, but this set no pattern of opposition to imperial legislation. The West Indian planters basically wanted to preserve the imperial status quo, not to reform or dismember it. When the Jamaican slaves revolted in 1776, many West Indians beyond

Jamaica blamed the uprising on the North American mainland for inspiring the island insurrection; for the vast majority of whites, the revolt bolstered their loyalty to Great Britain.

IRELAND

Ireland was another "colony" that the Americans had some hope of attracting to their revolution. No less a person than William Pitt told the British House of Commons in 1775 that "Ireland" the Americans "have to a man."[6] In truth the Irish Catholic community was at best divided over the issue. Its small middle class, along with the few remaining Catholic peers, had decided that their best interests lay in establishing their loyalty to the crown by supporting the war effort by offering bounties for those enlisting for service in America (even though Catholics were still barred from military service). In the end the Irish Parliament's opinion was the only one that mattered, and that body's loyalty to the crown, the overlords in London made sure, was as safe as money could make it. As Daniel Carroll's brother-in-law, Thomas Attwood Digges, wrote John Adams from London, "The [Irish] Commons have been touchd with English gold or English paper, & have proved themselves as corrupt as another parliament nearer me."[7] Still, there was concern about the allegiance of the people—that scores of thousands of Irish Catholics might be moved to emigrate to America to seize the revolutionary opportunity to improve their condition. So British authorities orchestrated a bill through the Irish Parliament in 1778 that provided some modest relief from penal legislation for Catholics. In time the Irish Parliament turned Britain's American crisis to its advantage, first by forcing the crown, by the familiar colonial legislative tactic of refusing to fund its share of the prosecution of the American war, to restore free trade for the country in 1779. A little more than three years later it secured legislative indepen-

---

6. Quoted in William Thackeray, *Life of Chatham* (London: 1827), 2:286, in "The Irish Parliament and the American Revolution," by Leo Francis Stock, *Historical Records and Studies* 30 (1939): 16.

7. William Ross to John Adams, April 28, 1780, in *Letters of Thomas Attwood Digges (1742–1821)*, edited by Robert H. Elias and Eugene D. Finch, 201 (Columbia: University of South Carolina Press, 1982).

dence when the crown and the English Parliament acknowledged that only the king and the Irish Parliament had the power to enact laws for Ireland.

MARYLAND: THE

MOST RELUCTANT

REBEL COLONY

"That is so eccentric a Colony," John Adams remarked of Maryland in 1776, "sometimes so hot, sometimes so cold… that I know not what to say about or to expect from it." Still, he felt that "when they get going, I expect some wild extravagant Flight or other from it. To be sure they must go beyond every body else when they begin to go."[8] Adams's admission of his inability to predict how Maryland would decide finally on the question of declaring its independence from Great Britain was an honest appraisal of the ever-shifting, increasingly complex political landscape in Maryland, which of all the colonies that formed the Continental Congress moved the most slowly toward formal separation from the mother country. But Adams *was* prophetic in sensing that whatever direction Maryland decided to take it would do so in a radical fashion, even though the nature of that radical turn likely caught him by surprise. Maryland's extremism proved to be its Catholic factor: the unique role that Catholics in Maryland played in shaping the forces that eventually moved the colony to become a full member of the revolutionary coalition and in their contributions to the formal war that followed.

As the Maryland convention pondered what course to pursue and measures to adopt as part of the colonies' resistance to Great Britain, social unrest grew, particularly on the lower Eastern Shore, where a disaffected coalition that spanned class and race had openly rebelled against the de facto ruling Patriot party. At times during the winter and spring of 1775 and 1776, the colony seemed to be teetering on the brink of anarchy. Realizing that such incipient disorder was the worst possible setting for revolution, the convention in May had instructed its delegates to the

8. Brugger, *Maryland*, 85.

Continental Congress to oppose any move toward independence. Into this cautious chamber Charles Carroll and Samuel Chase returned from Philadelphia in mid-June. Despite the disappointing outcome of their Canadian mission, despite the risks to their property and wealth that revolution clearly involved, the pair was fully committed to achieving independence and creating a new republic. Carroll once again took to the pages of the *Maryland Gazette* to make his case to the colony's shapers and the public in general. Under the nom de plume "CX," Carroll argued that the war they were already engaged in was inevitably bringing about changes, the chief one of which would be independence. What they needed to do was to create a tripartite government for the republic that independence would provide the need for. Radical change was inevitable; they had to seize the moment to attempt to manage its course. Within a fortnight of their return Carroll and Chase had turned around the convention's sentiment about independence. On July 3 the convention formally voted to declare the colony's independence from Great Britain. The following day it selected delegates to the Second Continental Congress, which appropriately included Chase and Carroll. By the time the Maryland delegation reached Philadelphia on July 17 the Congress had already (on July 2) voted for independence; Carroll, along with the other Maryland delegates, got to sign the declaration on August 2.

The man whom Daniel Dulaney had mocked three years earlier for not even being a citizen had now played perhaps the most important role in moving Maryland from colony to statehood and had become one of its signers to the declaration that became the cornerstone of a new nation. In doing so Carroll had transcended the religious and ethnic tribalism that had defined his ancestors to establish a new commonweal that would embody much of the spirit of the Maryland experiment that the Calverts had boldly undertaken nearly a century and a half before. The revolution that Carroll and the other signers were formally committing themselves to through the Declaration of Independence promised to restore the full citizenship that Catholics had lacked in Maryland for the last three-quarters of a century and elsewhere for the lifespan of the respective colonies.

MARYLAND CATHOLICS AND
THE PATRIOTS' CAUSE

The 25,000 to 30,000 Catholics in the thirteen colonies that revolted in 1776 represented but about 1 percent of the general population. Most of them were in Maryland and Pennsylvania, with Maryland containing the largest bloc, some 16,000. Maryland Catholics were also the most committed patriots. Catholic loyalists were hard to come by in the state. Catholics, along with Presbyterians and Baptists, were on the militant, or patriot, side of the spectrum among religious denominations (Anglicans and Methodists being the major occupiers of the loyalist, or noncommitted, side). If there were virtually no Catholic loyalists in Maryland, in Pennsylvania there were far many more, probably in excess of 20 percent of the Catholic population in that colony. In New York the loyalists among the relatively few Catholics in the state would appear to be a far greater proportion.

Maryland Catholics like Carroll were quick to seize the opportunity for public service that had been denied them. Beatriz Hardy discovered that more than 40 percent of the Catholic gentry who had come of age between 1750 and 1775 were serving in government by 1777.[9] As early as late 1774 Catholics in significant numbers served on the Committees of Observation in St. Mary's and Prince George's counties, at least thirteen being on the St. Mary's committee in 1776 alone. Other Catholics served on the Committees of Correspondence in several counties. Carroll, Benjamin Hall, Ignatius Fenwick, and Jeremiah Jordan were the four Catholics elected (of seventy-six) as delegates to the provincial convention in the summer of 1776.

When the delegates convened in Annapolis, Carroll was appointed to the committee to draft a constitution and declaration of rights for the new state. Over the past year resistance to the revolution, both internal and external, had continued to mount in forms ranging from slave and militia insurrections, particularly on the Eastern Shore, to the taunting threat from British warships commanding the Chesapeake and its trib-

9. Hardy, "Papists," 314.

utaries. In this unnerving climate Carroll and his fellow Patriot Party leaders decided to pursue, in Ronald Hoffman's apt phrase, "a policy of institutional conservatism and economic radicalism."[10] Despite the enormous turnover in the composition of the convention (fifty of the seventy-six delegates were new), the party still controlled the group and dominated the committee chosen to write the constitution. The franchise was restricted to those with a minimum of a fifty-acre freehold or £30 in current money. A scale of property holding was set as a requirement for the level of office sought. So the higher the office, the more property was required in order to be a candidate, on the principle that the higher the office held, the greater should be the stake in the society one sought to govern. But if property continued to serve as a gatekeeper of governance, religion no longer did. Catholics, Quakers, even nonbelievers were now free to run for any office. This constitution that Charles Carroll had helped to create affirmed, in effect, the unwritten historical one that Peter Atwood and George Hunter had previously extolled in their treatises.

To gain popular support for this highly conservative frame of government as well as to assuage debtor unrest, Carroll, Chase, and their party associates enacted a measure that required creditors to accept paper currency rather than sterling money as payment for all debts. That inflationary step proved a galling one for many of the state's investors, none more so than Charles Carroll's father, who found the bill the equivalent of property confiscation. To his son it was the price one needed to pay for the revolution to succeed. "No great revolution," he wrote, "can happen... without revolutions or mutations of private property."[11] Absorbing steep financial loss was the price of retaining political power. Nor was that the whole of what the elder Carroll took to be the assembly's assault on property. To fund the war in a politically palatable way, they also drastically shifted the tax burden onto large property holders.

The impact of the debt relief and tax restructuring was quick and

10. Hoffman, *A Spirit of Dissension: Economics, Politics, and the Revolution in Maryland* (Baltimore and London: The Johns Hopkins University Press, 1973), 2.
11. Quoted in Hoffman, *Spirit of Dissension*, 124.

profound upon the finances of the Carrolls and others in their class. By 1779 the Carrolls' taxes had increased by about 75 percent, to nearly £7,000 annually. That same year the substitution of paper currency for sterling in redeeming debts cost father and son no less than £4,000. In vain the elder Carroll twice petitioned the legislature to repeal the legislation. Meanwhile, two British raids on their Poplar Island plantation had forced them to discontinue operating that portion of their network of plantations. Their loss in revenue from Poplar Island as well as from the debt relief act was substantially offset by the windfall profits they realized in 1779 from having withheld their tobacco from the market for three years until more favorable shipping conditions arose. The alliance with France provided the friendly bottoms to carry their crop safely to Europe, with the Carrolls realizing more than £4,400 in the transactions. Still, the younger Carroll confessed to his father at the end of 1779 that "If the war Should continue much longer we may be robbed of our lands, as well as money."[12] Fortunately for the Carrolls and the other large creditors in the state, in 1780 the assembly rescinded the legal tender bill. The Carrolls had survived one major threat to their wealth. But, so long as the outcome of the war remained uncertain (and in 1780 the prospects for an American victory were less than promising), their situation remained a precarious one.

Following Carroll, Maryland Catholics quickly seized the opportunity to serve in the various levels of the newly created government, most notably in Charles, Anne Arundel, and St. Mary's counties, where they became a prominent part of the governing elite. By 1781 Catholics (George Plater, Charles Carroll, and Daniel Carroll [brother of John Carroll]) made up a fifth of the fifteen state senators representing the Western Shore, consistent with the Catholic proportion of the population in that section of the state.

Daniel Carroll was one of five members elected to the Council of State by both houses of the legislature in 1777, which had, among its responsibilities, the provision of supplies for the Americans' armed forces in the South, where the major fighting during the latter half of the war

12. Hoffman, *Princes of Ireland*, 328.

occurred. Maryland, along with Virginia, became the chief supplier of
the troops in the Southern theater. To Carroll fell the task of ensuring
that the military units would have sufficient salt, wheat, flour, clothing,
and equipment. He served in that office until 1781, when the Maryland
General Assembly chose him to be a delegate to the Continental Congress, a post he held for three terms, the maximum allowed.

Of all the Maryland Catholics involved in public service during the
war, none was as controversial as Thomas Attwood Digges. The Digges
family had a distinguished history in both Virginia and Maryland. Digges's great-great-grandfather Edward had been the governor of Virginia
in the 1650s. His grandfather had been one of the Catholics summoned
in vain to appear before the Maryland Council in 1720. His sister, Elizabeth, was the wife of Daniel Carroll. In 1766 he was persuaded by friends
to quit the country for some scandal that had led his parents, according
to John Carroll, to disinherit him.[13] He took himself to Portugal, from
where he published in 1775 Adventures of Alonso, the first novel by an
American. Moving to London just before the outbreak of hostilities between Great Britain and the colonies, Digges in 1777 became a member
of a committee charged with distributing relief to Americans held pris-
oner in England. John Carroll, presumably from information obtained
through his brother, was convinced that Digges had misappropriated the
funds entrusted to him for relief. American authorities evidently never
had cause to distrust Digges as a reliable agent. He apparently went beyond his charge of providing relief by risking his own freedom to assist
prisoners in escaping. In any event, beginning in 1776, he secretly pro-
cured munitions for the Continental Army. Three years later, after taking
the oath of loyalty in John Adams's presence, Digges began serving the
Congress as both informant and diplomatic courier. In regular letters
to Adams and others, under various fictitious names, Digges communi-

13. John Carroll to James Thomas Troy, April 16, 1792, in John Carroll Papers, edited by Thomas
O'Brien Hanley (Notre Dame: University of Notre Dame, 1976), 2:25–26. If Digges's novel Adventures of Alonso is truly autobiographical, as many believe, then the scandal consisted of his involvement with a married woman.

cated his readings of the shifting moods of the public as well as of Parliament and crown. He also reported information he had come by on troop movements and diplomatic maneuvering. Finally, in 1782 he was the conveyer of a peace feeler from Lord North that led some, including John Carroll, to conclude that he was a double agent. But his appraisals of the popular and governmental sentiment about the war seem straight enough. So in the summer of 1780, with the principal Southern cities of Charleston and Savannah in British hands and Cornwallis's army beating a seemingly unstoppable path through the Carolinas, Digges reported the unity of feeling, from the crown to the street, that "America is again ours," that they were more determined than ever to reduce America to submission.[14] By summer's end he was able to report a much chastened public mood in the face of British setbacks in the West Indies. "The minds of the people," he wrote Benjamin Franklin, "are getting reconcild apace to the Independence of America." There was a rising desire in England for peace. He sensed, he told Adams, that the British ministry would soon be making overtures toward peace.[15] A month later, after news of Cornwallis's victory at Camden, South Carolina, and of the failure of the French to pursue their advantage in the West Indies, Digges had to substitute his prediction of an imminent peace with the judgment that the British cabinet was intent on renewing all-out war, both in the Caribbean and the North American mainland. Indeed, it was not until a year and a half later, in March of 1782, that Digges became the chief intermediary in the initial negotiations that led eventually to the Peace of Paris. By that time he had become convinced that the British had realized that American independence was a reality; the only question was how they would publicly acknowledge it.

Limited evidence indicates that the service of Maryland Catholics in the military during the war matched the strong one of those in government. Sonia Johnston found that about 40 percent of the eligible Catholic

14. W. S. Ch[urch] to John Adams, July 12, 1780; cited in *Letters of Thomas Attwood Digges*, edited by Elias and Finch, 234–36.

15. T. D. to Franklin, September 18, 1780, in *Letters of Thomas Attwood Digges*, edited by Elias and Finch, 273; W. S. C. to Adams, September 20, 1780, in *Letters*, 277–78.

males in Charles and St. Mary's counties joined the neighborhood-based state militia or Continental Army units. If her figures are representative of Catholic participation throughout the state, then Catholic involvement was strong, even before the introduction of conscription by the state in 1776 for all males between sixteen and fifty, and continued so throughout the conflict. At the very least, she concluded, Catholics, who had been barred by law from the militia for three decades, once again had a presence consistent with their proportion of the state's general population.

St. Mary's County, with its extensive shorelines, was particularly vulnerable to the British naval raids that, as the war went on, became increasingly numerous and destructive in attempting to severely disrupt, if not destroy, the food and supplies that southern Maryland was providing for the military. That perennial harassment from 1776 to 1783 may account for the high and growing rate of enlistments, including those of Catholics, in the two battalions of the St. Mary's militia, whose "Flying Camp," also with heavy Catholic representation, was organized to provide a rapid response against the marauders from the sea. By 1780 the battalions numbered nearly 1,550 men, remarkably about as many eligible males as there were in the county. Catholics dominated the officers' ranks; among the rest of the county militia, they were likely at least a strong minority. Resistance to British incursions grew more effective with greater experience, organization, and numbers.

On the Eastern Shore Catholics did not adopt the loyalist bent that the Methodist-dominant majority in the region did. That Joseph Mosley, whose circuit ministry included most of the Catholics on the Maryland portion of the Delmarva peninsula, eventually (in 1777) became an advocate of the patriot cause to his scattered congregations may have been a factor in Catholics choosing to cast their lot with the revolutionaries. All of his 250 or so male parishioners, Mosley reported, had, at his "direction," taken the required loyalty oath. Joseph Callahan, at the advanced age of forty-five, enlisted in the militia, as did his sons. Other St. Joseph members to serve in the Talbot and Caroline militia included John Corkrill, Nathan Besswicks, Henry and Edward Downes, Thomas Orell, James Summers, John and James Keene, John Butler, and Dennis Carey. Dr. Thomas Bennett Willson II served as surgeon to the 20th

Battalion of the Talbot County militia. Charles Blake and James Seth were lieutenants in the Caroline County militia; John Sayer Blake II was a captain in Queen Anne County's militia.

Maryland Catholics also constituted at least a proportionate element of the "Maryland Line," the state's contribution to the Continental Army. The initial unit of 1,100 men, headed by Col. William Smallwood, consisted of troops mainly from southern Maryland and the Eastern Shore, where the vast majority of Catholics were concentrated. William Clarke, James Semmes, and Henry Neale were among the southern Maryland Catholics to become officers in the Maryland Line. Its initial testing in the disastrous Battle of Long Island in late August 1776 proved a devastating one. The Line's losses beginning at Long Island and culminating at the Battle of Princeton five months later reduced the regiment to 60, the size of a company. Nonetheless, Maryland continued to supply more than its share of manpower to the Continental Army. By 1780, when the major fighting shifted to the Carolinas, Marylanders made up a third of the patriot force. Catholics accounted for a significant minority of the Maryland contingent.

Two Virginia Catholics served as officers in the Continental Army. George Brent of Woodstock, the nephew of Daniel and John Carroll, was a lieutenant of cavalry. John Fitzgerald, an Irish immigrant merchant residing in Alexandria, became a secretary to George Washington in 1776. Wounded in the battle of Monmouth in 1778, Colonel Fitzgerald resigned from the army.

Many of the ex-Jesuits in British America were not only English in birth but had strong, continuing ties with their mother country. Joseph Mosley was probably not the only English immigrant who found himself "between hawk and buzzard" when war broke out between Great Britain and the colonies in 1775. "I know not what step I best take."[16] Mosley eventually took the oath of loyalty to the new government, as did all of his fellow ex-Jesuits. The ex-Jesuits in Maryland provided supplies for the patriot forces but no chaplains. There were virtually no priests avail-

16. Mosley to Dunn, Tackahoe, August 16, 1775, Maryland Province Archives, Georgetown University Special Collections.

able for such service and no regiment heavily Catholic enough to warrant a chaplain of that denomination, if there had been any to appoint. The main Jesuit plantations on the Western Shore, on the other hand, could be food suppliers for the patriot forces. St. Thomas Manor in Charles County, for one, supplied wheat, beef, and tobacco to the army, beginning in 1779; Newtown sold bacon to purchasing agents for the military. It was not surprising that, as important supply centers, St. Thomas, St. Inigoes, and Newtown became the objects of British shelling and raids that resulted in burned or damaged buildings; slaves, horses, and livestock appropriated, and crops plundered. The manor house at Newtown was converted into a hospital for wounded military.

As Charles Metzger summed up the Maryland Catholic contribution to the war effort, "As regulars in the Continental Army, as militia, as sailors, as diplomats, as civil officials on a local or state, even a national, level, and as humble providers of food and other essential commodities, they rivaled their neighbors of other faiths."[17]

PENNSYLVANIA CATHOLICS:
LOYALISTS, PATRIOTS,
AND NEUTRALS

John Adams's remark about the American Revolution being a civil war in which the people were equally divided in portions of those supporting, opposing, and indifferent about the rebellion caught the central character of the conflict, even if it erred in appraising the strength of the respective stances of the American people about it. As a reflection on the Catholic community in Pennsylvania, Adams's comment very probably came very close to the reality. The strong majority of Catholics in Pennsylvania were Germans, but they made up but a minority of those Catholics committed to the patriot cause. The vast majority of Catholic patriots were of Irish origin. Martin I. J. Griffin estimated from the available evidence that approximately 300 of them served in Pennsylvania's Continental military force. He simply assumed that there was a compa-

17. Metzger, *Catholics and the American Revolution*, 206–7.

rable German Catholic response, producing a total Catholic participation on the patriot side that represented at least one-third of the eligible Catholic population. But, from all we know, it seems far more likely that the proportion of German Catholic patriots fell a good deal short of that percentage and that there were more loyalists and neutrals taken together than there were patriots among them. German Catholics, settled in largely rural areas of the colony, tended to be politically isolated. The war itself impacted them much less than their Maryland counterparts; their heartland concentration rendered them far less vulnerable to British raids than those in tidewater Maryland were.

Pennsylvania's Irish were a formidable ethnic bloc. Most of these Irish, however, were from Ulster, of Scotch origin and Presbyterian. Philadelphia's Society of the Friendly Sons of Saint Patrick, organized in 1771, boasted a hundred members, but only seven Catholics, including Stephen Moylan, who was its first president. Moylan, a merchant from County Cork (his brother was the bishop of that diocese), led a military company to Boston to join the Continental Army three months after the outbreak of hostilities in 1775 and shortly afterward became George Washington's secretary. In June 1776 Congress appointed him Quartermaster General of the army. Washington subsequently asked him to organize a regiment of cavalry, and in 1778 all the Continental Army cavalry were placed under his command. Moylan led the cavalry forces for the remainder of the war, culminating with the Yorktown campaign. In 1783 Congress made him a brigadier general. Three of Moylan's brothers also served the patriot cause as diplomatic and commercial agents of the Congress, both in America and abroad, in France and Spain.

Another Irish merchant, Thomas FitzSimmons, became the first Catholic to hold public office in Pennsylvania when he was elected to the provincial convention in 1774 and later that year served in the Continental Congress. FitzSimmons, along with his partner and brother-in-law George Meade, raised a battalion for the Continental Army. Meade provided vital financial support to the army during the critical winter of 1776 and 1977. Yet another Catholic merchant, James Mease, had a decidedly less distinguished record of service. Mease, in the course of the war, acquired a reputation as a sharp dealer who at least occasionally

John Barry

put personal profit-making over meeting the country's needs, as when he conspired with Benedict Arnold to make a killing in selling military supplies to the army.

Philadelphia Catholics made extraordinary contributions to the prosecution of the war on the seas, either through service in the navy or through privateering. At least fourteen of St. Mary's Irish parishioners, including Meade and FitzSimmons, engaged, with considerable success, in the pursuit and capture of British supply ships and transports on the high seas. Joseph Cauffman, an Austrian-American physician, volunteered to serve as a surgeon aboard naval vessels. In 1778 he was aboard the *Randolph* when the ship, during an engagement with a British cruiser off Barbados, was blown up by a shell misfired from an American ship. All hands, including Cauffman, perished.

No one made a greater contribution to the establishment of the new country's navy than did the Philadelphia Irish Catholic John Barry. Barry, a native of County Wexford, Ireland, had been involved in maritime commerce, mostly with the West Indies, for nearly a decade when he was given command of one of the two cruisers the Congress had just commissioned in October of 1775 as the initial ships in the military service of the united colonies. It was the first of several commands for Barry. No commander in the proto-navy was more active over the entire course of the war, engaging in his last hostile naval engagement in 1783. In that regard, he is appropriately called "the father of the American navy."

Unlike Maryland, there was a strong loyalist element among Pennsylvania's Catholics, not only among the Germans, but among the Irish and Scotch, as well. This became all too clear when Alfred Clifton, a wealthy Anglo-Irish parishioner of St. Joseph's Church in Philadelphia, organized the Roman Catholic Volunteers for service of the crown shortly after the British occupied the city in the late fall of 1777. This was a consequence of the British decision, once it became clear that their forces would not be able to put down the rebellion in short order, to change their policy and recruit Catholics in Ireland and America for military service. The Volunteers were mainly merchants, professionals, and artisans, heavily Irish, with a sprinkling of Scotch and Germans. By the end of 1777 they numbered about 144. Ferdinand Farmer was providing religious services for them, although he claimed not to have been their chaplain. When the British abandoned the city in 1778 the Roman Catholic unit moved with the army to New York, where they recruited an additional 150 men, bringing their total to 330. The remnants of the Volunteers, plagued by discipline problems and desertion, were all too soon absorbed into an Irish regiment.

CATHOLICS, RIGHTS, AND
THE REVOLUTION

In 1775 a letter writer, signing himself "Protestant," reported in an English journal that an Irish Catholic peer was offering a bounty to his fellow Catholics to enlist in the British army to oppose the American uprising. Just as King James II had tried to raise Catholic armies in England and Ireland to preserve the "popery" he had forced upon the English people, so too the present crown was hoping to use Catholics to make war on the civil and religious liberties of the Americans. It was the Glorious Revolution *redivivus*. The no-popery theme was raised in America, particularly early in the war, as a justification for revolt and as a recruiting tool. When Daniel Barber of Claremont, New Hampshire, enlisted in a militia company, he remembered, "The real fear of popery stimulated many people to send their sons to join the ranks. The common word then was: 'No King, no Popery.'"[18] But even in New England, where anti-Catholicism had its deepest hold on the culture, the vicissitudes of war forced people to reconsider their prejudices. That was especially so when the traditional *bête noire* of New Englanders, the French, became in 1778 the Americans' principal European ally. The Congregational minister Samuel Cooper, the notorious anti-Catholic polemicist, suddenly preached toleration of Catholics as a distinct virtue. That he was receiving $1,000 a year from the French government to be in effect a propagandist no doubt had something to do with his change of attitude, but it reflected a broad shift in public opinion, which in general was more liberal in its thinking about Catholics than was that of the clergy.

The revolution did bring about fundamental changes in the legal status of Catholics throughout the new states. In February 1779 John Carroll wrote his English friend and fellow ex-Jesuit Charles Plowden that "almost all the American states" had adopted the "fullest and larg-

18. Daniel Barber, *The History of My Own Times* (Washington: 1827): in *No King, No Popery: Anti-Catholicism in Revolutionary New England*, by Francis D. Cogliano, 53–54 (Westport, Conn.: Greenwood Press, 1995). Barber, who later became an Anglican minister, eventually converted to Catholicism and was ordained a Roman Catholic priest.

est system of toleration." Indeed, Carroll thought that the United States was becoming a model for the recognition of religious rights that England and Ireland would soon adopt.[19] The pathbreaker was the Virginia legislature, which in June 1776 enacted a bill of rights that included the principle of religious freedom as well as that of the separation of church and state. Three months later Pennsylvania in its Declaration of Rights included freedom of religion among them, but restricted officeholding to Christians. Two months after Pennsylvania, Maryland declared that all Christians should enjoy religious liberty as well as the full rights of citizens, including the right to vote. Other states were more restrictive regarding the rights of Catholics. In the Carolinas as well as Georgia and New Jersey, Catholics could vote but not hold office. Massachusetts and Connecticut eventually extended freedom of religion to all, but maintained the Congregational Church in its established position. Massachusetts is a good example of how military needs affected the recognition of religious rights. By 1779 leaders in that state had come to the conclusion that religious toleration, including that of Catholics, was simply a *sine qua non* for the military success that only a durable alliance with Catholic France could make possible. So John Hancock and Samuel Cooper both argued publicly that religious toleration was a necessary step toward the defeat of the British. It is perhaps worth noting that the sailors of the French fleet then anchored in Boston harbor made up no less than a fifth of the population of the city.

Ironically, anti-Catholicism during the war proved most virulent in Great Britain itself. In June 1780 the lifting by Parliament of some of the penal legislation affecting Catholics led mobs to rampage through the Catholic sections of London, then spread out in an orgy of targeted arson and destruction of public buildings, including the Bank of London and Newgate Prison, that paralyzed the city for several days. "No Popery" signs papered the walls of buildings throughout the besieged sections of the city. The most powerful government in the world, the "power which are to bring America to unconditional Submission," Thomas At-

19. Carroll to Plowden, February 28, 1779, in *John Carroll Papers* 1:53.

twood Digges commented to John Adams, had been taken hostage by a few hundred "Rioters & plunderers."[20]

OTHER CATHOLICS IN BRITISH SERVICE

Despite the persistent anti-Catholicism in England, some English observers gauged that George III, like his Stuart predecessors, would need to get his military manpower from the peripheral regions of Great Britain, particularly Scotland and Ireland, including the Catholics there. In 1775 the sheriff of London was convinced that if "the Ministry... get men at all it must be from Scotland, or among the Irish Roman Catholics, for the American War is really so odious and disgusting to the common people in England, that no soldiers or sailors will inlist."[21] The two kingdoms, Scotland in particular, proved to be fertile recruiting grounds, as both Irish Catholic nobles and gentry and Scottish lairds sought to utilize military service as a means of demonstrating their loyalty. In any event, the Scotch dominated the British forces engaged in the North American conflict. Ten of the thirteen regiments sent from Great Britain were Scotch. In addition, four regiments were raised from the Scotsmen in the colonies themselves. Since Scottish law prohibited Catholics from serving in the military, there were likely few Catholics among the Great Britain–based Scottish regiments. That was certainly not the case with at least one of the colonies-based regiments.

Some 400 to 500 Scottish Highland Catholics had chosen in 1773 to emigrate to New York, where Sir William Johnson, an Irish-born, Old English Catholic who had converted to the Anglican Church, was seeking settlers for the huge tract of land he had acquired decades earlier in the Mohawk Valley over which he ruled as a feudal lord. The Catholic Highlanders were part of a large body of Celts whom Johnson had recruited from the Scottish Highlands and Ireland, mostly from the former. In the summer of 1775 a large portion of the Mohawk Valley settlers were under arms in behalf of the crown to which they had all taken a

---

20. Alexander Brett to John Adams, June 8, 1780.

21. William Lee to Richard Henry Lee, London, July 13, 1775, in *Letters of William Lee* (Brooklyn: Historical Printing Club, 1891), 1:164; cited in Griffin, *Catholics* 3: 254.

pledge of loyalty before they had sailed for America. Finding themselves an isolated loyalist pocket, the community decided to send their Irish priest, John McKenna, to Canada to seek asylum there. He arrived in Montreal just ahead of the invading American army of Richard Montgomery, which occupied the city in November. Eventually most of his parishioners managed to join him in Canada, where the adult males formed two companies, the Royal Highlanders and the Royal Yorkers, with McKenna as their chaplain, and eventually returned to the Mohawk Valley in 1777 as part of Barry St. Leger's regiment in a failed attempt to regain the area.

The Mohawk Valley Scots and Irish were not the only Catholic loyalists in New York. In New York City several Irish merchants and innkeepers, both male and female, let their commercial interests in serving the British occupiers during the war dictate their allegiance to the crown. Exceptions were Margaret Smith, Catherine Barry, and John Kelly. Smith and Barry were imprisoned for attacking and wounding a British soldier. Kelly fled the city just before the British arrived in 1776 and remained in exile until the British finally abandoned New York seven years later.

Lacking sufficient troops within its empire to put down the American rebellion, Great Britain, as early as 1776, resorted to recruiting some 30,000 mercenaries from the rulers of several German states, including Frederick II, the Catholic landgrave of Hesse-Cassel, who provided more than half the German soldiers who saw action in the conflict. As a result of this majority all the German soldiers, despite being from six principalities, became known as "Hessians." At least 3,000 of the nearly 17,000 Hessians were Catholics from Westphalia.

EUROPEAN CATHOLIC
VOLUNTEERS AND THE
DECISIVE CATHOLIC
ALLIANCES

Three professional soldiers, two Poles and a Frenchman, made extraordinary contributions to the American war effort: Tadeusz Andrezej

Bonawentura Kościuszko, Count Casimir Pulaski, and the Marquis de Lafayette (Marie Joseph Paul Yves Roch Gilbert du Motier). Kościuszko, appointed by Congress as an engineer in the Continental Army in the fall of 1776, a year later selected the ground at Saratoga, upon which the Americans made their stand that led to the critical surrender of General John Burgoyne. When the war shifted to the Southern theater in 1780, Kościuszko became chief engineer under General Horatio Gates. Pulaski secured an appointment as a brigadier-general of cavalry in 1777. For two years Pulaski led the American cavalry in battles ranging from Brandywine to Savannah. In leading an attack on the latter city in October 1779, the Polish count was mortally wounded. The Marquis de Lafayette, arriving in America about the same time as Pulaski, was appointed a major general by Congress and served under Washington from Brandywine in 1777 to Yorktown in 1781, except for a brief return to France in 1778, when he successfully lobbied for more aid for the Americans.

The alliance with France that the United States entered into in February 1778 proved to be the turning point of the war. From the beginning of the conflict France had been a covert supplier of money, supplies, and arms to the Americans. The alliance made the relationship one that promised not only the financial and material support of the Catholic power, but formidable military forces, as well. That the country had turned for its salvation to the power that had represented the epitome of Catholic despotism throughout colonial history did not escape the bitter criticism of American loyalists. The Pennsylvania *Ledger* reminded its readers that a mere four years previously, "the bare toleration of the Roman Catholic religion in Canada... was treated as a wicked attempt to establish a sanguinary faith, which had for ages filled the world with blood and slaughter." Now the rebel Congress had made a pact with "the most powerful and ambitious enemies of the Reformation." It could conceive of nothing worse toward the "universal re-establishment of Popery through all Christendom."[22] Benedict Arnold attempted to justify his treason as a proper response to the American bedding down with this

---

22. *Ledger*, May 13, 1778; cited in Griffin, *Catholics* 1:39.

prime enemy of "the Protestant Faith."[23] But the majority of Americans saw the alliance with France (and the later one with Catholic Spain) not as an international plot to subvert Protestantism, but as the best hope for winning the war.

Over the next four years that hope was slowly borne out. The French West Indies became America's chief trading partner as French forces increasingly gained control over the Antilles isles and the Caribbean waters. The entry of France on the side of the Americans clearly reversed the opinion of the French Canadian clergy regarding the war. As British authorities in Canada reported, whereas few of the priests had been favorable to the rebellion before 1778, once France became involved and Louis XVI reminded his former subjects in Canada that they could "never cease to be French," the clergy became supportive. In the Ohio Valley a French priest, Pierre Gibault, together with several hundred French settlers, joined the American forces under George Rogers Clark in February 1779 in the successful campaign to win control of that vital region.

Five regiments of nearly 7,000 soldiers, including a regiment of 1,400 Irishmen in French service, accompanied the French fleet to America. Over 100 chaplains came with them. Their presence quadrupled the number of priests in the area covered by the thirteen former colonies. The French steadily captured much of the British West Indies, from St. Kitts to Grenada. At the same time Spanish forces were seizing Florida from the British.

The military power that the French fleet and regiments provided was crucial in bringing about the entrapment and surrender of the principal British Army at Yorktown that effectively marked the war's end, although peace did not formally come until a year and a half later. Less than a month after Yorktown, on the eve of the no-longer-celebrated Pope's Day, there was a very odd official celebration that would have been unthinkable just a few years before: a Mass of thanksgiving held at St. Mary's Church in Philadelphia, attended by the Continental Congress, the Pennsylvania Assembly, other government officials, and the French minister who had

23. Cogliano, *No King, No Popery*, 83.

initiated the event. A French chaplain delivered the sermon in which he declared the victory at Yorktown a modern miracle, a new Jericho in which "the wonderful work of that God who guards your liberties" had brought together a French-American army from the north and a French fleet from the south to besiege and overcome the main British force in North America. Only providence could explain how two such antagonistic "nations" as the Americans and French had been able to unite so effectively to achieve victory and independence for the Americans. The dreaded "papist" power had become God's instrument for achieving the liberty that most Americans had always considered a Protestant preserve.[24]

24. *American Museum* 4 (July 1788): 28–29; cited in Griffin, *Catholics* 1:314.

EPILOGUE

THE COLONIAL
LEGACY

THE MARYLAND TRADITION

Seven months after the signing of the Peace of Paris at the end
of November 1782, John Carroll prodded John Lewis, the last
formal superior of the Maryland mission, to call a meeting of
the twenty-three priests in the new republic to consider a plan
that Carroll had devised for organizing the American Catholic
community. The suppression of the Society of Jesus and the
American Revolution had created an institutional vacuum for
American Catholics, but the Revolution itself, if it had severed
the Catholic community from its direct ecclesiastical authority in London, had also created an unprecedented opportunity
to organize the church openly throughout the former colonies,
now become states. Through the newly framed constitutions of
the states, the American Revolution, Carroll noted in a sermon,
had changed the status of Catholics from that of aliens to citizens; had transformed their situation from living "in a Country no longer foreign or unfriendly to us" to one "now become
our own."[1] That change in status for American Catholics was
a direct consequence of the extraordinary contributions, Car-

1. Undated Carroll Sermon, American Catholic Sermon Collection, Georgetown
University Special Collections.

roll suggested elsewhere, that the Catholic community, more united in its support of the Revolution than perhaps any other religious group in America, had made to the creation of the new republic. The attainment of full citizenship by Catholics was consistent with the establishment of a republic in which the state no longer privileged a particular religion or imposed a certain socioeconomic bondage upon those not professing it. Carroll extolled the neutral state, the intellectual child of the Calverts' experiment, which based government "on the attachment of mankind to their political happiness, to the security of their persons and their property, which is independent of religious doctrines, and not restrained by any."[2] No surprise then that he joined Presbyterians, Methodists, Baptists, and Quakers in successfully opposing the attempt of the Maryland Assembly in 1784 to establish a tax to provide financial support for all religions. The state had no business involving itself in the religious sphere, even as a universal benefactor. For the church there was a troubling corollary: if religion was to be a private affair in which the state had no part, then the religious community, as such, had no jurisdiction to promote the public good. This was a presupposition that would increasingly guide the institutional church in its social teaching as the nineteenth century wore on. At the same time such a leveling of the religious playing field promoted an ecumenism in which members of the different faiths could dialogue, worship together, and nurture a common culture.

Lacking close episcopal government for the century and a half that constituted the colonial period, the Catholic community in America developed a certain ecclesial independence. The clerical republican body that the subsequent meeting of clergy representatives produced reflected that tradition. The meeting, involving six priests, took place at Whitemarsh, a Jesuit plantation in Prince George's County and a central location in the Chesapeake region that had defined Catholic America during the colonial era. These representatives adopted Carroll's proposal to organize themselves into a republican body that would be charged with their financial support, both through overseeing the administration of

2. *Gazette of the United States;* cited in *Catholics in Colonial America,* by John Tracy Ellis (Baltimore: Helicon, 1965), 452.

the plantations and farms previously the property of the Society of Jesus and with the pursuit of policies that would promote "the good of Religion." The Select Body of the Clergy consisted of six representatives chosen from three districts spanning Pennsylvania and Maryland. Inherent in Carroll's rationale for the Select Body was the affirmation of a clear-cut separation of spiritual and temporal realms of the church, along with a deep distrust of the reach of the Holy See's authority. They petitioned Rome for the formal appointment of a superior with faculties to administer Confirmation and to exercise religious jurisdiction to a limited extent. But they specifically urged that the Holy See not make that superior a bishop, given the adverse feeling in American society toward prelates. Linked to this separation of realms was Carroll's belief in the fundamental right to property that helped shape the responsibilities of government and that was intrinsic to citizenship in a republic, since possession of property was the surest safeguard of the liberty a citizen needed to be independent. As with the beliefs regarding freedom of religion and the separation of church and state, this one very much grew out of the Maryland tradition that Peter Atwood and others had shaped.

That a major responsibility of the Select Body was providing the financial support for the priests' ministry was a clear indication that Carroll and the others were still assuming that the plantations would be the principal source of revenue for the institutional church, as they had been in Maryland and Pennsylvania during the colonial period. It would soon become all too evident that the plantations could not bear that burden, particularly as the number of mission stations grew exponentially, not only in cities (Boston, New York, Baltimore, the newly created District of Columbia), but in the trans-Appalachian territory that Catholics, along with other Americans, began to pour into at war's end. The congregational support that the Jesuits had first adopted as a source of funding in the parishes of Philadelphia in the late colonial period became increasingly commonplace in Catholic churches, both urban and rural, in the early nineteenth century.

As urban parishes were established in Boston, New York, Baltimore, and elsewhere, laity and (usually) their priests in those cities, as well as in Philadelphia, where churches had been organized long before the Revolution, pressed for local, or congregational, control of their religious lives. The requirements of American law, the tradition of the congregational-centered Protestant denominations, and Catholic enlightenment ideology all tended to foster the trustee system that developed as a governing structure in the public organization of Catholic churches that took place after the country achieved its independence. Carroll all too quickly realized the need for episcopal authority to put down this move toward ecclesiastical democracy. Carroll went to New York in the summer of 1787 to attempt to settle a dispute in the recently formed congregation between the parish's trustees and its pastor, Charles Whelan, the Irish Capuchin who had come to America as a chaplain with the French fleet. For his efforts, while trying to say Mass, Carroll was *twice* routed from the church by opponents of Whelan and forced to conclude the liturgy at the nearby home of the Spanish minister. He was experiencing in the ecclesiastical realm what the makers of the American Revolution were experiencing in the political: the lack of central authority to maintain order and direction. That authoritative vacuum precipitated, within the leaders of the American Catholic community, the move to create an episcopal-based hierarchy, just as it provided the motivation for the founding fathers, through the Constitution, to establish a powerful central government.

INSTITUTIONAL DEVELOPMENT

The institutional development of Catholicism very much grew out of the experience of the colonial period; it included the selection of the first American prelate by the priests in the new republic, the foundation of the first community of religious women, the creation of the first Catholic schools, the establishment of the first seminary in the United States by French Sulpicians, and the restoration of the Society of Jesus's presence in Maryland by five ex-Jesuits who had survived the suppression.

The lack of a spiritual leader with effective authority was one of the reasons that the Select Body appealed to Rome in 1788 for the appointment of a bishop. In recognition of America's republican sensibilities about independence, the petition stressed, the prelate should be an American priest elected by his peers. Rome, aware that in America it was confronted with the unprecedented situation of a tiny group of Catholics in a Protestant-dominant society that had just adopted a republican form of government, consented to the request and authorized "as a special favor and for the first time" to elect a bishop from among themselves.[3] Carroll was the overwhelming choice, receiving all but two of the twenty-six votes cast. For his see Carroll chose Baltimore, which the Revolution had made the most important urban area in the Chesapeake region, which contained the vast majority of American Catholics.

In 1790, five years after the beginning of the great migration of Maryland Catholics, Charles County became the site of the first women's religious community in America. At the end of the American Revolution, American women Mary Margaret Brent and Bernardine Teresa Matthews headed the English Carmelite monasteries at Antwerp and Hoogstraet, respectively. The two American Carmelites had been receiving pleas from Catholic clergy and laity in Maryland for the Carmel to begin a foundation there. After much deliberation the American-born superiors decided to honor the requests by sending a group of Carmelites to Maryland. As Ann Louisa Hill, a Carmelite at Hoogstraet, wrote her cousin John Carroll in August 1790, "it is a subject of joy to me to hear our Holy Faith & Religion flourishes so much in my native country; & that Religious are permited to make establishments.... I am glad our Holy Order is the first."[4] By that time Mother Bernardine had already set sail with three other Carmelites, accompanied by the ex-Jesuit Charles Neale, a native of Charles County who had been the chaplain at the Hoogstraet Carmel, to establish a monastery at Port Tobacco, close by the Neale family estate. Three of the four Carmelites, including Matthews, were Marylanders, women who had gone from Maryland in the late colonial period to pursue their education and enter the convent. Now they were returning home to establish something that had been unthinkable for Catholics to do when they had last been there. The

3. *Atti* (1789), 369–78; quoted in Peter Guilday, *The Life and Times of John Carroll: Archbishop of Baltimore, 1735–1815* (New York: Encyclopedia Press, 1922), 1:352. In fact, there were two other episcopal elections, in 1793 and 1794, of coadjutors to succeed Carroll as ordinary.
4. August 8, 1790, Archives of the Archdiocese of Baltimore, 4-G-4, Associated Archives of St. Mary's Seminary and University.

trans-Atlantic recusant education that Maryland Catholic gentry sought for their children now, in a way, became the source for the introduction of formal religious life for females in America.

Four years before Neale led the quartet of Carmelites to Charles County, John Carroll had written a Roman official that a shortage of priests had led him to conclude that "a school where boys will be trained in piety and in the discipline of the *litterae humaniores*" was an absolute prerequisite as a nursery for vocations to the priesthood. As the convent schools on the Continent had prepared scores of Maryland girls for the religious life, so St. Omer's and other recusant schools had served as the minor seminary for Maryland boys who had entered the Jesuits and other religious orders. Thanks to the religious liberty that Catholics were finally enjoying, Carroll planned to open at Georgetown an academy to provide for the Catholics of the new republic what the recusant schools had offered to Carroll and his fellow Marylanders during the colonial period, but now on a much larger scale to meet a much larger need in a rapidly expanding nation. Carroll also was concerned about providing an American Catholic education for girls. When the Carmelites decided in 1790 to begin a foundation in Maryland, Carroll secured for them a dispensation from Rome in order that the contemplative nuns might open a school for girls. The mother superior, Bernardine Matthews, politely but firmly informed the bishop that they had come to America not to teach, but to pray. Teaching was not congruent with the contemplative nature of their vocation. Carroll had to wait another decade for Catholic education to become available for young women. In 1799 the Poor Clares began a school next to Carroll's academy that eventually became the Georgetown Visitation School.

The creation of an indigenous seminary for the training of American priests had a serendipitous origin. When Carroll was in England for his consecration as bishop, the superior of the Sulpicians, clearly seeking a refuge for his imperiled members in a France now itself torn apart by revolution, offered to provide personnel to establish a seminary in the new see of Baltimore. Carroll was quick to accept the offer. The Sulpicians came to Baltimore in 1790 to establish St. Mary's, as well as to provide much of the faculty for Georgetown during the decade.

In the sixteenth and seventeenth centuries France had been a major haven for Catholic refugees from the revolution that was the English Reformation. Now, in the last decade of the eighteenth century French Catholics fleeing from a new revolution found refuge in the most unlikely of places: the former British colonies that had had, on the whole, no place for Catholics in their societies. This new set of French clergy would be but the first wave of French priests and religious that, over the course of the next two generations, would play a disproportionately large role in molding the institutional matrix and culture of the expanding American Catholic community.

In 1802 six ex-Jesuits in Maryland petitioned John Carroll to solicit the superior general of the Society of Jesus in Russia (where the society had survived the suppression because Catherine the Great valued the Jesuit schools in Byelorussia too much to allow the papal brief to be promulgated and carried out) for permission to rejoin the Society. When Carroll failed to act upon the request, the six renewed their plea eight months later, now joined by four other priests and five seminarians from St. Mary's. This time Carroll took action and secured the Jesuit general's approval for the ex-Jesuits to renew their vows and to receive new members. In 1805 five of the ten surviving Jesuits in America reentered the Society. A year later, at Georgetown, a novitiate was established. Eight of the first novices were alumni of Georgetown College.

THOSE BEYOND THE PALE

The institutional presence of Catholicism in British America was geographically a very limited one, confined, with the exception of Philadelphia, to the rural areas of southern and Eastern Shore Maryland as well as southeastern Pennsylvania. Such a limited presence, in all likelihood, reached but a minority of the Catholics who settled in the colonies that became the United States of America. For too many colonial Catholics there was no priest or church available to provide for the central life passages of birth, marriage, and death. In such an institutionless environment, intermarriage promoted conversions to other faiths that did have an institutional footprint. The endemic discrimination that Catholics

faced throughout the colonies merely abetted the trend. The negative
result was the loss of a Catholic identity for the thousands of Irish and
other ethnics who, for varying reasons, put down stakes in places beyond
the pale of the institutional church. For many Irish Catholics, particularly in the southern colonies, this loss of Catholic identity manifested itself in the name-changing to an English- or Scotch-sounding one. David
Doyle estimates that somewhere in the neighborhood of 45,000 Irish
Catholics (35 percent of all Irish Catholic immigrants, who were a small
minority [25 percent or so] of all Irish immigrants) became Protestants
during the colonial era. That constituted about 12 percent of the Irish
population in the country in 1790.[5]

THE MARYLAND DIASPORA

Central to Catholic penetration into the new lands south and west was
the Maryland Catholic diaspora that originated immediately following
the Revolution. The overpopulated southern Maryland region with its
tobacco-exhausted land found itself in the 1780s in a severe economic
depression that struck particularly hard at the majority who were small
farmers. For more and more people of the region, the virgin land to the
west that the Peace of Paris had just opened up proved to be a powerful
magnet. Charles County in just one decade, the 1790s, lost 7 percent of
its residents, and the exodus continued in force over the next half century. Between 1790 and 1850 the county lost approximately 45 percent of
its white population. In the two decades between 1790 and 1810, Thomas
Spalding estimated, between one-quarter and one-third of the Maryland
Catholic community abandoned the state. The emigration began on a
large scale in 1785 when twenty families headed to central Kentucky and
its rich lands available "for almost nothing."[6] Multi-family migrations
from Maryland to Kentucky became a spring ritual over the next two
decades, with the scale of migration becoming larger after 1795, when

5. David Doyle is cited in *The Irish Diaspora: A Primer,* by Donald N. Akenson (Toronto: P. D.
Meany, 1993), 250.
6. Stephen Badin; quoted by Thomas W. Spalding in "The Maryland Catholic Diaspora," *U.S.
Catholic Historian* 8 (Fall 1989): 164.

the Treaty of Greenville eliminated the threat of Indian attacks upon the caravans. By 1807 Stephen Badin was ministering to 972 families in twelve counties of Kentucky. In just fifteen years Catholic settlement in Kentucky had tripled. Virtually all were transplants from Maryland. For many Catholic families with deep roots in Maryland, by 1830 a remarkable majority of their members had made the move across the mountains to Kentucky. Thus the census of that year recorded twenty-one Mudd households in Kentucky and only eight remaining in their native Charles County. For the Mattinglys of St. Mary's County, the removal was much greater, with nearly six times as many households in Kentucky as in Maryland. The Coomeses, Spaldings, Lancasters saw a similar pattern of displacement. In general this was a migration of small farmers, as the few slaves they took with them reveals. A more affluent family, such as the Jenkinses, experienced much less movement. As for the elite Catholic families—the Fenwicks, Brookes, Diggeses, and Neales—they had the means to stay and, with few exceptions, did so.

Out of the Catholic settlement around Bardstown came no fewer than three of the earliest sisterhoods produced in Catholic America: the Sisters of Loretto, the Sisters of Charity of Nazareth, and the Dominican Sisters. Those religious communities also became educational pioneers in the trans-Appalachian region by establishing female academies. Within a radius of twenty miles, Dominican fathers and diocesan priests founded three colleges for males between 1808 and 1821.

For many, Kentucky proved to be but the way station to further migrations that took Maryland Catholics into Illinois, Missouri, Indiana, and eventually Texas. Nor was Kentucky the only destination that Marylanders set out for, beginning as early as the 1770s, when Joseph Hamilton of Charles County moved his family to Louisiana. Other Maryland Catholics followed the Hamiltons; still others chose Georgia and Mississippi to begin life anew. The family migrations persisted throughout the antebellum era. And Catholic institutions tended to follow these Catholic communities as they expanded west- and southward.

Many of the 20 percent of the Maryland Catholic community in 1785 who were African slaves had their own diaspora experience—not originating in their own free decisions to seek a better life elsewhere,

but rather from forced migrations that were either part of owners transplanting themselves, their families, and their slaves to the new lands of
the south and west or, much more often, as the result of being part of
the slave trade that shifted a large portion of the slave population from
the Chesapeake region to the deep South in the early nineteenth century.
Ironically the biggest slave trader proved to be the Maryland Jesuits, who
by the antebellum period were among the largest slaveholders in the nation. Shifting priorities and pressing financial difficulties forced the Jesuit superiors in Maryland to engage in a series of slave sales, culminating
in 1838 with the disposing of nearly 300 slaves to Louisiana. That event,
scandalizing Protestants and Catholics alike, provided fodder for the
anti-Catholicism restirring in the 1830s.

RESURGENT MEMORIES

The Catholic colonial experience had embedded a deep memory of being
regarded and treated as inside aliens, a community representing a threat
to the beliefs and interests of the larger society. Catholics would initially
suppress that memory in the flush of the good feelings that Catholics,
both American and European, had awakened in America by the decisive
part they had played in the creation of the republic. By the second quarter of the nineteenth century that memory would be all-too-painfully
revived as Catholic immigration (40 percent of the total), Catholic expansion in general, and a new evangelical awakening set loose once more
the specter of "Papist devils" that would haunt the popular mind until
the Civil War and cause the Catholic community, once more in reaction,
to close in on itself. One of the victims of this assault and inward turning
would be the Maryland tradition.

BIBLIOGRAPHY

PRIMARY SOURCES

Brown, William Hand, ed. *Archives of Maryland.* 72 vols. Baltimore: Maryland Historical Society, 1883–.

Curran, Robert Emmett, ed. *American Jesuit Spirituality: The Maryland Tradition, 1634–1900.* Rahway, N.J.: Paulist Press, 1988.

Elias, Robert H., and Eugene D. Finch, eds. *Letters of Thomas Attwood Digges (1742–1821).* Columbia: University of South Carolina Press, 1982.

Griffin, Martin I. J. *Catholics in the American Revolution.* 3 vols. Philadelphia: The Author, 1907–11.

Hall, Clayton Colman, ed. *Narratives of Early Maryland, 1633–1684.* New York: Charles Scribner's Sons, 1910.

Hanley, Thomas O'Brien, ed. *John Carroll Papers.* 3 vols. Notre Dame: University of Notre Dame, 1976.

Hughes, Thomas. *The History of the Society of Jesus in North America. Vol. I.* Documents. London: Longmans, Green. Part I, 1908; Part II, 1910.

Miller, Kerby A., Arnold Schrier, Bruce D. Boling, and David N. Doyle. *Irish Immigrants in the Land of Canaan: Letters and Memoirs from Colonial and Revolutionary America, 1675–1815.* New York: Oxford University Press, 2003.

Onuf, Peter, ed. *Maryland and the Empire, 1773: The Antilon-First Citizen Letters.* Baltimore: The Johns Hopkins University Press, 1974.

White, Andrew. *Declaratio Coloniae Domini Baronis de Baltimore.* Baltimore: Maryland Historical Society, 1874.

———. *Relatio Itineris in Marylandium.* Baltimore: Maryland Historical Society, 1874.

SECONDARY SOURCES

Books

Anderson, Fred. *Crucible of War: The Seven Years' War and the Fate of Empire in British North America, 1754–1766.* New York: Alfred A. Knopf, 2000.

Akenson, Donald H. *The Irish Diaspora: A Primer.* Toronto: P. D. Meany, 1993.

———. *If the Irish Ran the World: Montserrat, 1630–1730.* Montreal and Kingston: McGill-Queen's University Press, 1997.

Aveling, Hugh. *Northern Catholics: The Catholic Recusants of the North Riding of Yorkshire, 1558–1790.* London and Dublin: Chapman, 1966.

Balmer, Randall H. *A Perfect Babel of Confusion: Dutch Religion and English Culture in the Middle Colonies.* New York: Oxford University Press, 1989.

Beckles, Hilary. *White Servitude and Black Slavery in Barbados, 1627–1715.* Knoxville: University of Tennessee Press, 1989.

———. *A History of Barbados: From Amerindian Settlement to Caribbean Single Market.* New York: Cambridge University Press, 2006.

Beitzell, Edwin W. *The Jesuit Missions of St. Mary's County, Maryland.* Abell, Md.: Edwin W. Beitzell, 1960. Revised edition 1976.

Beneke, Chris, and Christopher S. Grenda, eds. *The First Prejudice: Religious Tolerance and Intolerance in Early America.* Philadelphia: University of Pennsylvania Press, 2011.

Bossy, John. *The English Catholic Community, 1570–1850.* New York and Oxford: Oxford University Press, 1976.

Brebner, John Bartlet. *New England's Outpost: Acadia Before the Conquest of Canada.* Master's thesis, Columbia University, 1927. Reprint, New York: Burt Franklin, 1973.

———. *The Neutral Yankees of Nova Scotia: A Marginal Colony during the Revolutionary Years.* New York: Russell and Russell, 1937. Reprint, New York: Columbia University Press,1970.

Brugger, Robert J. *Maryland: A Middle Temperament, 1634–1980.* Baltimore: The Johns Hopkins University Press, 1988.

Burnard, Trevor. *Creole Gentlemen: The Maryland Elite, 1691–1776.* New York: Routledge, 2002.

Campbell, Kenneth L. *The Intellectual Struggle of the English Papists in the Seventeenth Century: The Catholic Dilemma.* Lewiston, Maine: Mellen, 1986.

Caraman, Philip. *The Years of Siege: Catholic Life from James I to Cromwell.* London: Longmans, 1966.

Carr, Lois Green, and David William Jordan. *Maryland's Revolution of Government, 1689–1692.* Ithaca: Cornell University Press, 1974.

Carr, Lois Green, Russell R. Menard, and Lorena S. Walsh. *Robert Cole's World: Agriculture and Society in Early Maryland.* Chapel Hill: University of North Carolina Press, 1991.

Carr, Lois Green, Philip D. Morgan, and Jean B. Russo, eds. *Colonial Chesapeake Society.* Chapel Hill: University of North Carolina Press for the Institute of Early American History, 1988.

Casway, Jerrold I. *Owen Roe O'Neill and the Struggle for Catholic Ireland*. Philadelphia: University of Pennsylvania Press, 1984.

Clarke, Aidan. *The Old English in Ireland, 1625–42*. Ithaca: Cornell University Press, 1966.

Clemens, Paul G. E. *The Atlantic Economy and Colonial Maryland's Eastern Shore: From Tobacco to Grain*. Ithaca: Cornell University Press, 1980.

Codignola, Luca. *The Coldest Harbour of the Land: Simon Stock and Lord Baltimore's Colony in Newfoundland, 1621–1629*. Kingston and Montreal: McGill-Queen's University Press, 1988.

Cogliano, Francis D. *No King, No Popery: Anti-Catholicism in Revolutionary New England*. Westport, Conn.: Greenwood Press, 1995.

Curran, Robert Emmett. *Shaping American Catholicism: Maryland and New York, 1805–1915*. Washington, D.C.: The Catholic University of America Press, 2012.

Cushner, Nicholas P. *Why Have You Come Here? The Jesuits and the First Evangelization of Native America*. New York: Oxford University Press, 2006.

Davis, Cyprian. *The History of Black Catholics in the United States*. New York: Crossroads, 1990.

Dolan, Frances E. *Whores of Babylon: Catholicism, Gender, and Seventeenth-Century Print Culture*. Ithaca and London: Cornell University Press, 1999.

Dolan, Jay P. *The American Catholic Experience: A History from Colonial Times to the Present*. New York: Doubleday, 1985.

Duncan, Jason K. *Citizens or Papists? The Politics of Anti-Catholicism in New York, 1685–1821*. New York: Fordham University Press, 2005.

Dunn, Richard S. *Sugar and Slaves: The Rise of the Planter Class in the English West Indies, 1624–1713*. Chapel Hill: University of North Carolina Press for the Institute of Early American History and Culture, 1972.

Elliott, Marianne. *The Catholics of Ulster: A History*. New York: Basic Books, 2001.

Ellis, John Tracy. *Catholics in Colonial America*. Baltimore: Helicon, 1965.

Faragher, John Mack. *A Great and Noble Scheme: The Tragic Story of the Expulsion of the French Canadians from their American Homeland*. New York: Norton, 2006.

Farrelly, Maura Jane. *Papist Patriots: The Making of an American Catholic Identity*. New York: Oxford University Press, 2012.

Fergus, Howard A. *Montserrat: History of a Caribbean Colony*. London: Macmillan Caribbean, 1994.

Fitzpatrick, Brendan. *Seventeenth-Century Ireland: The War of Religions*. Totowa, N.J.: Barnes and Noble, 1989.

Foley, Henry. *Records of the English Province of the Society of Jesus*. 8 vols. London: Burns and Oates, 1877–1883.

Foster, R. F. *Modern Ireland: 1600–1972*. New York: Penguin, 1988.

Fraser, Antonia. *Faith and Treason: The Story of the Gunpowder Plot*. New York: Doubleday, 1997.

Geiger, Mary Virginia. *Daniel Carroll: A Framer of the Constitution*. Washington. D.C.: The Catholic University of America Press, 1943.

Gillespie, Raymond. *Devoted People: Belief and Religion in Early Modern Ireland*. New York: Manchester University Press, 1997.

Gragg, Larry Dale. *Englishmen Transplanted: The English Colonization of Barbados, 1627–1660*. New York: Oxford University Press, 2003.

Guilday, Peter. *The Life and Times of John Carroll: Archbishop of Baltimore, 1735–1815*. New York: Encyclopedia Press, 1922.

Haigh, Christopher. *Reformation and Resistance in Tudor Lancashire*. New York: Cambridge University Press, 1975.

Hamshere, Cyril. *The British in the Caribbean*. Cambridge, Mass.: Harvard University Press, 1972.

Hanley, Thomas O'Brien. *Their Rights and Liberties: The Beginnings of Religious and Political Freedom in Maryland*. Chicago: Loyola University Press, 1959. Reprint, 1984.

———. *American Revolution and Religion, 1770–1800*. Washington, D.C.: The Catholic University of America Press, 1971.

———. *Charles Carroll of Carrollton: The Making of a Revolutionary Gentleman*. Chicago: Loyola University Press, 1982.

———. *Revolutionary Statesman: Charles Carroll and the War*. Chicago: Loyola University Press, 1983.

Hanson, Charles P. *Necessary Virtue: The Pragmatic Origins of Religious Liberty in New England*. Charlottesville: University of Virginia Press, 1998.

Hatch, Nathan O. *The Sacred Cause of Liberty: Republican Thought and the Millennium in Revolutionary New England*. New Haven: Yale University Press, 1977.

Havran, Martin J. *The Catholics in Caroline England*. Stanford, Calif.: Stanford University Press, 1962.

Hennesey, James. *American Catholics: A History of the Roman Catholic Community in the United States*. New York: Oxford University Press, 1981.

Hibbard, Caroline M. *Charles I and the Popish Plot*. Chapel Hill: University of North Carolina Press, 1983.

Hoffman, Ronald. *A Spirit of Dissension: Economics, Politics, and the Revolution in Maryland*. Baltimore and London: The Johns Hopkins University Press, 1973.

———. *Princes of Ireland, Planters of Maryland: A Carroll Saga, 1500–1782*. Chapel Hill: University of North Carolina Press, 2000.

Hoffman, Ronald, and Peter J. Albert, eds. *Religion in a Revolutionary Age*. Charlottesville: University of Virginia Press, 1994.

Holmes, Peter. *Resistance and Compromise: The Political Thought of the Elizabethan Catholics*. Cambridge and New York: Cambridge University Press, 1982.

Horn, James P. P. *Adapting to a New World: English Society in the Seventeenth Century Chesapeake*. Chapel Hill: University of North Carolina Press, 1994.

Hughes, Thomas. *The History of the Society of Jesus in North America: Colonial and Federal.* Text. Vol. 1, *From the First Colonization till 1645.* London: Longmans, Green, 1908. Vol. 2, *From 1645 till 1773.* New York: Longmans, Green, 1917.

Kerr, Wilfred Brenton. *The Maritime Provinces of British North America and the American Revolution.* New York: Russell and Russell, 1941.

Kidd, Thomas. *The Protestant Interest: New England After Puritanism.* New Haven: Yale University Press, 2004.

————. *God of Liberty: A Religious History of the American Revolution.* New York: Basic Books, 2010.

Krugler, John D. *English and Catholic: The Lords Baltimore in the Seventeenth Century.* Baltimore and London: The Johns Hopkins University Press, 2004.

Kupke, Raymond J., ed. *American Catholic Preaching and Piety in the Time of John Carroll.* Lanham, Md.: University Press of America, 1991.

Land, Aubrey C. *Colonial Maryland: A History.* Millwood, N.Y.: KTO Press, 1981.

Lee, Jean B. *The Price of Nationhood: The American Revolution in Charles County.* New York and London: W. W. Norton, 1994.

Linck, Joseph C. *Fully Instructed and Vehemently Influenced: Catholic Preaching in Anglo-Colonial America.* Philadelphia: St. Joseph's University Press, 2002.

Lippy, Charles H., Robert Choquette, and Stafford Poole. *Christianity Comes to the Americas, 1492–1776.* New York: Paragon, 1992.

Main, Gloria L. *Tobacco Colony: Life in Early Maryland, 1650–1720.* Princeton: Princeton University Press, 1982.

McGrath, Patrick. *Papists and Puritans Under Elizabeth I.* London: Blandford, 1967.

McGreevy, John T. *Catholicism and American Freedom: A History.* New York: Norton, 2003.

Melville, Annabelle M. *John Carroll of Baltimore: Founder of the American Catholic Hierarchy.* New York: Charles Scribner's, 1955.

Metzger, Charles H. *The Quebec Act: A Primary Cause of the American Revolution.* New York: U.S. Catholic Historical Society, 1936.

————. *Catholics and the American Revolution: A Study in Religious Climate.* Chicago: Loyola University Press, 1962.

Meyers, Debra. *Common Whores, Vertuous Women, and Loving Wives: Free Will Christian Women in Colonial Maryland.* Bloomington: Indiana University Press, 2003.

Mullett, Michael A. *Catholics in Britain and Ireland, 1558–1829.* New York: St. Martin's Press, 1998.

Murphy, Thomas. *Jesuit Slaveholding in Maryland, 1717–1838.* New York: Routledge, 2001.

Norman, Edward. *Roman Catholicism in England from the Elizabethan Settlement to the Second Vatican Council.* Oxford and New York: Oxford University Press, 1985.

O'Callaghan, Sean. *To Hell or Barbados.* Dingle: Brandon, 2000.

O'Farrell, Patrick. *Ireland's English Question: Anglo-Irish Relations, 1534–1970*. New York: Schocken, 1971.

O'Rourke, Timothy, J., ed. *Colonial Source Records: Southern Maryland Catholic Families*. Parsons, Kans.: Brefney Press, 1981.

———. *Catholic Families of Southern Maryland: Records of St. Mary's County in the Eighteenth Century*. Baltimore: Genealogical Publishing Co., 1985.

Osborne, Francis J. *The History of the Catholic Church in Jamaica*. Chicago: Loyola University Press, 1988.

O'Shaughnessy, Andrew Jackson. *An Empire Divided: The American Revolution and the British Caribbean*. Philadelphia: University of Pennsylvania Press, 2000.

Peterman, Thomas Joseph. *Catholics in Colonial Delmarva*. Devon, Penn.: Cooke, 1996.

Pointer, Richard W. *Protestant Pluralism and the New York Experience: A Study of Eighteenth-Century Religious Diversity*. Bloomington: Indiana University Press, 1988.

Questier, Michael. *Catholicism and Community in Early Modern England: Politics, Aristocratic Patronage and Religion, 1550–1640*. Cambridge: Cambridge University Press, 2006.

Quinn, David Beers, *England and the Discovery of America, 1481–1620*. New York: Alfred A. Knopf, 1974.

———, ed. *Early Maryland in a Wider World*. Detroit: Wayne State University Press, 1982.

Rawlyk, George A. *Nova Scotia's Massachusetts: A Study of Massachusetts–Nova Scotia Relations, 1630 to 1784*. Montreal and London: McGill-Queen's University Press, 1973.

Riordan, Timothy B. *The Plundering Time: Maryland and the English Civil War, 1645–1646*. Baltimore: Maryland Historical Society, 2004.

Ritchie, Robert C. *The Duke's Province: A Study of New York Politics and Society, 1664–1690*. Chapel Hill: University of North Carolina Press, 1977.

Rose, Elliot. *Cases of Conscience: Alternatives Open to Recusants and Puritans under Elizabeth I and James I*. Cambridge: Cambridge University Press, 1975.

Schultz. Edward T. *History of Freemasonry in Maryland*. Baltimore: J. H. Medairy, 1884.

Shea, John Gilmary. *The History of the Catholic Church in the United States*. Vol. 1. New York: J. G. Shea, 1886.

Smith, John Talbot. *The Catholic Church in New York*. Vol 1. New York: Hall and Locke, 1908.

Spalding, Thomas W. *The Premier See: A History of the Archdiocese of Baltimore, 1789–1989*. Baltimore and London: The Johns Hopkins University Press, 1989.

Steffen, Charles G. *From Gentlemen to Townsmen: The Gentry of Baltimore County, Maryland, 1660–1776*. Lexington: University of Kentucky Press, 1993.

Tavard, George H. *The Seventeenth-Century Tradition: A Study in Recusant Thought.* Leiden: E. J. Brill, 1978.

Tomlins, Christopher. *Freedom Bound: Law, Labor, and Civic Identity in Colonizing English America, 1580–1865.* New York: Cambridge University Press, 2010.

Walch, Timothy. *Catholicism in America: A Social History.* Malabar, Fla.: R. E. Krieger, 1989.

———, ed. *Early American Catholicism, 1634–1820: Selected Historical Essays.* New York: Garland, 1988.

Walsh, Richard, and William Lloyd Fox, eds. *Maryland: A History, 1632–1974.* Baltimore: Maryland Historical Society, 1974.

Whitman, T. Stephen. *Challenging Slavery in the Chesapeake: Black and White Resistance to Human Bondage, 1775–1865.* Baltimore: Maryland Historical Society, 2007.

Articles, Dissertations, and Theses

Abromitis, Carol N. "Catholicism in Maryland in the Seventeenth Century." *Recusant History* 29 (May 2009): 355–66.

Akenson, Donald Harman. "Why the Accepted Estimates of the Ethnicity of the American People, 1790, Are Unacceptable." *William and Mary Quarterly* 41 (January 1984): 102–29.

Alpert, Jonathan L. "The Origin of Slavery in the United States: The Maryland Precedent." *American Journal of Legal History* (July 1970).

Axtell, James. "White Legend: The Jesuit Missions in Maryland." *Maryland Historical Magazine* 14 (July 1986): 1–7.

Balmer, Randall H. "Traitors and Papists: The Religious Dimensions of Leisler's Rebellion." *New York History* (October 1989): 341–72.

Beckles, Hilary McDonald. "A 'Riotous and Unruly Lot': Irish Indentured Servants and Freemen in the English West Indies, 1644–1713." *William and Mary Quarterly* 47 (1990): 506.

Bergmann, Mathias D. "Being the Other: Catholicism, Anglicanism, and Constructs of Britishness in Colonial Maryland, 1689–1763." Ph.D. diss., University of Washington State, 2004.

Binzley, Ronald A. "Ganganelli's Disaffected Children: The Ex-Jesuits and the Shaping of Early American Catholicism, 1773–1790." *U.S. Catholic Historian* 26 (Spring 2008): 47–77.

———. "Ganganelli's Disaffected Children: The Suppressed English Jesuit Province and the Shaping of American Catholicism, 1762–1817." Ph.D. diss., University of Wisconsin-Madison, 2011.

Buomi, Patricia U., and Peter R. Eisenstadt. "Church Adherence in the Eighteenth-Century British American Colonies." *William and Mary Quarterly* 39 (April 1982): 245–86.

Burnard, Trevor. "A Colonial Elite: Wealthy Marylanders, 1691–1776." Ph.D. diss.,
The Johns Hopkins University, 1988.

———. "A Tangled Causiary? Associational Networks of the Maryland Elite,
1691–1776." *Journal of Southern History* 61 (February 1995): 17–44.

Carr, Lois Green, and Russell R. Menard. "Wealth and Welfare in Early Maryland:
Evidence from St. Mary's County." *William and Mary Quarterly* 56 (January
1999): 95–120.

Carr, Lois Green, and Lorena S. Walsh. "Inventories and the Analysis of Wealth
and Cosmopolitan Patterns in St. Mary's Country, Maryland, 1658–1777." *Historical Methods* (Spring 1980).

Carragielo, Michael L. "Runnymeade or Rome? Thomas Copley, Magna Carta, and
In Coena Domini." *Maryland Historian* (Fall and Winter 1985): 59–69.

Casino, Joseph J. "Anti-Popery in Colonial Pennsylvania." *Pennsylvania Magazine of
History and Biography* 105 (1981): 279–309.

Clancy, Thomas H. "English Catholics and the Papal Deposing Power, 1570–1640."
Recusant History 6 (October 1961): 114–40.

———. "Papist-Protestant-Puritan: English Religious Taxonomy, 1565–1665."
Recusant History 21 (October 1976): 227–53.

Clark, Michael D. "Jonathan Boucher and the Toleration of Roman Catholics in
Maryland." *Maryland Historical Magazine* 71 (Summer 1976): 194–203.

Cogliano, Francis D. "To Obey Jesus Christ and George Washington: Massachusetts, Catholicism, and the Eastern Indians during the American Revolution."
Maine Historical Society Quarterly 32 (1992): 108–33.

Conley, Rory T. "Robert Cole's Religion: The Religious Practice of Maryland's First
Catholics." *Catholic Historical Society of Washington Newsletter* (July–December
2001): 2–16.

Curran, Robert Emmett. "The Jesuits as Educators in Anglo-America." In *Jesuit
Encounters in the New World: Jesuit Chroniclers, Geographers, Educators and Mis-
sionaries in the Americas, 1549–1767,* edited by Joseph A. Gagliano and Charles E.
Ronan, 195–207. Rome: Institutum Historicum, Jesuit Institute of History, 1997.

Duncan, Jason K. "A Most Democratic Class: New York Catholics and the Early
American Republic." Ph.D. diss., University of Iowa, 1999.

Ebeling, Robert. "Education and Religious Toleration in Seventeenth-Century
Maryland." Ph.D. diss., University of Maryland, 1991.

Everstine, Carl N. "Maryland's Toleration Act: An Appraisal." *Maryland Historical
Magazine* (Summer 1984): 99–116.

Farrelly, Maura Jane. "Papist Patriots: Catholic Identity and Revolutionary Ideology
in Maryland." Ph.D. diss., Emory University, 2002.

Fausz, J. Frederick. "Present at the 'Creation': The Chesapeake World That Greeted
the Maryland Colonists." *Maryland Historical Magazine* 79 (Spring 1984).

Feist, Timothy Philip. "'A Stirring Among the Dry Bones': George Whitfield and the Great Awakening in Maryland." *Maryland Historical Magazine* 95 (Winter 2000): 388–408.

Feres, Angela. "Father Andrew White, the Jesuit Order, and the Marketing of Colonial Maryland." Ph.D. diss., Claremont Graduate University, 2011.

Flanagan, Charles M. "'The Sweets of Independence': A Reading of the 'James Carroll Daybook,' 1714–1721." Ph.D. diss., University of Maryland, College Park, 2005.

Fogarty, Gerald P. "Property and Religious Liberty in Colonial Maryland Catholic Thought." *Catholic Historical Review* 72 (October 1986): 573–600.

Francis, Charles Ellias. "Anti-Catholicism in Maryland, 1632–1776." Ph.D. diss., Howard University, 1942.

Frost, J. William. "Religious Liberty in Early Pennsylvania." *Pennsylvania Magazine of History and Biography* 105 (October 1981): 419–51.

Gleissner, Richard A. "Religious Causes of the Glorious Revolution in Maryland." *Maryland Historical Magazine* 64 (Winter 1969).

Graham, Michael. "Lord Baltimore's Pious Enterprise: Toleration and Community in Colonial Maryland, 1634–1724." Ph.D. diss., University of Michigan, 1983.

———. "Churching the Unchurched: The Establishment in Maryland, 1692–1724." *Maryland Historical Magazine* 83 (Winter 1988): 397–426.

———. "Meetinghouse and Chapel: Religion and Community in Seventeenth-Century Maryland." In *Colonial Chesapeake Society*, edited by Lois Green Carr, Philip D. Morgan, and Jean B. Russo. Chapel Hill: University of North Carolina Press for the Institute of Early American History, 1988, 242–74.

———. "'The Collapse of Equity': Catholic and Quaker Dissenters in Maryland, 1692–1720." *Maryland Historical Magazine* 88 (Spring 1993): 5–25.

———. "Popish Plots: Protestant Fears in Early Colonial Maryland, 1676–1689." *Catholic Historical Review* 79 (April 1993): 197–216.

Grimes, Robert R. "The Emergence of Catholic Music and Ritual in Colonial Maryland." *American Catholic Studies* 114 (Summer 2003): 1–35.

Hardy, Beatriz Betancourt. "Papists in a Protestant Age: The Catholic Gentry and Community in Colonial Maryland, 1689–1776." Ph.D. diss., University of Maryland, 1993.

———. "Religious Practices of Maryland Catholics, 1689 to 1776. *American Catholic Studies Newsletter* (Spring 1993): 10–12.

———. "A Papist in a Protestant Age: The Case of Richard Bennett, 1667–1749." *Journal of Southern History* 60 (May 1994): 203–28.

———. "Roman Catholics, Not Papists: Catholic Identity in Maryland, 1689–1776." *Maryland Historical Magazine* 92 (Summer 1997): 138–61.

———. "Women and the Catholic Church in Maryland, 1689–1776." *Maryland Historical Magazine* 94 (Winter 1999): 397–418.

———. "The Papists . . . have shewn a laudable Care and concern': Catholicism,

Anglicanism, and Slave Religion in Colonial Maryland." *Maryland Historical Magazine* (Spring 2003): 4–33.

Heinz, Helen. "'We are all as one fish in the sea…': Catholicism in Protestant Pennsylvania, 1730–1790." Ph.D. diss., Temple University, 2008.

Hennesey, James. "Several Youth Sent from Here: Native-Born Priests and Religious of English America, 1634–1776." In *Studies in Catholic History in Honor of John Tracy Ellis*, 1–26. Wilmington, Del.: Michael Glazier, 1985.

———. "Catholicism in the English Colonies." In *Encyclopedia of the American Religious Experience: Studies of Traditions and Movements*, edited by Charles H. Lippy and Peter W. Williams, 1: 345–55. New York: Charles Scribner's Sons, 1988.

Hoffman, Ronald. "'Marylando-Hibernus': Charles Carroll the Settler, 1660–1720." *William and Mary Quarterly* 45 (April 1988): 207–36.

Hughes, Thomas. "Educational Convoys to Europe in the Olden Time." *American Ecclesiastical Review* 29 (1903): 24–39.

Johnson, Whittington B. "The Origin and Nature of African Slavery in Seventeenth-Century Maryland." *Maryland Historical Magazine* 73 (Fall 1978): 238–45.

Johnston, Shona Helen. "Papists in a Protestant World: The Catholic Anglo-Atlantic in the Seventeenth Century." Ph.D. diss., Georgetown University, 2011.

Jordan, David W. "A Plea for Maryland Catholics." *Maryland Historical Magazine* 67 (Winter 1972): 429–35.

Keane, James Patrick. "The Status of Catholics in Maryland, 1689–1760." Master's thesis, The Catholic University of America, 1950.

Kempski, Leonard John. "A History of Catholicism in Delaware, 1704–1868." Master's thesis, University of Delaware, 1955.

Koning, Gretchen Z. "The Transformation of the Catholic Community: Maryland, 1750–1840." Ph.D. diss., Harvard University, 1993.

Krugler, John B. "Lord Baltimore, Roman Catholics, and Toleration: Religious Policy in Maryland During the Early Catholic Years, 1634–1649." *Catholic Historical Review* 65 (January 1979): 49–75.

———. "'With Promise of Liberty in Religion': The Catholic Lords Baltimore and Toleration in Seventeenth-Century Maryland, 1634–1692." *Maryland Historical Magazine* 79 (Spring 1984): 21–43.

Krugler, John B., and Timothy B. Riordan. "'Scandalous and Offensive to the Government': The 'Popish Chappel' at St. Mary's City, Maryland and the Society of Jesus, 1634 to 1705." *Mid-America* (October 1991): 187–208.

Lahey, Raymond J. "The Role of Religion in Lord Baltimore's Colonial Enterprise." *Maryland Historical Magazine* 72 (Winter 1977): 492–511.

Lowe, William W. "The Master of the Ark: A Seventeenth-Century Chronicle." *Maryland Historical Magazine* (Fall 2000): 261–89.

Lurie, Maxine N. "Theory and Practice of Religious Toleration in the Seventeenth

Century: The Proprietary Colonies as a Case Study." *Maryland Historical Magazine* 79 (Summer 1984): 117–25.

Maloney, Eric John. "Papists and Puritans in Early Maryland: Religion in the Forging of a Provincial Society, 1632–1665." Ph.D. diss., State University of New York, Stonybrook, 1996.

McAleer, Margaret H. "Conewago, Pennsylvania: Transmission of Catholic Culture in Rural Pennsylvania, 1741–1901." Master's thesis, Georgetown University, 1984.

———. "Civil Strangers: The Irish in Philadelphia During the Early National Period." Ph.D. diss., Georgetown University, 1997.

McConville, Brendan. "Pope's Day Revisited: 'Popular' Culture Reconsidered." *Explorations in Early American Culture* 4 (2000): 258–80.

McGrath, Patrick. "Elizabethan Catholicism: A Reconsideration." *Journal of Ecclesiastical History* (July 1984): 414–28.

McMaster, Richard K. "Parish in Arms: A Study of Father John Mackenna and the Mohawk Valley Loyalists, 1773–1778." *Historical Records and Studies* 45 (1957).

Menard, Russell R. "Maryland's 'Time of Troubles': Sources of Political Disorder in Early St. Mary's." *Maryland Historical Magazine* 76 (June 1981).

———. "Population, Economy, and Society in Seventeenth-Century Maryland." *Maryland Historical Magazine* 79 (Spring 1984).

Merrell, James. "Cultural Continuity Among the Piscataway." *William and Mary Quarterly* 36 (October 1979): 548–70.

Miller, Henry M. "Baroque Cities in the Wilderness: Archeology and Urban Development in the Colonial Chesapeake." *Historical Archeology* 22, no. 2 (1988): 57–73.

Muldoon, Andrew R. "Recusants, Church-Papists, and 'Comfortable' Missionaries: Assessing the Post-Reformation English Catholic Community." *Catholic Historical Review* 86 (April 2000), 242–57.

Mullaney, William Francis. "Oliver Pollock: Catholic Patriot and Financier of the American Revolution (1737–1823)." Master's thesis, The Catholic University of America, 1933.

Muller, Herman J. "Jesuit Writings of the Seventeenth and Eighteenth Centuries and British-American Trade." Ph.D. diss., Loyola University of Chicago, 1950.

Murrin, John. "English Rights as Ethnic Aggression: The English Conquest, the Charter of Liberties of 1683, and Leisler's Rebellion in New York." In *Authority and Resistance in Early New York*, edited by William Pencak and Conrad Edick Wrights, 56–94. New York: New York Historical Society, 1988.

Muser, Edgar A. "Old Saint Mary's of Lancaster, Pennsylvania: The Jesuit Period, 1741–1785." *Journal of Lancaster County Historical Society* (Easter 1967).

Newman, Paul Douglas. " 'Good Will to all men ... from the King on the throne to the beggar on the dunghill': William Penn, the Roman Catholics, and Religious Toleration." *Pennsylvania History* 61 (October 1994): 457–79.

Pomerenk, Kathleen Orr. "Faith in Art: Justus Engelhardt Kuhn's Portrait of Eleanor Darnall." Master's thesis, Georgetown University, 2009.

Pyne, Tricia T. *The Maryland Catholic Community, 1690–1775: A Study in Culture,
Region, and Church.* Ph.D. diss., The Catholic University of America, 1995.

———. "The Politics of Identity in Eighteenth-Century British America: Catholic
Perceptions of their Role in Colonial Society." *U. S. Catholic Historian* 15 (Spring
1997): 1–13.

———. "A Plea for Maryland Catholics Reconsidered." *Maryland Historical Magazine* 92 (Summer 1997): 162–81.

———. "Ritual and Practice in the Maryland Catholic Community, 1634–1776."
U.S. Catholic Historian 26 (Spring 2008): 17–46.

Ray, Mary Augustina. "American Opinion of Roman Catholicism in the Eighteenth
Century." Ph.D. diss., Columbia University, 1937.

Riley, Arthur Joseph. "Catholicism in Colonial New England, 1620–1788." Ph.D.
diss., The Catholic University of America, 1936.

Rose, Lou. "Ebenezer Cooke's *The Sot Weed Factor* and Its Uses as a Social Document in the History of Colonial Maryland." *Maryland Historical Magazine* 78
(Winter 1983).

Rossi, Joseph S. "Jesuits, Slaves and Scholars at 'Old Bohemia,' 1704–1756. As
Found in the *Woodstock Letters*." *U.S. Catholic Historian* 26 (Spring 2008): 1–15.

Shaw, Jenny. "Island Purgatory: Irish Catholics and the Reconfiguring of the English Caribbean, 1650–1700." Ph.D. diss., New York University, 2009.

Schwartz, Sally. "William Penn and Toleration: Foundations of Colonial Pennsylvania." *Pennsylvania History* 50 (October 1983): 284–312.

———. "*A Mixed Multitude*": *The Struggle for Toleration in Colonial Pennsylvania.*
Ph.D. diss., New York University, 1987.

Shugg, Wallace. "The Baron and the Milliner: Lord Baltimore's Rape Trial as a Mir-
ror of Class Tensions in Mid-Georgian London." *Maryland Historical Magazine*
83 (Winter 1988): 310–30.

Sikora, Barbara. "Colonial Catholic Chapels in Prince George's Country." *Catholic
Historical Society of Washington Newsletter* (July–September 1995): 5–11.

Spalding, Thomas W. "The Maryland Tradition." *U.S. Catholic Historian* 8 (Spring
1989): 51–58.

———. "The Maryland Catholic Diaspora." *U.S. Catholic Historian* 8 (Fall 1989):
163–74.

Stanwood, Owen Charles. "Creating the Common Enemy: Catholics, Indians, and
the Politics of Fear in Imperial North America, 1678–1700." Ph.D. diss., Northwestern University, 2005.

Steiner, Bruce E. "The Catholic Brents of Virginia: An Instance of Political Toleration." *Virginia Magazine of History and Biography* 70 (1962).

Stock, Leo Francis. "The Irish Parliament and the American Revolution." *Historical Records and Studies* 30 (1939): 11–29.

Stone, Garry Wheeler. "Manorial Maryland." *Maryland Historical Magazine* 82 (Spring 1987): 3–36.

Terrar, Edward. "Was There a Separation between Church and State in Mid-Seventeenth-Century England and Colonial Maryland?" *Journal of Church and State* (Winter 1993): 61–82.

Towles, James Lawrence. "Anti-Catholic Passions in Maryland during the French and Indian War." Master's thesis, The Catholic University of America, 1968.

Usherwood, Stephen. "Conquered Canada: General James Murray's Impressions, 1762." *History Today* 29 (1979).

Walsh, Lorena S. "Land, Landlord, and Leaseholder: Estate Management and Tenant Fortunes in Southern Maryland, 1642–1820." *Agricultural History* 59 (July 1985): 373–96.

———. "Staying Put or Getting Out: Findings for Charles County, Maryland, 1650–1730." *William and Mary Quarterly* 44 (January 1987): 89–103.

Whelan, Frances Mary. "The Influence of the Roman Catholics in Pennsylvania and Maryland in the Eighteenth Century." Master's thesis, University of Chicago, 1926.

Wise, Mary Charles. "History of the Catholic Church in St. Mary's Country, Maryland." Master's thesis, The Catholic University of America, 1944.

Ziegler, Edith. "The Transported Convict Women of Colonial Maryland, 1718–1776." *Maryland Historical Magazine* 97 (2002): 5–32.

INDEX

Calvert, George: death of, 29; early life,
21–22; interest in colonization, 24; and
Newfoundland, 24–26 obtaining a
charter, 28–29; petitions king for land
in Chesapeake area, 27; reconversion
to Catholicism, 22–24; as secretary of
state, 22; supporter of English Jesuits'
controversy with secular clergy, 30–31; in
Virginia, 28
Calvert, Leonard: and Calvert-Jesuit
controversy, 52–53; death of, 67; fears
concerning Indians, 48; as privateer, 61;
and religion in Maryland, 41; and retak-
ing of Maryland, 65, 68–69, 154–55; and
Richard Ingle, 62–65; voyage to Mary-
land and settlement, 33, 35; and William
Claiborne, 59
Calvert, Philip, 72, 112
Calvert County, 118–19, 132, 158
Calverts: commitment to religious liberty,
xiii, 43; and Glorious Revolution,
133; plan Maryland venture, 31; regain
province, 65
Cambridge University, 58
Camden (South Carolina), 261
Canada, 226, 233
Canary Islands, 74
Cape Breton Island, 210–11
Carberry, Elizabeth, 188
Carew, Henry, 112
Carey, Thomas, 262
Caribbean, 75, 94, 261
Caribs, 75, 89–91
Carmelites, 186, 279–80
Caroline County (Maryland), 262–63
Carr, Lois Green, 38
Carroll, Charles, of Carrollton: and
Continental Congress, 239, 256; and
Dr. Charles Carroll, 205–6; drafts Mary-
land Constitution, 257–58; as "First
Citizen," 236–38; mission to Canada,
248–50; prodder for independence, 256;
Provincial Convention, 239; renovation
of Annapolis mansion, 194–95; return to

America, 230; shapes Catholic participation in American Revolution, 245; social
life, 194–95, 230–31; and Stamp Act,
234–35; in state senate, 259
Carroll, Charles, Dr.: co-founder of
Baltimore Company, 191; convert to
Anglicanism, 156; urges enforcement of
penal laws, 205–6
Carroll, Charles, the Settler: biography, 152;
and birthday salute, 164–65; on Calverts'
regaining control of Maryland, 134;
death of, 171, 188; dismissed as Calvert
agent, 167; emigrates to Maryland,
126–27; imports Irish servants, 146,
159; as leader of Catholic opposition to
penal legislation, 149, 159, 162, 167–68;
and oath-taking, 165; patronage from
Calverts, 163–64, 172; power play with
Hart, 165–66; as public counsel, 147
Carroll, Daniel, 191
Carroll, Daniel, of Rock Creek, 177, 254,
259–60
Carroll, James, 164, 167, 177, 190, 205
Carroll, John: and American Revolution,
268–69, 275–76; on church and state,
276; elected bishop, 279; establishes
seminary, 280; Georgetown Academy
and education, 280; mission to Canada,
249–50; need for episcopal authority,
278; organizing American Catholic
community, 275; restoration of Society
of Jesus, 281; suppression of Jesuits, 240;
on Thomas Digges, 260–61
Carrolls: at Bohemia school, 185; British
raids on Poplar Island 259; chapel
building, 177; economic impact of Revolution, 258–9; economic success, 155; and
proprietary offices, 172
Castillo, James, 102
Catherine the Great, 281
Cauffman, Joseph, 267
Cecil, Robert, Sir, 22
Cecil County, 158, 177, 185
Central America, 94

Lotbinière, Michel Chartier, Marquis de, 250
Louis XIV, 138
Louis XVI, 273
Louisbourg, 203, 210–12, 215
Louisiana, 216, 224–25, 284
Lower Resurrection Hundred, 175
Lowes, 110
Lynch, Nicholas, 92, 101

MacDonald, John, 252
Macnemara, Thomas, 167, 171
Macquacomen, 48
Maine, 19
Manners, Mathias, 199
Manners, Peter, 111
Manorial court in Maryland, 39
Manorial system in Maryland, 31–32, 37–40, 65
Mansell, Thomas, 159
Manual of Catholic Prayers, A, 198
Marians, 6
Martha's Vineyard, 121
Martinique, 91, 99, 209
Mary, queen of James II, 128
Mary of Guise, 11
Mary of Orange, 128, 130, 132, 135, 138
Maryland: and the American Revolution, 255–57, 260; and Catholic Colonial history, xi; currents of change in early eighteenth century, 150–52; decline of tobacco economy, 151; demographics, 37, 104–5; diversification of economy, 151; economic boom, 188–89; economic depression, 116, 174–75; enacts bill of rights, 269; enforcing religious toleration, 44–45; establishment of Church of England, 144, 175; fur trading, 37; immigration to, 36–37; "Marianus," 29; military provider during Seven Years' War, 221n10; mortality in, 36, 106; opposition to Calverts' rule, 118–19; opposition to Stamp Act, 234; outmigration, 104; population, 65, 104,

106, 150; Provincial Court, 59; rebellion of *1676*, 118–19; rebellion of *1681*, 119–20; religious diversity, 117–18; religious rights granted to minorities, 258; socioeconomic mobility in, 40, 151; tradition, 277, 284; turn to slave labor, 151–52
Maryland Catholic community: acceptance of Protestant accession, 171–72; and American Revolution, 244–45, 255, 257–64; compared with England, 149, 228; composition of, 173–74; days of fast and abstinence, 184; defiance of Provincial Council, 168–71; on the Eastern Shore, 177–78; education, 111, 185; expansion, 228–29; feast days and manual labor, 183–84; gentry compared with Irish, 155–56; Irish immigrants, 144–46, 159, 178; marriage patterns, 181; "Mass Houses," 110; outmigration, 282–83, petition against appointment of bishop, 227; planter-merchants, 152–56, 188–89, 194; political nadir, xv; political reentry, 239, 257, 259–60; proliferation of chapels, 176–77, 228; reaction to penal laws, 145, 148–49, 157, 160, 206–7, 223–24; reaction to Stamp Act, 234; relief from penal legislation, 225; religious culture in eighteenth century, 176–78, 180–84; and Seven Years' War, 221–225; size, 40, 112, 158, 173, 188, 229; slavery, 156, 177, 283–84; and Society of Jesus, 240; in Somerset County, 110; 283–84; status and roles of women, 107–8, 180, 183; St. Mary's County, 175; transatlantic education of gentry's children, xv, 112, 185–88, 279–80; the unchurched, 177–78; vocations to religious life, 112; under William and Mary, 143; women's religious vocations, 187–88
Maryland Gazette, 192, 219–20, 224, 229, 235–36, 242, 256
Maryland General Assembly: and Acadians, 214; declaration on religion, 44, 59, 60; disfranchises Catholics, 167–68;

INDEX 309

elections of *1773*, 238; establishes Church
of England, 144; on financial support for
churches, 276; legislation on Irish immigration, 145, 148; and Margaret Brent,
67; penal legislation in Seven Years' War,
220–22, 225; penal legislation upheld in
London, 167; rescinds Suspending Act of
1704, 168; revolt of *1659*, 72; struggle with
Provincial Council, 118; Toleration Act
of *1649*, 70–71
Maryland Jesuits: adapting ministry,
175–76; and American Revolution, 243,
263–64; arrest of, 166; as circuit riders,
178–79; as clerical planters, 45, 109;
conversions by, 46, 111; demographics,
158, 173–74; establishment of missions,
46, 197; flee to Virginia, 71, 133; German
missioners, 198–200, 218; maintaining
libraries, 182; manor houses as liturgical
centers, 46; ministry to native Americans, 46–51; ministry in St. Mary's City,
45; mortality rate, 66, 104, 109; in New
York, 124–25; option of returning to
England, 179–80; possible termination
of mission, 108–9; as proselytizers, 46,
51, 111, 144; retreats to laity, 46; and
slaves, 284; status of mission, 65, 73;
and Tobacco Fees Controversy, 235;
trading with Piscataway, 49–50; use of
sodalities, 183
"Maryland Line," 263
Maryland Provincial Convention, 239,
255–58
Maryland Provincial Council: and Acadians, 214; as counterforce to lower house
in Seven Years' War, 221–22, 225; disarms
Catholics, 204; eligibility, 39; invitation
to Catholic gentry, 168–70; membership,
68, 118; and rebellion of *1681*, 119–20;
rejects rescission of Suspending Act,
207; summons Carroll of Annapolis, 165;
summons Jesuits, 147; and test oaths, 160
Massachusetts, 213, 269
Massey, Thomas, 112

Mattapany, 38–39, 49–50, 112, 133
Matthews, Bernardine Teresa, 279–80
Matthewses, 186
Mattingly, John, 178, 180
Mattinglys, 283
McKenna, John, 271
Meade, George, 200, 244, 265–67
Mease, James, 244, 265–66
Mendoza, Bernardino de, 18
Merrimack River, 129
Methodists, 276
Metzger, Charles, 244, 264
Mexico, 94
Mikmaq, 209
Minas, 212
Missouri, 283
Mohawk Valley, 243, 270
Molyneux, Richard, 204–05
Molyneux, Robert, 198
Monhegan Island, 19
Monocacy River, 195
Montgomery, Richard, 248, 250, 271
Montgomery, Thomas, 136
Montreal, 248, 250, 271
Montserrat: and American Revolution, 251;
colonization, 80; and Glorious Revo-
lution, 137; Irish outmigration, 137–38;
Irish population, xii, 76, 89–91, 97; and
Maryland adventurers, 74–75; origin
of Irish settlement, 89–90; practice of
religion, 98, 101; rebellion of *1666*, 91;
socioeconomic mobility, 91–92; sugar as
staple crop, 90–91; white population, 138
Mortmain, statutes of, 53, 55, 109
Mosley, Joseph: and American Revolution,
243, 262–63; as circuit rider, 178–80; de-
scription of Maryland, 174; on libraries,
182; on suppression, 240
Moylan, Stephen, 200, 244, 265
Moylans, 265
Mudds, 283
Mullett, Michael A., 6
Munster, 16

Nanticokes, 132
Nantucket, 121
Navigation Acts, 116
Neale, Anne Brooke, 186
Neale, Bennet, 187
Neale, Charles, 187, 240, 279–80
Neale, Henrietta Maria, 108
Neale, Henry, 263
Neale, Henry, SJ, 187, 198
Neale, James, 73
Neale, Leonard, 187
Neale, William, 186
Neales, 155, 185–87, 283
Netherlands, 2
Nevis, 80, 89
New England: Catholics in, 229–30; and
    Nova Scotia, 247; opposition to "Intol-
    erable Acts," 239; as recruitment area for
    Maryland, 68
New English, 16
Newfoundland, 18, 210, 230, 252
Newgate Prison, 269
New Jersey, 122–23, 199–200, 269
New Netherland, 121–22, 130
Newport, 230
New Survey of the West Indies, A, 94
Newtown Hundred, 175
Newtown Manor: 178–79; and American
    Revolution, 264; chapel, 176; established,
    109; plantation, 156
Newtown Neck, 109, 111
New York City, 121–23
Nicholson, Francis, 129–30, 143–46
Nine Years' War, 14
Nixon, George W., 196
Norman, Edward, 6
North, Lord Frederick, 261
Northern Neck (Virginia), 104
Nova Scotia: and Acadians, 209–14; and
    American Revolution, xv, 246–47, 251;
    resettlement, 215–16, 247

Oath of Supremacy, 16, 28
Objections Answered Touching Maryland, 44

O'Dougherty, Cahir, Sir, 14–15
Ogle, Samuel, 206
Oglethorpe, James, 202
Ohio River, 241
Ohio Valley, 208, 273
O'Kelly, John, 230
Old English: in Barbados, 88; and Irish
    Parliament, 15–16; on Montserrat, 90,
    93; origin of, 13; and Rebellion of 1641,
    77–78; in South America, 79
O'Neill, Hugh, 14
O'Queely, Malachy, 97–98
Orell, Thomas, 262
Orkneys, 252
Oxford, 57

Paca, William, 195, 231, 234, 238
Paine, Thomas, 242
Palatine Germans, 199, 243–44
Pale, 13–14, 77
Paris, 230
Parliament, English: abrogation of slave
    trade monopoly, 152; Act of Uniformity,
    2; Anti-Popery Act (1704), 206; and
    George I, 161; and Glorious Revolution,
    128; 232; and Gunpowder Plot, 4–5; and
    "Intolerable Acts," 239; and James II, 127;
    and penal laws, 25; rationale for Sugar
    and Stamp Acts, 232–33; repeal of Stamp
    Act, 235; virtual representation, 234
Parliament, Irish, 15, 138–39, 254–55
Parnham, Anna Maria, 185–86
Patapsco River, 191
Patriot Party, 255, 258
Patuxent, 48, 71
Patuxent River, 45, 50, 120, 132
Patuxent tribe, 45, 48
Peace of Paris, 261, 275, 282
Peckham, George, Sir, 17–18
Pemberton, Ebenezer, 216–17
Pembroke, 213
Penal Laws: Catholic resistance to, 2; as
    deterrents of Catholic socioeconomic
    power, xiv; in England, 2, 127; after

Stamp Act, 231–35, 242, 253

Stapleforts, 110

Stapleton, William, 93–94

Staten Island, 121

St. Clement, 34–35

St. Clement's Bay, 38

St. Clement's Hundred, 175

St. Clement's Island, 35, 41–42, 70

St. Clement's Manor, 105–6

Stede, Edwyn, 136

St. Francis Regis Mission, 199

St. Francis Xavier (Newtown), 228

St. George River, 19

St. Inigoes Creek, 62

St. Inigoes plantation: and American
  Revolution, 264; attacked, 62; overseer
  fined for religious intolerance, 44–45; as
  parish center, 176; patented, 56; supporting ministry, 109; tenants on, 156

St. John's, xii, 246, 251–52

St. John's River, 213

St. Joseph's (Philadelphia), 197, 214–15,
  229, 267

St. Joseph's Mission (Tuckahoe), 179

St. Kitts (St. Christopher's): and American
  Revolution, 273; Catholic population of,
  xii, 97; and Glorious Revolution, 136–37;
  immigration into, 89; and Jamaica,
  94–95; and Maryland adventurers, 75,
  80–81; practice of religion, 97–99, 101;
  rebellion of 1666, 91

St. Lawrence River, 140, 241

St. Leger, Barry, 271

St. Mary's (Lancaster), 218

St. Mary's (Philadelphia), 229, 273

St. Mary's City: Bennett and Claiborne at;
  captured by Puritans, 71; chapels, 46,
  110, 159; concentration of settlers, 37;
  development, 38, 112–15; founding, 36;
  Franciscans working in, 112; Glorious
  Revolution, 133; Jesuit property in, 56;
  return of Jesuits, 65–66; and Richard Ingle, 60–62; 70; as royal capital, 142–43;
  site of Jesuit school, 111–12, 185

St. Mary's County: and American Revolu-

tion, 257, 259, 262; as backwater, 174–75;
  Catholic gentry, 155–56; Catholic
  population, 158, 228; circuit riding in,
  178; outmigration, 283; and Protestant
  Association, 132; reported murders, 120;
  religious women, 188

St. Mary's Seminary, 28

Stock, Simon, 25–26

St. Omer's: and Calverts, 162; founding,
  9; Maryland Catholics, 185–86, 230; as
  minor seminary, 280

Stone, William, 68, 70–72

Stones, 157

St. Peter's (Baltimore), 214

Stritch, John, 98–99

St. Thomas Fort. See Fort Thomas

St. Thomas Manor (Portobacco): and
  American Revolution, 264; attacked, 62;
  blacks gathering at, 205; devotional life,
  182; as parish center, 176; patented, 66;
  projected development, 229; supporting
  ministry, 109

St. Vincent, 251

St. Xaverius Mission. See Bohemia

Stuart, Charles I: becomes king, 1, 20, 22,
  25; Catholic expectations, 1, 25; and
  English Civil War, 57–58, 66; improved
  position of Catholics under, 32; and Irish
  Confederation, 78; revival of penal laws,
  25–26

Stuart, Charles II, 70, 155; grants New
  Netherland to brother, 121; grant to
  William Penn, 195; orders brother from
  England, 124; upholds Cecil Carroll, 72

Stuart, Charles Edward, 204–5, 227

Stuart, Henry, Cardinal York, 227

Stuart, James I: Catholic hopes for, 4; and
  George Calvert, 22; and Ireland, 16, 76;
  as James VI of Scotland, 11

Stuart, James II: compared to George III,
  268; conversion, 121–22; flees to France,
  128; impact of ascension on West Indies,
  86, 101–2; loses Ireland, 138–39; and
  New York, 123–25; pro-Catholic policies,
  126–27; and William Penn, 195

Washington, George: addresses Canadians, 247; and American Revolution, 263, 265, 272; at Fort Necessity, 208, 219; guest of Charles Carroll, 195
Watten, 187
Waymouth, George, 19–20
Welsh, Nicholas, 136
Wentworth, Thomas, Sir, 22, 26
Western Shore (Maryland), 158, 177–78
West Indies: and American Revolution, 246, 25–53, 261; Catholic institutional presence, 97; Catholic population, 81; demographics, 253; economic mobility, xiii–xiv; immigration, 88; lay-centered Catholicism, 100–101; outmigration, xiv; penal laws, 97, 99–100; recovering its Catholic history, xii–xiv; slave population, 82; trade to, 193
West Jersey, 123, 125
Whelan, Charles, 278
White, Andrew: 66; on Barbados, 83–84; celebrating Mass on St. Clement's Island, 41; crossing to Maryland, 34; gift from Mattapany, 48, 54; ministry to Indians, 48–49, 50n5; on Montserrat, 90; planning Maryland colony, 29–32, 54; taken captive to England, 62–64
White, Jerome, 113
Whitehall, 141
Whitemarsh, 176, 276

Whitfield, George, 217
Wicomico River, 110
Willcox, Thomas, 196
William and Mary College, 185
William of Orange: death of, 145 and Glorious Revolution, 128–30, 132, 135, 139; renewal of penal laws, 138; toleration for Maryland Catholics, 142–43
Williamsburg, 185
Willoughby, Francis Lord, 82, 84
Willson, Thomas Bennett, 262
Willsons, 110
Wiltshire, 56
Winslade, Tristam, 19
Wintour, Ann, Lady, 33
Wiseman, Thomas, Sir, 33
Worcestershire, 7
Wren, Christopher, 113
Wriothesley, Henry, Earl of Southampton, 18–19
Wye Chapel, 111
Wye River, 110, 179

Yaocomico tribe, 35–36
Yellow fever, 84
Yeo, John, 117
Yorkshire, 22
Yorktown, 272–74
Ysasi, Christóbal Arnaldo, 95

Papist Devils: Catholics in British America was
designed in Adobe Jensen Pro with Arvil display
type and composed by Kachergis Book Design
of Pittsboro, North Carolina. It was printed
on 55-pound Natures Natural and bound by
Sheridan Books of Ann Arbor, Michigan.